ESCAPE FROM THE GHETTO

Henry Carr in a kilt

ESCAPE

from the

GHETTO

A Story of Survival and Resilience in World War II

CHAIM HERSZMAN

(also known as Henryk Karbowski and Henry Carr)

AS TOLD TO HIS SON

JOHN CARR

PEGASUS BOOKS

NEW YORK LONDON

ESCAPE FROM THE GHETTO

Pegasus Books, Ltd.
148 West 37th Street, 13th Floor
New York, NY 10018

Copyright © 2022 by John Carr

First Pegasus Books cloth edition April 2022

Interior design by Maria Fernandez

ISBN: 978-1-64313-885-5

10 9 8 7 6 5 4 3 2 1

Printed in the United States of America
Distributed by Simon & Schuster
www.pegasusbooks.com

For Glenys Thornton

Author's Note

This book is written as far as possible in my father's own words, drawn from many hours of tape-recorded conversations and transcribed interviews which took place over many years. Haltingly at first, Dad eventually told me a full account of how he survived his extraordinary war years. I then set out to corroborate as much of it as I could through extensive additional interviews and research.

A key eye-witness to the seminal event, the escape itself, was his cousin Heniek. So in that spirit I have let him start the story. Heniek was in my dad's 'gang'. Unprompted and unsolicited, while we were both in the offices of the Jewish community in Lodz, Heniek's description of that day at the ghetto perimeter was almost identical to my father's account of how this scarcely believable adventure began. It was key to spurring me to investigate my father's story further.

Either on tape or in contemporary or near contemporary notes, I recorded everything Dad told me about his life and conditions in Poland before the war, about this journey away from there and finally what happened after he reached England, right up to the time of the divorce. Is every single word in this book exactly as he relayed it to me? No, it is not. For one thing, Dad could not remember the names of everyone he met en route. I had to give them names. The dialogue between the individuals who appear in the book reflects the content of conversations Dad recalled having, but the language is mine. However, all the key events I have described are events Dad remembered. If there is a gloss, it is the gloss of interpretation.

John Carr

ESCAPE FROM THE GHETTO

Part One

Heniek

I

There were three of us. We were a team. A gang. A tight clique. Not a band of brothers, but a band of two brothers with a cousin thrown in. Our mothers were sisters.

Chaim and Israel Herszman (pronounced 'Hershman') were the brothers. I was the cousin. My full Jewish name was Avrum-Hersh Lewkowicz, but at the time almost everyone who knew me, Jew and Christian, family, friend or foe, called me by my given Polish tag, which was 'Heniek'. 'Srulek' was the popular form of Israel's name, but Chaim, well, he was always Chaim, so that's easy enough.

We lived in western Poland, in Lodz, then the country's second city, a grimy, factory-filled, polyglot textile town frequently referred to as the Manchester of Poland. Some thought that a little unkind to Manchester. Lodz was not too far from the border with Germany. Not far enough as it turned out. On 1 September 1939, the German Army crossed the Polish border at multiple points, Danzig was attacked, and the Second World War was underway. Seven days later, an enormous swastika flew over Lodz town hall.

Up until just before the war started, the Lewkowicz and Herszman families lived in the same house, at 15 Zagajnikowa (pronounced 'Zaganicova'). We lived there longer than anywhere else I can remember. Consequently, in the intervening years, whenever I thought about Poland, which was not often, this is the place that came to mind as home. It was a mixed house in a mixed neighbourhood – that is to say, a house of twelve flats inhabited by Jews and Catholics, in a neighbourhood where Jews, Catholics and who knew what else lived cheek by jowl.

Number 15 was a large, visibly dilapidated two-storey building owned by Mirla Blumowicz, formerly Cendrowicz, our mother's mother, my grandma. A widow since 1902, she had been married to Nachman Blumowicz, an enterprising man who had established a portfolio of properties and businesses that allowed Mirla to live comfortably on the income they generated.

Mirla let her daughters and their families live at number 15 rent free. Mind you, it wasn't easy to find anybody, family member or no, willing to hand over money for the privilege of being there. In fact, a few months before the war started the municipal authorities in Lodz said number 15 had to be abandoned because it was no longer fit for human habitation. Everyone had to move out. I believe most of the tenants, including us, ended up in places also owned by Grandma. The majority went to Baluty, the district at the heart of the city's main Jewish quarter, about three kilometres from Zagajnikowa. The Herszmans got a flat on Wawelska, and we were not that far away on Zielna.

Mirla also lived on Zagajnikowa but in another house she owned further down the street. She stayed put for a while after we all left number 15. Finally, when the war started, she came to stay with us in Baluty. Mirla's somewhat diminutive stature belied a giant rasping tongue, as sharp as a crocodile's teeth. Her nickname was 'Beelzebubska'. This was meant affectionately, usually, and owed much to the fact that whatever was on her mind she just said it out loud and with no obvious attempt to spare the feelings of the listener, adult or child, rich man or poor. The concept of sugar-coating and Grandma were on permanently divergent paths.

The Lewkowicz family consisted of my dad Moishe, my mum Liba-Sura, big brother Yehuda, little sister Rutka and, of course, me, making five in total. We were on the ground floor at number 15. The Herszmans were in the flat immediately above us. The grown-ups in the Herszman family were Uncle Chil and Aunt Chaja-Sura and, with a final tally of six children, they were a noisy bunch. I'm sorry, but even at the time I could never remember the names of all the Herszman offspring. There were three girls. Nathan, Chaim and Srulek, the boys, were the ones I knocked about with, played football with and did all the other things that were truly important in our lives.

Among the youngsters in our neighbourhood, Chaim, Srulek and I were known collectively as the 'Holy Trinity'. This name was the invention of Cesek Karbowski, a Catholic boy who was a great friend of Chaim's. The Karbowskis also lived at number 15. Cesek had been present one day when the three of us, the cousins, were discussing whether or not we should adopt a name and, if so, what it might be. Cesek said the Holy Trinity was the obvious choice, and when he explained what it meant to the majority Catholic population of Poland, the irony of three little Jews using such a revered Catholic concept to refer to themselves was completely and instantly irresistible. It stuck. Mind you, if I ever referred to the existence or activities of the Holy Trinity by name in the presence of my parents, a vigorous shellacking would usually swiftly follow. They didn't get the joke or, if they did, they emphatically did not like it.

Chaim and I sat next to each other in the same class at the Jewish school on Magistracka Street. There was no question Chaim and I were close, but in the Holy Trinity there was always a special bond between the brothers. I never tried to break, weaken or loosen it, not least because I knew I couldn't. As an operational unit we all got along just fine.

There had been some talk of us asking Chaim's older brother Nathan to join the gang. Chaim was absolutely devoted to and hero-worshipped him. However, Nathan was that bit older, and it was plain he really didn't want to get too involved in 'kids' stuff', as he saw it. Despite this, difficulties with Srulek arose, Chaim would ask Nathan to give an opinion or advice, and whatever that opinion or advice was it became a definitive ruling. Neither Chaim nor Srulek would argue with Nathan, so he was sort of a shadow member of the gang. The main upside of Nathan not actually being a member was we never had to think of a new and similarly irreverent or amusing name for what would have become a gang of four. Maybe we would have had to insult a completely different religion.

Polish was the everyday language of the Holy Trinity, as it was at home and school, but, naturally, practically every Polish Jew I knew, me included, also spoke Yiddish. This was because Yiddish had been the communal language of the Jews in Poland for the thousand or so years we'd been there, although I gathered some of the wealthier and the assimilated Jews refused to speak our historic tongue even if they knew it. My mum and dad said, leaving aside the poor lost souls who were assimilated and trying not to be Jews, the rejection of Yiddish for everyday use was usually more about snobbery and social climbing than it was about rejecting the faith. Since I had no contact with either wealthy or assimilated Jews, this was never an issue for me. What did I care what language people spoke or why? If we could communicate with each other, I was fine with that.

When the Holy Trinity was out on the street, if we needed to speak in code and there were no other Jewish kids in the vicinity, we would often talk to each other in Yiddish. We needed to be careful if Germans were around. The closeness of the Yiddish and German language meant the smarter ones could sometimes catch the drift of a conversation even if they didn't get it all. There had been a few awkward moments when a German boy worked out what we were up to.

When I say a 'German boy', I am generally referring to a descendant of German settlers, most of whom had come to Lodz towards the end of the nineteenth century when it was a textile boomtown at the westernmost edge of the Russian Empire. By 1939, ethnic Germans made up about a third of the entire population of the city, so we were completely accustomed to Germans in the flesh. Several of the Holy Trinity's good friends came from German families. We played football with Germans and Catholic Poles all the time. They couldn't be blamed for what the idiot adults in their lives were doing or believed. Football transcended the trivial concerns of what passed for politics in Poland in the 1930s.

Of course, the great bulk of the Jews in Lodz were also Poles, but we always thought of ourselves and talked about ourselves first as Jews, simply to distinguish us from Poles who were not Jews. It didn't mean we were any less patriotic or cared any less about the fate of Poland. Jews had helped create modern Poland, had fought and died for it. Referring to ourselves as Jews was just shorthand, at least it was as far as I was concerned.

★   ★   ★

Chaim had been born in Zyrardow (pronounced 'Jeerardoof'), not far from Warsaw, whereas Srulek and I were Lodzers soup to nuts. Born in April 1928, Srulek was the baby of the trio. His nickname was 'Little Srulek'. He wasn't always happy about that. Occasionally, when we had to introduce ourselves to strangers, calling him Little Srulek struck them as being absolutely hilarious, because none of us were what you would call over-endowed in the height department, even among others of the same vintage. Pronounced shortness was part of our common genetic inheritance.

I was the next oldest, having arrived in September 1926. Chaim was at the top of the chronological tree, if only by five months. He made his debut on the planet Earth in April 1926, on Hitler's birthday – the twentieth of that month.

As Hitler loomed larger and larger in the lives of everyone living in Poland, but particularly in the lives of the Jews, more information about him became known. This obviously included information about his birthday. When Srulek and I, and everyone else in the family, at school and in our broader social circle, made the connection between Hitler and Chaim, it caused a mixture of *schadenfreude*-tinged raucous merriment and low-level bemusement, or, alternatively, anxiety that it betokened some kind of evil omen. All the Jews I knew then were deeply superstitious. All the Jews I have ever known were deeply superstitious.

Yet with Chaim there was zero ambiguity, zero amusement and definitely no merriment when it came to his link with the Führer. He hated it. Kids are easily embarrassed. They don't want to be different, at least not in any way that might help someone poke fun at them, particularly if it is felt to be unjust. Chaim became quite obsessed with suppressing any knowledge of his real birthday and concocted all kinds of complicated evasions and untruths to conceal it. At a rational level Chaim must have known sharing a birthday with someone was a completely meaningless coincidence, but where is it written that everyone, kids included, always has to be rational about everything?

Before the war, we were all members of Hashomer-Hatzair, a secular Zionist youth group, a bit like the Boy Scouts only it was decidedly left wing, with boys and girls participating on the same basis. We all looked forward to helping build a socialist homeland and paradise for the Jews in Palestine. Hashomer-Hatzair organised camps and other activities where, apart from learning about socialism, we were taught the practical skills our leaders thought would be useful when we eventually went to the Promised Land. These practical skills were soon going to double as survival skills.

After the German Army arrived in Lodz, on 8 September 1939, things immediately started getting bad, very bad, for every kind of Pole, be they Jew or Christian. For the Christian Poles, it was terrible; for the Jews, it was horrific. We quickly realised the stories that had been coming out of Germany, Austria and elsewhere about the way the Nazis treated Jews were not just propaganda or the product of a newspaper reporter's fevered imagination. That was what we'd often been told by supposedly worldly-wise adults, although it is possible they were only trying to shield us from the ugly truth.

What we saw and heard on the streets was now our present and indeterminate future. Nothing had prepared us for the scale of the ferocious, random brutality. The writing was not so much on the wall as painted in vivid, blood-red, mile-high letters in the sky.

At the time the 'big thing' happened, Chaim was nearly fourteen, I was thirteen and a half, and Srulek was almost twelve. What did that make our average age? Too young. But there is never really a right age for what we witnessed or were party to back then. Today we say 'shit happens'. That expression doesn't get anywhere near capturing the awfulness of it all.

There's something about Srulek you need to know. It will help you to better understand what was going on when the big thing took place, maybe even explain what caused it or at any rate contributed to it, because to this day I am still not clear about the precise causal chain or what weight or importance to attach to any individual part of it.

Srulek had a club foot. This gave him a slightly twisted, foreshortened leg and a limp. It singled him out. Chaim insisted on Little Srulek being in our gang so he, or rather 'we', could keep an eye on him, look after and protect him, be his guardian angels. I have a suspicion Nathan had insisted Chaim take on this duty, maybe even suggested he form the gang with me in the first place, as a way of disguising its essentially protective purpose in respect of Srulek. We had to be a trio not a duo. I didn't have a problem with that even if it could sometimes be a bit of a pain. I liked Srulek's defiant determination not to let his disability get in the way.

Neither Chaim nor I could bear to see Srulek being abused or bullied because of his leg, so on the street or in the parks, where much of our lives were lived, we frequently and instinctively formed a defensive barrier to counter any verbal or physical attacks on him. Street life for kids in Lodz could be rough, and gangs were a big part of it.

Next important piece of information. All of the Holy Trinity had light complexions and light-coloured hair. None of us looked obviously Jewish or wore clothes or insignia that broad-cast our religious affiliations. On the contrary, if you galloped by on horseback, or even stood close up, you would imagine we were just another bunch of urchins from Polish or German backgrounds and therefore, if you thought about it further or at all, probably Catholic or some sort of Christian. There were many Protestants in Lodz, mainly Germans, but the Jews, or at least this bit of juvenile Lodz Jewry, tended to eschew fine theological distinctions and refer to everyone who wasn't Jewish as 'Catholic'.

In theory, everyone knew not all Jews looked like the classic stereotype of a Jew, but unless there was a reason to enquire more deeply mostly people reacted instantly and instinctively to what was in front of their eyes. Outward appearances there-fore mattered hugely, and in our case we all looked like, or could easily be mistaken for, *goyim* (gentiles). I have no doubt this helps explain the otherwise inexplicable: how Chaim survived past 1945.

Chaim had blue eyes and strikingly blond, almost white hair. If he hadn't been such a skinny little short arse, he could easily have been a poster boy for the Nordic League. This was another reason why his birthday connection to Herr Hitler irked him. Chaim looked about as un-Jewish as it was possible to be. While he was also known as 'Blondie', his most commonly used nickname among our co-religionists was *Yoisel*, which in Yiddish means 'Jesus'.

Even the Polish and German kids in our circle would call him Yoisel. Some got the gag, some didn't. Chaim didn't mind, or he accepted it as being inevitable, and he was definitely OK about using his looks to his advantage. But in no sense, other than in moments of extreme danger on the street, did I ever pick up even a whiff that he wanted to deny being a Jew or put distance between himself and his Jewishness.

Anyway, the point here was when the Holy Trinity was together roaming the city, Chaim, our leader, was emitting a strong aura of *goyness* that somehow enveloped and, more often than not, helped protect everyone around him, at least from being attacked by anti-Semites, of which there were many in those pre-war years. It didn't mean we avoided all trouble on the street. Gangs of young Germans or Poles, or the odd gang containing both, could still come at us, intent on inflicting injuries or stealing from us, as they would any rival gang or bunch of unknowns whom they could over-power. We would still hurt, still bleed, still be deprived of any property the aggressors took. No one said life was fair for us Jews, even when we weren't being attacked for being Jews!

Unfortunately, if the belligerent street gang we ran into were themselves Jews, perhaps looking for a bit of payback, it could get interesting. When this happened, and it happened quite a few times when we were outside our normal territories, we knew it was almost certainly Chaim's looks that had attracted their attention. Here his appearance was working against us. His shock of almost white hair was like a klaxon. In these circumstances, to assert his status as a Jew, Chaim would imme-diately start cursing and speaking very loudly in Yiddish. That generally did the trick and diverted them. A peremptory or demanded flash of Chaim's dick might nevertheless occasion-ally still be necessary to seal the deal. Sometimes all three of us would have to show them what we had. Very undignified, but better than a beating. Three circumcised penises hanging together could only mean one thing: Jews.

Sealing the deal in this way didn't necessarily mean we always got away without being thumped, although I like to think if we were still smacked it wouldn't be as comprehensively or viciously as might have been the case if our fellow Jews thought we actually were *goyim*. What probably annoyed or irked them was our non-Jewish appearances implied pathways from or out of the kind of persecution Jewish-looking Jews had to put up with on a daily basis. Several comments I heard suggested being a Jew who didn't look like one was cheating: a cowardly contrivance adopted only to avoid their own unenviable fate.

Although we wanted to protect Little Srulek, the fact is he usually didn't need much of what you might call 'looking after'. Despite his bad leg and club foot, he was able to move fast when necessary. On the football field, he could sometimes dazzle, even if his movements were a little awkward. Srulek was also quick-witted and had the gift of the gab to talk his way out of trouble. Srulek and Chaim were very much alike in that regard. I like to think I did not do too badly myself.

No, it was often more a matter of Srulek being held back. For all his street smarts, the club foot and gammy leg had undeniably created an extra layer of chippiness which could easily and quickly translate into false bravado or recklessness – for example, when being patronised or teased about his deformity. Srulek was determined not to be sidelined or laughed at.

The Nazis eventually declared Baluty to be part of the core of what we all understood would become a sealed-off ghetto. Jews from other parts of the city and the surrounding area were required to go and live there. After murdering several prominent members of different Jewish leadership bodies and

community organisations in Lodz, the Nazis had appointed
Chaim Rumkowski as the top dog, or 'Eldest of the Jews' to
give him his full, formal title. He was to be solely responsible
for all Jewish affairs in the city, and for all communications
between the Germans and the Jews. Rumkowski appointed a
few advisers to help him, but really the ghetto was his show, at
least as far as the soon to be incarcerated Jews were concerned.

As the ghetto got going, Rumkowski was responsible for
making arrangements to accommodate the huge influx of
newcomers, in terms of sorting out accommodation, distribut-
ing the all-important food rations and signing people up, children included, for various kinds of work in the many different
factories that carried on at full tilt or were created to produce
goods to help with the German war effort.

In an area of around four square kilometres, overcrowding
was chronic and oppressive. According to the best available
estimates before the war, there were about 60,000 Jews in
Baluty. On the day the ghetto was finally sealed on 1 May
1940, there were more than 160,000. Over its four-year life-
span, the official records show more than 240,000 people lived
there. The population would fluctuate from day-to-day according to the level of deportations and arrivals.

Rumkowski was also in charge of the ghetto hospital and an
impressive range of the kind of civic and cultural activities you
would associate with the functioning of any large settlement of
human beings. There was a court, a prison and a police force
made up entirely of Jews who lived in the ghetto. All were part
of Rumkowski's fiefdom.

A German order was issued requiring all Poles and any
Aryans to vacate Baluty by the end of February 1940. I suppose
Cesek Karbowksi and his family joined this exodus. I never

saw him around Baluty after that. The Karbowksis wouldn't have had a choice about leaving Baluty. And so it was that while most Jews in Poland and elsewhere in Europe would be obliged to up and carry what they could of their worldly possessions to a new home in a ghetto some distance from where they previously lived, by a twist of fate and pre-war municipal fiat the ghetto came to us.

When we realised we were going to be living in an official ghetto that would be sealed off, we talked about ditching the Holy Trinity brand name. Cesek was gone, so he'd never know, but we were sure he wouldn't have minded. 'Ghetto Commandos' was put forward by Srulek as the replacement. I liked that, and while it might not have fitted our physical size or our years, somehow it matched our mood and the lion-sized shared sense of grievance and righteous mission. Yet, among the other Jewish kids from Lodz who were in the ghetto with us, our sacrilegious identity was already firmly implanted. For practical purposes, Holy Trinity it remained.

From the very beginning of the German occupation of Lodz, food, or the lack of it, became a constant source of worry and anxious chatter for both Poles and Jews but especially for the Jews. It quickly became clear to most Jews, that relying solely on the official, coupon-based handouts from the new ghetto bureaucrats was never going to be enough to keep body and soul together. Our families had managed to create a stock-pile that was held in common, but it was pathetically small.

Hustling and trading for food within the ghetto had its risks, but before you could even do that you needed stuff with which to hustle and trade. The Lewkowiczs and Herszmans had little or nothing of that sort, and stealing from other ghetto residents was both difficult and wrong. Our parents forbade it, and the interdiction was sincerely meant and honoured by us. Largely.

A small number of heavily guarded and constantly patrolled official entry and exit points were established as, a bit at a time, the Nazis began a process of sealing-off the ghetto. In some places, this involved constructing a physical wall of stone, concrete, brick or wood, or putting up a high fence with barbed wire strung between stanchions. In others, at least temporarily, heavy-duty barbed wire was strung out in rolls between weighted posts.

If we were going to do anything to increase our store of food or tradeable goods in a significant way, we had to get into the city, which meant we needed to act soon. Who knew how solid or impenetrable the ghetto perimeter would become? Right then, it was clearly still porous, particularly where the rolls of barbed wire strung between the weighted posts remained the only physical delineator of the boundary.

Once a no-man's-land was officially declared on both sides of the perimeter, it became an offence even to approach the fence, whether from inside or outside the ghetto. 'Going to the wire' became a euphemism for committing suicide, because you would be shot if you did. In its favour, it normally meant death was quick and clean. Nobody would ask too many questions about a dead Jew found near the fence inside the boundary, or indeed pretty much anywhere in the ghetto, neither would they normally trouble over a corpse found near the perimeter on the outside, as whoever it was would very likely have been trying to communicate with a Jew or engaged in smuggling. Both strictly *verboten*.

Nevertheless, it was quite obvious, even when looking at the rolls of wire from a distance, that while the hooks and barbs were large and would be vicious if they caught you, in lots of places the rolls were not that tightly packed. With care and maybe a stick, or heavy gloves or hand coverings to manipulate the strands, it ought not to be too difficult for small guys like us to negotiate a passage. The ghetto was buzzing with rumours of children and small women who were regularly doing just that. These rumours persisted, but we tended to discount them until the day Chaim and I met someone from our Hashomer-Hatzair group who swore on everything that was dear to him he had already been through the wire and back a half-dozen times. That was the clincher. It was game on.

The Holy Trinity set about researching every possible breach point. If measured as a straight line, the ghetto's perimeter would have been approximately eleven kilometres, with lots of wiggles and curves, so, in those early days, there seemed to be plenty of scope to find a weak point. Rome wasn't built in a day. Neither was the Lodz ghetto. We quickly learned we were not the only people to have had the same idea. If we hung about a likely looking spot for too long, we were moved along, either by another larger gang or by adults who were concerned for our well-being or were sizing it up themselves, doubtless contemplating something similar and not wanting us to muck it up for them.

We finally found a section of the ghetto perimeter consisting of not very densely packed barbed-wire rolls that appeared not to have been claimed by a rival group. We knew this could change at any time. We were not going to dither.

The site had an additional, extremely attractive feature. Just by our stretch of perimeter was a deserted building which almost brushed up against the ghetto fence. Presumably the building was waiting to be assigned a use by Rumkowski or one of his cronies, but in the meantime its second-floor landing had a partially sheltered spot with a clear view of the streets outside the ghetto and the surrounding area, as well as of the interior of the ghetto. This was important.

If the ghetto police force were to spot us, it was hard to know how they would react. I guessed some would look in the other direction and walk away or else just shout at us and move us along. Unfortunately, others seemed to have bought into Rumkowski's philosophy. He maintained that if we all obeyed the Germans' rules and made ourselves useful, not only would they leave us alone, but it might bring about a new era of opportunity and prosperity: a self-governing, self-sufficient Jewish homeland right here in Poland, at least until those who were so minded could go to Palestine.

It was never clear if Rumkowski genuinely believed what he was saying or if, to give Jewish people hope, he was just making the best of what he knew was an awful but inescapable situation. Whatever the truth, in those early days many ghetto residents, not just the police, had signed up to and either acquiesced in or seemed to support the new order. We had to be careful. It wasn't just the coppers who could do for us. From where we stood inside the ghetto looking out, those mounds, trees and alleyways could not have been much more than 100 metres distant. So near, yet so far.

From our vantage point on the second floor of the deserted building, we could see there was a little piece of land on the city side containing what looked like several substantial mounds of grass. If they had been on a beach, you might have called them dunes, with some trees standing off a few metres behind. We named it 'Freedom Park'.

Freedom Park abutted a large complex of tenements which

seemed thinly populated – perhaps they were completely empty, as we never saw anyone at any windows. That was good. We could also see there were alleyways and openings at street level that led to a courtyard, or it might have been the midden, with views of another street on the other side. We all sort of knew the area anyway because we had sometimes played football close by.

There was a sentry box positioned on a pavement at, what to us from the second floor was, the left-hand end of Freedom Park, and it was possible to observe the behaviour of the occupant. Usually, it was a German soldier or, if he wasn't a soldier, he wore a uniform which marked him out as a guard, a sentry or a police officer – something official and therefore dangerous. Different guards came on at different times, but they all followed the same routine. A rifle was normally carried over the shoulder, always in plain view. They wanted everyone to know they meant business and the business was killing. The guard patrolled a section of the perimeter of the ghetto both to the left and the right of his station. Ambling might be a better word. It wasn't marching.

There was nothing very exact about it, but three times every hour the guard set off to the left or the right of the sentry box, and it was never fewer than four minutes before he came back to where he started. We didn't have watches or anything like that. We counted the seconds. Carefully. We knew our lives might depend on getting this right. From inside the ghetto, we were able to shadow a major part of the route. Because of the contours of the perimeter in both directions, after roughly ten seconds, we realised the guy would no longer have sight of the area in front of the sentry box from where he had started his journey and would eventually end it. This would be our optimal point of egress and return. The sentry box was the beacon, our marker.

As a result of our observations, we knew if we left it for, say, twenty seconds after the guard had started to walk in either direction, we would have the best part of four minutes to negotiate the wire and get across the street into the invisibility of Freedom Park or the alleyways. Likewise coming back to the ghetto. Twenty seconds after the guard set off, we would have the best part of four minutes to complete the return trip. In fact, we discovered not infrequently there would be a lot more than four minutes available before the guy returned to his starting point because if, at either end, he met up with his counterpart who was patrolling the adjoining stretch they could stop and share a cigarette or chat.

There was always a chance a guard could change his routine, but up to now that had not happened. The odds seemed strongly in our favour. Anyway, we were invincible. Completely unstoppable.

The Holy Trinity never really discussed, or rather we skirted around, the subject of who would actually go out into the city on the excursions we were planning, but the unspoken assumption was it would be best if there were two of us. If you are going to nick anything from a shop, or anywhere else, an extra pair of eyes is essential, but we also needed someone to stay on the second floor, our command post, to act as lookout, and to signal when the guard started walking and when the coast was clear.

We agreed an approximate time when the two who went out would return. For a large part of the year, even before the ghetto was created, 5 p.m. was when the Germans had decreed Jews were meant to be off the streets. Our curfew. We therefore agreed we had to aim to be back at the ghetto perimeter well before then to allow for possible hitches or delays. And if there were any problems on the outside, the lookout would just wait until they saw a familiar head bob up from behind one of the mounds of grass in Freedom Park. The possibility that both of them might never make it back was not mentioned. That wasn't on our agenda.

I had assumed all along that Chaim and I would be the two who went out. I should have known better. Everything involving the Holy Trinity was always surrounded by a penumbra of uncertainty because of Srulek's determination not to be treated differently. That argument was still to come.

Despite the underlying certainty that we were unbeatable, our conviction was nevertheless moderated by a degree of practicality. We agreed there had to be a trial run. A proof of concept. Maybe we had missed something, some important detail. Who knew what life was like these days 'out there'? It was a while since any of us had been in or around the main shopping areas of Lodz. If for some unforeseen reason this thing wasn't going to work, we needed to know sooner rather than later so we could devise another and better strategy.

Inside the ghetto, we had found unused coils of the same barbed wire that made up the sections of the perimeter we were planning to cross, so we had all had the chance to do a sort of dress rehearsal of how we might negotiate our way through. A stick proved unnecessary, but we did improvise some gloves made from a felt-like heavy cloth. However, we knew an unhurried experiment was never going to be quite the same as the genuine article. We needed to check out the ease with which we could get through the actual fence at the precise chosen spot, and how long it would take to get out the other side and over to the cover of the alleyways or Freedom Park. However for the trial run we agreed only one of us need go.

Who would go? I've already told you the three of us didn't dress, or very obviously look, like Jews. None of us had a noticeable Jewish accent, so there was little or nothing to separate us on that score. Srulek did not make the case for himself to be the solo artist, and while I really didn't want it to be me, at the same time I didn't want to make a thing of it, so I was hugely relieved when Chaim insisted it should be him because of his excellent spoken German. Srulek and I raised no objections. The die was cast.

This was the plan.

Chaim would go behind a wall that was part of a yard attached to the lookout building near the wire. This would shield him from the view of anyone inside or outside the ghetto – in fact, from everyone except me and Srulek. The two of us would position ourselves on the second floor in the building and prepare to give Chaim three signals. The first would indicate it was all clear inside the ghetto: that there were no signs of police officers, potential witnesses or busybodies who might try to halt, disrupt or report the proceedings. The second would be when the sentry was starting his patrol and everything was clear on that side too. The final signal would indicate that still nobody was in sight on either the ghetto side or the Polish side so the journey should start immediately.

Having agreed all that, we decided we would give it a go the following day at 11 a.m. and, come what may, Chaim would be back at 3 p.m. the same afternoon. That would give us a comfortable margin within the curfew. On his return, Chaim would hide behind one of the mounds in Freedom Park and watch for us to become visible in the lookout building. He would give a signal to tell us he was there, in no danger and ready. We would give a signal to acknowledge we'd seen him. Our next and final wave would indicate the conditions were right for him to come back over.

The fateful moment arrived. It was bitterly cold, but at 11 a.m. Chaim took off his warmer, bulkier clothes and put them in a knapsack. Srulek and I both noticed he was wearing a crucifix. I had seen it before, although judging by his reaction I am not sure Srulek had. Chaim looked at us, winked, smiled and said, 'Why be Yoisel if you can't wear a crucifix?'

Srulek and I went up to the second floor as Chaim moved to crouch behind the wall and wait for the signals. When I gave the last one, with no hesitation Chaim walked straight to the wire and threw the knapsack over it before starting to negotiate his way through the barbs and snags. We hadn't talked beforehand about the throwing thing, but obviously Chaim had given it some thought or was improvising. That was encouraging. He was obviously feeling confident. When he emerged on the other side of the wire – it took a count of just over fifteen seconds – Chaim picked up the bag then ran straight away into one of the alleyways, where I assume he took out the warmer clothes and put them back on. The knapsack would then become his receptacle for collecting, concealing and carrying the contraband. From start to finish, Chaim was through and out of sight in less than a minute. Perfect.

As the day wore on, Srulek and I stayed together, on tenterhooks, barely able to speak as we tried to avoid imagining the huge number of things that could be going wrong for Chaim. Maybe he had been spotted and betrayed by someone from our old neighbourhood who knew he was Jewish and shouldn't have been outside the ghetto. Or, since he had no money to buy anything, he had been caught stealing, and, with no means to prove who he was, the cock-'n'-bull story he had prepared for just such an eventuality might have fallen apart. He was dead already, or he'd been captured and tortured, revealing who his co-conspirators were. We'd be next and just hoped they spared the rest of our families.

We stayed away from those parts of the ghetto where we were most likely to bump into any of our relatives or people who knew us. We didn't want to be interrogated about Chaim's whereabouts. By 2.50 p.m., we made sure we were back in the building overlooking the wire. It seemed like ages before Chaim's head finally bobbed up from behind the mound, but bob it did. We gave a wave to indicate we had spotted him, and he signalled back to tell us he was waiting for us to let him know when it was safe to make his move.

It worked like a dream. On our signal, Chaim came running out from behind the mound, straight up to the wire with the knapsack in one hand and a bundle of clothes in the other. He threw both over, danced daintily through the wire, picked up the knapsack and the bundle of clothes then headed for the building where we fell into each other's arms cheering and screaming.

What couldn't be disguised or supressed was the way we were all shaking with a mixture of fear and relief. I asked Chaim what happened on his odyssey.

'We know thieving from shops before the war was not easy at the best of times,' he said. 'Now it's ten times worse. To start with, there is not much in the shops, or nothing like what you used to see, and it was the same whether the shops were Polish-owned or German-owned, although maybe the German places had a bit more gear in them. Anyway, in all the places selling food, it looked like they were being super vigilant, especially if any kids were milling about. Without someone else there to keep watch, stealing anything is just too dangerous. We were right to conclude this is a two-man job.'

Chaim then tipped out the contents of the knapsack. It was a small, dismal haul. He had brought back a child's shoe, a bit worn but not too bad. One of our parents or maybe Chaim's older sister would be able to trade it for something. There was a German newspaper, two ends of a stale loaf of bread and then, the best bit, ten apples that looked past their best but were nevertheless perfectly good to eat, certainly by ghetto standards. We had definitely shown our plan worked.

My first question to Chaim was, 'The apples? How come?'

'They didn't come from a shop. When I realised how hard it was going to be to get anything decent to eat, I decided to go and visit Mrs Jawinski. You know she has an orchard at the back of her house? Well, she collects all the apples that haven't been stolen by local kids or eaten by her family and keeps them in a barrel in her cellar. I just told her my family were very short of money and I was trying to find things to eat. Without a word and no questions asked she took me down to the cellar and gave me the apples. I don't think I can go there again, but anyway tonight and tomorrow both our families will eat well. On apples.'

I had a million questions about why Chaim thought it was safe to go to Mrs Jawinski's, but I thought I'd let it go for now.

The next day, Chaim went out again, coming back with more and better stuff. I made it plain there was no way I was going to go out solo. However, we agreed two trial runs were enough. Time was moving on. We were ready for the main event, the real thing.

That's when Srulek got started. He was determined. Whichever of us two went out, he would be the other one. Srulek suggested I could perform the lookout job. Chaim and he would go. I was stunned. Neither Chaim nor I had anticipated this turn of events. Srulek's previous reticence, his failure to push himself forward for the experimental first run, I thought was a tacit acknowledgement that there were limits to what a boy with a twisted limb and a club foot could do. All that was now blown away. Chaim and I saw it as madness, but we also knew from past experience we would need to handle this situation with great care.

We tried everything. First, we told Srulek he was too young; then we said he looked too Jewish and his Polish was heavily accented. None of this worked, so, of course, in the end we referred to his leg. This was a bad mistake. Srulek had a complete, almost foaming at the mouth, meltdown.

An argument raged, but finally we gave in. We didn't have the heart to insist that a venture of this sort was beyond Srulek's capacity. Srulek would have been completely crushed.

The outcome was I agreed to act as lookout and give the signals. Chaim would go through first and this time rather than heading straight into an alleyway, as he had done twice before, he would take cover behind one of the mounds in Freedom Park. On the next cycle, Srulek would go through and make his way into the alleyways. Once Srulek was out of the wire, Chaim would leave Freedom Park and follow close behind Srulek. When they were both in the alleyways, they could change into warmer clothes and set off towards the city centre.

The moment arrived. I went up to the second-floor obser-vation point. I saw Chaim and Srulek's outer garments go into the knapsack. Once again, the crucifix was there around Chaim's neck, only this time no one remarked on it. Chaim carried the knapsack to the wire and threw it over. So far so good. Chaim went through, picked up the bag and got to the mound in Freedom Park. He ducked behind and signalled he was in position. As the sentry disappeared on his next perambulation, I signalled Srulek to move. He approached the wire and gingerly began to negotiate the coils in the way we had all discussed, practised and seen Chaim do twice. Srulek had even dared to go up close to the wire on Chaim's second excursion just to see how it went from nearer at hand.

Disaster struck. Somehow or other, and I was never able to work out if it had anything at all to do with his club foot and twisted leg or if it was just bad luck, Srulek's trousers on his good leg got caught by the wire. At first, from my perch on the second floor, I could see he did not panic. Srulek calmly tried to disentangle himself. I went down from the second floor and crouched behind a wall. I was a lot closer to Srulek now, but I stayed put, out of sight, hoping Srulek would free himself and come back into the ghetto or carry on. That four-minute margin was ticking away.

Srulek probably imagined they were hours, and as the precious seconds went by, panic finally did set in. Srulek tried what looked like an inelegant ballet move, but this had the effect of dragging the hooks and barbs into his flesh. He let out a terrible scream that I think someone on the moon could probably have heard. I still didn't move. I crouched there will-ing Srulek to free himself.

I heard Chaim shout to Srulek, telling him to calm down and concentrate on slowly removing the hooks, but there was then an even louder scream. This would have been heard on the outer planets of the solar system. I guess more hooks and barbs had gone in or gone deeper. I then saw Chaim make a sudden move, and I lost sight of him.

Next, I realised the guard was coming this way, moving towards the section of wire where Srulek was, for all practical purposes, trussed up and trapped. Judging by the sentry's state of undress, I'd guess he had been taking a dump somewhere along his route or stopped for a piss when he heard the screams. Whatever the explanation, as he moved along he was wrestling with buttons, hauling his greatcoat over his tunic, which was flapping about, exposing his vest. And he was talking to someone who was obviously also outside the wire but close. He was talking to whoever it was in German. I was astonished to realise the person with whom he was having a conversation was Chaim, who had left the shelter of the mound and was walking purposefully towards the soldier laughing and pointing at Srulek. The soldier, in turn, continued towards Srulek while simultaneously beginning to remove his rifle from his shoulder. It was clear how this was going to end. Badly. He was going to shoot Srulek, and I had no idea what the hell Chaim was doing or was planning to do. It looked to me like a determined attempt to get himself killed along with his brother.

The soldier was by now right next to the wire on the city side, still advancing towards Srulek, getting ready to take aim. Chaim was gabbling away to him as he too drew nearer. Srulek's eyes were darting between Chaim and the soldier, utterly bewildered, uncomprehending and deeply terrified. Between

Chaim and the young man in uniform with the rifle I caught a reference to a 'little Jewish rabbit'.

The sentry clearly believed, given his looks and his fluency in the language, Chaim was a young German, like him attracted to the scene by the Jew's screams and now intent on enjoying the sport. Without missing a step, as he got nearer to Srulek he told Chaim he shouldn't really be this near to the wire, but he could understand why he wanted to watch a Jew die.

As the talk continued, Chaim got almost next to the man. Just as the guard was raising his rifle, in a single fluid movement, Chaim swung his knapsack round, reached into it and withdrew a large knife, which he immediately plunged deep into the exposed vest covering the soft fleshy area of the sentry's lower abdomen. It was done in a second. The man let out a huge roar, his face instantly transformed into a look broadcasting uncomprehending horror. He dropped his rifle and fell to the ground clutching his stomach. But he was not dead. Death arrived soon afterwards. Chaim jumped on the prone man then used the knife again. This time he tore open the guy's jugular. Afterwards, I remember thinking, 'How did Chaim have the presence of mind to do that?' And, 'I didn't even know he had a knife in the bag.'

I saw an enormous spurt of blood coming from the neck wound, which instantly acted as a trigger for me to act. I ran out from behind the wall and rushed over to the wire to try to get Srulek free. Chaim had the same idea. From the other side, he went partly in among the tangles to where Srulek was impaled. Between us we got Srulek out of the mess. Removing the metal did not generate the same loud screams as before, because while Chaim did the crude field surgery, I held my hand over Srulek's mouth. He bucked and writhed, but no noise escaped. Srulek was obviously distressed and in agony, but he hadn't passed out. He was holding it together. Srulek and I stood on the ghetto side of the wire looking at Chaim, still in the midst of it, edging backwards covered in, actually drenched in, blood and now outside the ghetto again. The sentry's face was hardly more than a metre or so away. It seemed to be whitening fast as more and more blood pulsed out of him, though at a less fierce, eruptive rate. If the sentry wasn't already gone, he was fading fast and incapable of any coherent speech or movement.

For a moment, we were stock-still, rooted to the spot. The enormity of what we had just done was starting to sink in. Chaim spoke first: 'We better get away from here as fast as we can. If the Germans find out who did this, not only will they kill us, probably very painfully and slowly, they will also kill our families and likely as not our neighbours as well, just for the hell of it. We owe it to them all and to ourselves to disappear. Let's go. Now!'

'Now' was more shouted than spoken.

After the German Army had arrived in Lodz, we'd all witnessed awful things on the streets, but rarely had we been this close to them, and never had any of us been the instigators or active participants. Even if the guard probably was a Nazi, seeing someone die so quickly and by our own hand, or at any rate Chaim's hand, was sending us into deep shock. With so much blood everywhere, and with Chaim still standing in among the wire, looking like an apprentice vampire, Srulek and I at least were petrified by the uncertainty of what lay immediately ahead.

Straight off, no conferring, we both said a raging 'no'.

Truthfully, we were just too cowardly, too afraid. How would the Holy Trinity hold up out there, in German-occupied Poland? What the hell would we do? How would we survive?

No papers, no money. No one would help us. We would last a day, maybe not even that.

We tried to convince Chaim to come back inside. As far as we could tell, there were no witnesses. If we got out of there straight away, back into the welcoming familiarity of the ghetto, we would all be OK. Chaim tried to argue with us but quickly realised we were not going to change our minds. There was a dead guard at our feet. That wasn't going to change. Staying next to the wire wasn't helping. We could be spotted at any moment by someone on either side of the fence. We pleaded with Chaim to come back.

Chaim just shook his head, finally saying, 'If you are not going to come out right now, go back in as fast as you can and do not tell anyone at all about this. Nobody at all. No exceptions. I will find somewhere safe and somehow get you out of there.

With a promise that the Holy Trinity wouldn't be beaten, he completed his reversal out of the wire, took Srulek's clothes out of the bag and threw them over to us before hightailing it into an alleyway across the street. It would be almost fifty years before I saw Chaim again. And it wouldn't be anywhere near Poland.

The Holy Trinity was never beaten, but it dissolved on the barbed wire that day. In the years that followed, Srulek and I never discussed what had happened. Not even once.

I stayed in the Lodz ghetto until March 1944, working in a factory making shoes. One day, my dad received a notice telling him he must go to a work camp outside the ghetto. I established this was genuine and that he was not simply being sent to the extermination camp of Chelmno or to Auschwitz about which, by then, we all knew the score. The problem was my dad was now extremely weak. Without anyone to look after and out for him, I didn't think he would even survive the journey, never mind last long when he got to the work camp. I went to the Ghetto Administration and persuaded them to let me take Dad's place. They agreed. I was out.

After the war, I learned Dad died four months later in the ghetto hospital on 18 July 1944. He was forty-one. My mum, Rutka and Yehuda, were with him at the time. That was some comfort but not much. The day Dad died, I was in Buchenwald, working in a factory that made gears for Tiger tanks.

Mum, Yehuda and Rutka were deported to Auschwitz a month later, on 20 August 1944. At the selection, Yehuda went to the right, Mum and Rutka to the left. Yehuda lived. They didn't. After the war, when we were finally reunited, Yehuda told me Mum's last words to him were 'do not forget me'.

He never did and neither did I. I still weep when I think of them saying goodbye to each other in the punishing heat of the August sun.

I lived long enough to meet Chaim again, in London, England. I met all of his children too. The same as his Herszman family in Lodz, although Chaim's six were all boys. Oi! It wasn't until we met again that he was able to tell me the most remarkable story of what had happened to him after that fateful day at the wire.

Part Two

Chaim

II

My mum, Chaja-Sura Blumowicz, and dad, Chil Herszman, were born in 1896 and 1895 respectively. Mum was the eldest of the three daughters of Mirla 'Beelzebubska' Blumowicz. Aunt Ruchia was born in 1899 and went on to marry a man called Aron Levinson, and Liba-Sura, Heniek's mum, was the baby, born in 1902, just after her dad had died, the granddad I never knew. The Lewkowicz, Herszman and Levinson wives and mothers were a closely knit triumvirate within the wider Blumowicz matriarchy. Before she got married, Mum was making something approaching a living helping to run Beelzebubska's properties and as a part-time teacher of German, principally working for adults, Jews and Catholics, who had decided that improving their grasp of the language would be interesting or useful. Mainly useful.

By contrast with Mum's more middle-class status, Dad was from an altogether different stratum of society, a manual worker employed making cloth in a factory in Zyrardow, about fifty kilometres southwest of Warsaw, eighty kilometres from Lodz. Zyrardow was close to the village of Mszczonow (pronounced 'Mschonoof'), the long-established ancestral home of the Herszmans.

Beyond that we never really knew a great deal about Dad's side. He had relatives in Warsaw, and he often, very often, made references to a Herszman relative, a recent ancestor who had been a famous rabbi or some other sort of big shot in the Amshinov sect of Chassidic Jews. When he spoke about this religious man, there was generally a wistful, faraway look in his eyes, and a hint of regret. I think, deep down, Dad had always dreamed of becoming a Talmudic scholar, maybe even a rabbi, perhaps both, but he had been cheated somewhere along the line and couldn't quite put his finger on when and where it all went wrong, or why.

Dad didn't go in for all the trappings, clothing, habits and accoutrements of the Chassidim, but he was deeply religious and strictly observant. Or rather he was as deeply religious and strictly observant as he could be given his domestic circumstances, given he had somehow ended up being married to Mum. Perhaps she had once been more observant but gradually she was worn down by circumstances, principal among these being six children and poverty, always poverty.

Which takes us to how Mum and Dad came to be married in the first place, the story Mum shared with anyone and everyone who would listen or was within earshot. It goes without saying that I wasn't around when Mum and Dad first met, but within the family, the story of how it happened was aired and shared not daily . . . well, yes, on a bad day more frequently even than that. The reality was, whatever Mum's intentions, and these were not always altogether clear, the story was not only shared in the intimate, enclosed and otherwise privileged surroundings of chez Herszman. In all too frequently occurring moments of stress, usually linked to there not being enough money to do something or other, for example eat, the thin walls of our flat in the thin-walled wooden building we lived in meant the whole house, the whole street, the whole neighbourhood, perhaps the whole of Lodz and Poland might be favoured with snippets of my parents' prenuptial circumstances. A matchmaker helped them find each other. It couldn't have been done in any other way. First, it was traditional although in decline in and around the cities of twentieth-century Poland. Second, and crucially, they did not live anywhere near each other. And third, even if they had, without the intervention of a matchmaker, it's likely they would never have otherwise met. They were from such different backgrounds, socially and economically, maybe even religiously. These differences, differences which expanded and became magnified with time, added to the alleged mystery or peculiarity of how the matchmaker had put them together.

It preoccupied Mum: 'Why did I do it? Why did I marry him? I had a choice. What was I thinking? What was my mother thinking to allow it? Why didn't I stand up for myself? Lots of my friends refused marriages suggested by matchmakers. Why didn't I? My sisters didn't do so bad. What did I do wrong? The matchmaker must have been bribed, drunk, or bribed and drunk.'

Those were Mum's usual opening lines when she started to bemoan whatever was going wrong for her at any given moment. Everything she didn't like, every unfortunate event, was traceable to the original error of deciding to marry Dad, and the matchmaker had played a singular part in the whole dastardly business. According to Mum, bribery rather than drunkenness was the more likely explanation. Everyone sobers up eventually, whereas money changing hands is forever. She would wonder, again out loud, thereby making it another essentially communal event, who in the wider Herszman family had given the money to the matchmaker? It had to be a

Herszman, a kind soul wanting to put Chil out of his unmarried misery. Mum acknowledged this was a generous act on that unknown person's part even if the consequences for her were manifestly awful and permanent.

That was Mum's charitable view. Sometimes she was given to speculating about alternative, darker scenarios. Could it be it was Chil himself who bribed the matchmaker? If so, it couldn't have been with his own money because he never had any. Could he have extorted someone after discovering their part in a truly terrible deed. The extortion victim had fixed the matchmaker as the payoff, or 'maybe the matchmaker was the person whose terrible deed Chil had discovered and landing me was how the matchmaker got Chil off his back. It was blackmail, not a bribe.'

Dad dismissed all this as fantasy but seemed capable of letting it wash over him. Mum was not to be put off, much less silenced. All this was fixed in her head. As I got a bit older, I began to wonder what effect constantly hearing it had on Dad's self-esteem. It can't have helped and perhaps went some way towards explaining his permanent hangdog air of resignation. Life had dealt him a lousy hand of cards. There was nothing to be done about it. He had to play it as it was. My big brother Nathan assured me this was normal in Jewish families and I shouldn't fret or worry about it.

As Mum got going and turned up the volume, I only ever saw that familiar motion of Dad shrugging his shoulders, maybe as he offered a silent prayer asking God to intervene. I came to think Dad must have recognised and accepted an underlying truth. He hadn't got the life he wanted for himself. Mum hadn't got the life she wanted for herself, so her bellicosity and anger were only mirror images of his own sense of failure. Mum just expressed her feelings more exuberantly and more often.

Nevertheless, as an at least initially dutiful Jewish wife, after the wedding Mum uprooted herself from Lodz and moved to Zyrardow to be with her new husband. Dad may have been a manual worker, but he was a highly skilled manual worker – or at least he always told us he was. I have no idea what he actually did in the factory, but whatever it was his employers must have shared that opinion because they had found him a small terraced cottage to rent near the factory. Although the house was by all accounts tiny, it was theirs alone. No facilities or indoor spaces were shared with anyone else. This was unusual for a factory worker in those times. Dad obviously had happy memories of living in that house in Zyrardow. Whenever he spoke about it, the gloom would lift, even if only momentarily. He smiled. He was in a happy place. Three Herszman children would be born there. Nathan in 1923, sister Chana in 1924 and me in 1926.

In the end, Mum's sojourn in Hicksville lasted only five and a half years. That was about five and a half too many for her taste, but in early 1928 she was saved by another economic downturn in the world of fabrics. There were layoffs and this time Dad was one of them. It became impossible to make ends meet or pay the rent. Going to live in Dad's original home in Mszczonow was never going to happen. Mum had her limits. However, Grandma Blumowicz, Beelzebubska, stepped in to offer the Herszman family rent-free accommodation in one of the houses she owned in Lodz, at 15 Zagajnikowa. To Mum it seemed like a minor miracle, an offer that could not be refused. She was absolutely delighted to be heading back to Lodz, 'going home' and rejoining her family, above all her two sisters.

She was returning to what was, in her eyes, the sophisticated metropolis, the big shiny city.

As Mum would say, 'If Lodz isn't the centre of the universe, it will make a damn fine substitute until the centre of the universe shows up.'

She thanked whoever was responsible for whatever shortcomings of capitalism had rendered her husband unemployed, thus forcing the move back to Lodz and civilisation: 'A blessing in disguise. Something finally went right for me.'

In Lodz, another three Herszman children were born. Srulek in 1928, Czypa in 1932 and finally Golda in 1937. We siblings never understood Mum to regret giving birth to any of us, or so many of us, but her musings about Dad's inadequacies, her frequent reflections on her miserable life, did little to create a sense of domestic peace and tranquillity.

Dad was less than thrilled about the move from Zyrardow to Lodz, but he accepted needs must where the devil drives or, as in this case, where Beelzebubska beckons. When we got to Lodz, Dad had to earn a living, but the factories in Lodz had been hit by the same recession that had caused the layoffs in Zyrardow. No one was hiring. He ended up becoming even more dependent on the Blumowiczs. They took him into the family recycling business. He was given a space and a storage shed in the huge yard behind 15 Zagajnikowa to operate as a rag-and-bone man. Dirty, unskilled work. In a hierarchy of occupations or professions, it was not exactly the lowest of the low, but it wasn't far off. Later, in occasional depths of self-pity, when his customary stoicism momentarily deserted him, Dad acknowledged this was not the sort of career development path he had sketched out for himself. Things were made worse for him because he felt guilty about not always feeling unqualified and complete gratitude for the help offered him by Beelzebubska and other members of the Blumowicz clan. There were no adult Herszmans nearby with whom he could confide, confess or share these less than wholly admirable thoughts, but once or twice he let them slip to me and to Nathan. Dad was marooned among Blumowiczs, but he would soldier on because that is what a good Jew does. Fate could have been kinder. But it hadn't been. What can you do? Kismet.

The fact that each family in the Blumowicz clan had a stake in the recycling business did sometimes lead to tensions. There were often fights, not normally involving fisticuffs, although at times things could get very heated. While travelling around the city, one relative who specialised in, say, textiles, might pick up and bring back an abandoned piece of metal, which would be bartered with the relative who did metals. Trying to establish a fair rate of exchange between metals and textiles or between any disparate classes of materials was when the trouble usually started.

Dad's recycling speciality was paper and cardboard. When he was going out on the horse and cart to a neighbourhood where it was unlikely I would be seen by anyone I knew, I'd sometimes volunteer or allow myself to be press-ganged into going with him to help see what we could find. For the rest of my life, I could never pass a skip in the street or a rubbish dump without checking it out to determine if there wasn't something of value I could retrieve and put to good use or sell. I would soon discover that learning how to make the most of what might be overlooked by others as garbage would come in handy as an aid to survival.

15 Zagajnikowa Street was large, rackety and highly ecumenical. Seven of the twelve flats were rented by very poor

Catholics. They had to be very poor, desperate, to end up there. The other five flats were populated by Jews, these being the three Blumowicz sisters and their families, all of whom, like us, lived there rent free, then there was someone who definitely was not kin, and an elderly reclusive guy who might have been. That was never clear.

There was another young Blumowicz, Nachman, a cousin more than ten years older than me. He didn't live at number 15, but we'd see him around from time-to-time, although I barely remember him because he left Lodz in 1934 to go to Palestine. What was important about this guy was that once he got to Palestine, he wrote to all his relatives in the old country, us, saying we should join him on his kibbutz as soon as we could. No snow! Never! Or at least not so far, and he was getting on just fine with the local Arabs. Already he had mastered the basics of the Arabic language. There were to be many heartfelt regrets nobody took him up on that invitation.

The two largest flats at number 15 were on the ground floor. They were occupied by the Lewkowiczs and the Levinsons. We were upstairs on the first floor. Our flat was a tad smaller, and this did cause a tiny bit of friction between Mum, her sisters and Mirla, because the Herszmans increased to six children whereas the Levinsons and Lewkowiczs never went beyond three. OK, they had lived in number 15 longer than us, so they did have temporal seniority, but my parents thought that ought to count for less than fecundity.

The Catholic Karbowskis were also on the first floor. They were going to play a very important part in my life, in ways they would never know and could never have imagined. Their flat and ours shared a landing, being no more than a few metres apart. The doors were always open. Mum was very close to her sisters, but relationships with sisters can be complicated and they were downstairs, not immediately at hand like the Karbowskis. Mrs Karbowski, Jadwiga, was on the spot. Mum and Mrs K watched out for each other and looked after each other's children as circumstances required. This was a some-what uneven arrangement. The Karbowskis only had two children: Mieczyslaw, known as Mietek, the elder one, and Czeslaw, known as Cesek, the younger, almost exactly the same age and build as me. We became fast friends, sharing a deeply held passion for football and mischief.

I tried to get Cesek into my gang, the Holy Trinity. After all, he had come up with the name and explained its subversive meaning, but the other two vetoed the idea. I didn't make a big deal of it. Cesek often came on manoeuvres with us anyway, and if I wasn't with the Holy Trinity, I would be with Cesek. Things weren't terribly complicated. More than once at Christmas time I had gone carol singing with Cesek in the expectation of receiving hot doughnuts from an appreciative audience. This had provided me with my first detailed intim-ations of what it meant to be a Catholic, as well as my first taste of doughnuts. The songs were strange but easy to learn. More importantly, the doughnuts were delicious, so what did I care?

Lodz in the 1930s was a city of frequently fractious thirds: Poles, Germans and Jews. The German minority was probably not exactly a mathematical third, but they were a sufficiently numerous and substantial group to qualify as a major subset of the total population. The fractiousness was mainly among the adults, but, particularly as the 1930s progressed, older kids could get caught up in the nonsense too. Because of my blond hair and blue eyes I think I might have been spared some of the worst of it. Definitely not all of it, but I didn't get set upon or verbally abused as often as my more Jewish-looking friends and relatives.

Among the Poles, there were innumerable blue-eyed and blond youngsters. Too many to count. Young blue-eyed and blond Germans were similarly commonplace. Yet even among the final element of the urban human jigsaw that was Lodz, my element, the Jews, a child with blond hair and blue eyes, while definitely rarer, would hardly cause the editor of any local newspaper, Jewish or not, to hold the front page. I heard someone say as many as one in ten Jews, men and women, could be blond or of very fair complexion. I have no idea if that is true, but I had definitely seen other Jews in Lodz who looked more Nordic than Mediterranean or Middle Eastern, although I don't recall seeing many who were quite as blond as I was as a young child and well into my teens.

I am pretty sure the genetic wobble that made me blond came down through my mother's side, because Heniek Lewkowicz was also very fair. What did Heniek and I have in common? Cendrowicz blood, Cendrowicz being the maiden name of our shared grandmother, aka Beelzebubska. Dad was not that dark either, and neither were the handful of his relatives whom I recall meeting over the years, so who knows? It was probably the specific mixture of genes that produced such striking blondness in me. Whatever the explanation, I would eventually have every reason to be grateful, although as a kid I didn't always see it that way.

When combined with some of God's other gifts, chief among them my talent for languages, having blond hair and blue eyes was going to help ensure I did not die, at least not during the war.

As Mum told the story, my knack for languages became

44

apparent when I was very young. She would proudly say I could read and write in Polish before I started school, which I think was at the age of six. At home, we always spoke Polish, despite Dad's strong preference for Yiddish. All the Herszman children, like every Jew I knew as a kid, was fluent in Yiddish. But Mum was adamant. At home, it had to be Polish. I also went to an after-school class to learn Hebrew and about the Torah. I was getting on OK with Hebrew, but the war brought my studies to an abrupt and premature end.

However, it was when a Herszman relative who normally lived in France came to stay that Mum said my ability to pick up foreign languages truly shone and was noticed. I think the relative's name was Dinah Herszman. She came to Lodz a couple of times a year to visit Dad and see a friend of hers. Sometimes Dinah stayed several months if the friend had managed to find work for her teaching French to some of the city's better-off citizens and their children. For free, she also instructed any of her relations who were interested, and I got bullied into it by Mum, herself a confident German speaker who thought learning languages was hugely important. Long story short, I was soon declared to be one of the fastest learning, most precocious students of French Dinah had ever taught, anywhere. Ever. This was embarrassing, but, somehow, I managed to live it down.

Knowing a little French would certainly help me a lot later. In fact, I would become a highly proficient French speaker, but right then speaking German mattered a lot more. Mum had taught me well, and in a city with so many Germans there were lots of opportunities to practise. I deployed my talent with the German language usually to avoid trouble on the street with German kids and occasionally adults. This also led me to understand that a talent for subterfuge could be vital in keeping you safe. I realised the benefits of being a chameleon, a shapeshifter. I could switch at will between being a German or a Pole as the need or the whimsy arose. Occasionally, drawing on Yiddish could also be very helpful.

Like my nicknames. Yoisel or Blondie. They were interchangeable. I answered to either or both.

I knew when they called me Yoisel what my co-religionists were really saying was I didn't look like one of them – rather, I looked like 'one of them'. They were right, plus I never wore garments or artefacts that might suggest a connection with Judaism. This was not a deliberate or worked-out strategy on my part, at least not to begin with. The fact remains, I looked like a *goy*. There was nothing I could do about it. My looks had helped me get hold of Catholic doughnuts, a lesson well learned, but in what lay ahead, the Catholic Church and I were to become involved in many different ways, not always happily.

III

I cannot remember exactly when I first realised being a Jew was a life-threatening condition. In pre-war Poland, it often felt like danger was all around us all the time. Yet I remember with complete clarity the moment I began to appreciate being Jewish could have dire, indeed fatal, consequences, not just for Jews but also for the friends of Jews. It started with a game of football.

I was mad about football. As far as I could tell, pretty much every boy in Lodz was similarly inclined. Pole and German, Gentile and Jew. Weather permitting, during school holidays and every weekend, all across the city boys would gather around any available piece of reasonably flat land looking for a game or a kick-about. In my neighbourhood, the preferred venue was a stretch of flagstones that had once been the yard for a long-disappeared factory or large workshop.

The flatness and relative smoothness of the flags were important. This was because none of my footballing fraternity owned or could regularly borrow what you might call an actual, proper ball, which back then meant a leather ball. Way too expensive, but we were never going to let a little thing like destitution stop us playing.

47

Generally, one or more of the players who turned up would have something with them that approximated a ball. Because my dad and uncles were in the recycling business, I was generally able to acquire a sufficient quantity of rags which could be tightly fashioned into a near-perfect sphere. At the end of a match, if the ball hadn't already returned to its constituent parts by virtue of the kicking it had received, the remnants would be disassembled anyway. You might say we recycled the recyclables. Sometimes, when it was available, we would use a little straw at the core of our rag balls. This lightened the ball a little. Either way, our footballs would generally last long enough for a game, and if they didn't, we just stopped when they disintegrated past the point of unplayability.

These rag balls never had quite the aerodynamic properties of the genuine article, which among other things meant our games tended to feature fewer headers. We had more of a ground game, usually 'first to five' or 'first to ten' rather than full-length affairs. Rain was the bugbear. A ball made of cloth, no matter how tightly and expertly packed, soon became unusable if it became wet. That's another reason why the flattest, well-drained flagstones were preferred. Puddles were anathema. We only played on grass if the ground was bone dry and very firm, which seemed to be rarely. If mud started sticking to the ball, it quickly became too heavy, and its shape became even more irregular. Tarmac surfaces were acceptable, and cobblestones were OK, but their irregularity meant they were definitely inferior.

Naturally, there was a real ball at our school, but that was only brought out when we played against other schools or for practices just before a game. In other words, for most of the time the prized item was, according to school mythology, hidden away in a strongbox in a cupboard in the headmaster's room, under lock and key, protected by hexes and spells which were further reinforced by the intimidating knowledge that he knew and was trusted by our parents and all the rabbis between Lodz and Jerusalem. That ball might as well have been sitting alongside the Crown Jewels in the Tower of London.

It had often occurred to me that the fact the school had a football which was almost certainly made of pigskin meant somewhere along the line the rabbinical authorities must have said it was OK to touch, kick or head the porcine epidermis. As long as we avoided consuming anything it had once encased, we were in the clear.

There were also proper footballs nearby, several of them, dozens, who knew? The problem was they were up the road at the largest Catholic Church in the vicinity. The church's footballs were used exclusively by their youth groups. These consisted principally of a large pool of altar boys, many of whom, according to Cesek, only volunteered for religious duties to get to play with a real football. That seemed logical to me.

Many times, the Holy Trinity discussed where, exactly, the balls were likely to be kept. We even sometimes managed to talk about those balls without smirking or giggling. Sometimes. We were coveting our neighbour's goods, big time. Where were the balls stored between games? Where was the local Catholic Church's equivalent of the headmaster's room? Cesek tried to find out for us, but he came back with conflicting reports. In the end, though, we concluded that even assuming we found out where the footballs were kept, and even if we could figure out a way of getting to them and succeeded in acquiring one or more, we would then be in possession of such a conspicuously costly and rare object we would never be able to use it in public. For one thing, there was the matter of the large, white, witty little halo painted on every ball to empha-sise its sanctified status. We doubted we would be able to remove the markings without leaving a tell-tale scratchy, blanched, holy trace.

Nope. As soon as word got out that the Holy Trinity had a real, leather football, everyone in a two-mile radius would know about it, likely as not within the hour. Assuming some bigger kids didn't then immediately come and take it from us, with or without actual violence against our persons, if the Church reported the theft to the police our newly acquired notoriety would ensure we would quickly be identified as the likely felons and apprehended. The police in Lodz were not famously sympathetic to the Jews, and if they were given any reason to suspect Jewish involvement in a crime against a Catholic institution, they could be relied upon to put in a little extra effort. Even so, I was probably more worried about my mum and dad and the rabbi. Doubtless the headmaster would also find out and would have something to say about it. Stealing? Bad. Stealing from a Catholic Church, or a sporting adjunct of same! Unforgivable. The *goyim* didn't need excuses to give our community a hard time. Gifting them one like this was an absolute no-no.

In the end, with great regret, and showing a degree of wisdom and self-restraint uncommon among persons of our age, we agreed there was little point risking getting caught trying to steal something we couldn't actually use and probably couldn't even talk about. Chutzpah of the order of magnitude we had in mind had no meaning or purpose if it had to be kept hidden. That was an end to it. The 'great football theft of Lodz' never got off the ground. However, Catholic footballs and I were not yet finished with each other. Not by a long chalk.

When we were at the flagstones waiting for enough players to turn up to get a game going, the players tended to congregate in groups reflecting their religious or linguistic affiliation, but the key word there is 'tended'. It was definitely not true of all of them. In a mixed neighbourhood like ours, particularly among footballers, there were lots of friendships and relationships that reached across the divides that seemed to preoccupy so many adults. The war would change that, but it was still some way off.

In those pre-war days, on the playing field, among ten to fourteen year olds, the only thing that mattered was how well you could dribble a ball, or a proxy for a ball. You were judged by the ease with which you could take it from an opponent who was moving towards your goal or, in trying to build an attack, by how accurately and consistently you could pass it to someone on your own side. Perhaps above all else you were judged on the grace and frequency with which you might put the ball between the pile of clothes on the ground which normally represented the opposing team's goalposts. These were the important things in life. Politics? Religion? Who needs 'em?

However, even at the age of eleven you would have had to have been unbelievably thick if you hadn't cottoned on to the fact that in Poland in the 1930s there were a lot of bad things going on. It was a place where imperfectly understood tensions could have the direst of consequences, even as you tried to play a game of football. And if anyone in our circle didn't know that, they were about to find out.

Sunday, 20 June 1937. The summer holidays had just started. We were all feeling great about the prospect of no school for ages. A motley collection of kids was milling about near the local flagstone pitch. By late afternoon, just over twenty-two boys had assembled. Not everyone was going to get a game, but a match was in the offing. Cesek Karbowski and his big brother Mietek were there, as were both my brothers.

As I recall, and I would relive the events of this day many times, there were roughly five Germans, about eight Jews and around a dozen Poles. I remember the number of Poles because a new kid who hadn't yet quite got into the shared rebel spirit of our footballing endeavours pointed out that the Poles were the only group who could form a religiously, ethnically and linguistically homogenous team. Who cared about homogeneity of that kind? We didn't.

Not all of our parents would have objected to this sort of cross-community fraternisation. My mum knew and approved. If Mum was OK with it, Dad would acquiesce. However, I deduced from some of the talk that went on that several other parents might not have been so charitable or relaxed. Best not to take any chances. Losing Heinz, Bogdan or Moishe because he had to go and visit his grandmother in Warsaw or Frankfurt was one thing. Losing him because he had taken a bad knock in the previous day's game was the natural order of things. But we all knew we had to guard against the possibility of losing Heinz, Bogdan or Moishe because their parents had discovered what they considered to be a racial or religious transgression. Keeping schtum or being vague was the best policy. Consequently, there was an unspoken understanding that at one level we were all engaged in a conspiracy which involved keeping as many grown-ups as possible ignorant of the secret lives of the young football players of Lodz.

When the two teams lined up that day, as with every other day, they each had to be given names. It could be Poland versus the Rest of the World. Germany against America. Today we resorted to another frequently used and irreverent descriptor. Today we decided to play Palestine versus Rome. There were Germans and Poles on both sides, and almost as many Catholics played for Palestine as there were Jews playing for Rome.

Our pitch was close by an open expanse of green space – not really a park, more a neglected field that was making a determined effort to go wild. A rarely used path ran across the field and indeed went straight across the pitch. When a game was on, most people would politely leave the path's straight line to take a marginally longer route around the edge, thereby allowing the boys to continue their mock and actual sporting heroics uninterrupted. Having any kind of audience, however fleetingly, never failed to spur one or other of the players to ever more extravagant athleticism. Perhaps they imagined that the apparently casual onlookers were in truth undercover scouts on a sly mission for Poland's youth team or one of the big clubs. Sporting glory and fame, permanent access to a proper ball, were within touching distance.

As the game progressed on this particular day, I became aware of a group coming along the path, heading towards us. It looked like there were about ten of them. It was soon obvious as they swaggered, listed and swerved about, singing and swearing loudly, that most, maybe all of them, were off their heads, probably with alcohol.

Two elderly ladies had just passed us by and were now, with their backs to us, walking along the path in the direction of the yobs. Three young men, one of whom was obviously the leader of the pack, peeled away and made for the women. He knocked the shopping bags out of their hands, and he and his mates, with exaggerated bows and faux courtly gestures, invited the women to dance. When the women protested and made clear they weren't interested, preferring to carry on with their journey, they were greeted with more gestures, this time obscene. The air was filled with raucous, disrespectful laughter as the idiots marvelled at their own wit.

When the jerks abandoned their attempt at dancing with the ladies, they continued lurching forward. Towards us. Nathan shouted at everyone to carry on the game and try not to pay them any attention. I guess we all hoped they would either leave us alone or just disrupt the game momentarily as they decided little kids offered them no real fun. This was no big deal.

Things like this had happened several times before, although generally there weren't this many potential aggressors. Just the odd hooligan or two. In a couple of minutes, it would all be over. The world would keep on spinning. Play would resume.

It was not to be. As the group got closer, it became obvious they had absolutely no intention of politely or quietly walking on the sidelines. They weren't going to walk around it at all. The leader soon identified himself as Adolf. It had to be Adolf. His face was familiar. I'd seen him in the neighbourhood before. Later, we discovered his surname was Kazimierczak. He was wearing a leather apron replete with a collection of slots, flaps and pockets. It looked like Adolf was either a carpenter or was working in a carpenter's shop or something similar. Quite why he was wearing his work clothes on a Sunday I'll never know. Maybe he'd had to go into work that morning, meeting up with his pals afterwards for a drink – a great many drinks.

Adolf stood in the middle of the pitch, hands on hips, glaring at us as he announced the game must end. Straight away. It very quickly became apparent what was driving him mad was the sight of youngsters who were obviously Jews playing football with boys who looked like they might just have fallen from the ceiling of the Sistine Chapel. The spectacle of religious harmony being rehearsed before his vodka-inflamed eyes had to end. If he had known some of the seemingly non-Jewish boys were not Poles but ethnic Germans, it might have brought on a cardiac arrest. No such luck.

'It's a fucking disgrace. What the fuck are you Catholic boys doing playing football, or doing anything, with these filthy Yids? Get off to confession and beg the priest to forgive you.'

At first, the boys tried to ignore the stream of invective coming their way, not just from Adolf but also from the rest of the gang who were joining in with similar profanities while they scrambled about intent on catching some of the players to give them a kicking. They didn't succeed.

In their inebriated state, it was not too difficult to avoid their grasping hands, and this only made them angrier. Even so, many of the footballers simply fled, abandoning the match completely to make their way to the safety of their homes. Others removed themselves a comfortable distance so they could watch the drama unfurl. Unfurl it did.

There was a group which included me, Srulek, Nathan, the Karbowski boys and a couple of others. We did not exactly stand our ground, but we knew we couldn't be caught by these pissheads, so maybe we could have a few laughs at their expense. And there was the little matter of the ball. The louts had not been able to get hold of anyone, so they had decided to grab the ball, which was in a sort of no-man's-land. Mietek advanced a little and tried to kick the ball out of their grasp. It didn't go quite far enough. He went to kick it further away. Later, Mietek insisted he mishit it, and if it weren't for the twinkle in his eye when he said it, I might have believed him. Either way, from a short distance, Mietek sent our ball crashing into Adolf's nether regions. Adolf fell to the ground grasping himself as he screamed in pain.

As Adolf writhed in agony uttering a string of terrible threats and profanities, Mietek made a move towards him, intent on retrieving the ball, but a couple of Adolf's cronies came rushing towards him, so he retreated. They picked up the ball and began ripping it apart, laughing demonically as they did. It was all becoming a tad insane.

What was left of our cloth ball was delivered into Adolf's possession. As he struggled to his feet, he held the remnants aloft and laughed at what he called our 'raggedy piece of shit'.

Then from underneath his apron he pulled out a large chisel and stuck it in the ball. Using it as a lever and knife, he began to take apart the last bits. All that was left were strips of mangled cloth on the ground mingled with some of the straw that had been at its core.

At that point, it was clear to everyone there would be no more football that day. The game was wrecked. Its spirit was wrecked. Now the ball was wrecked. Beyond reach and beyond repair.

Nathan, Cesek, Little Srulek and I were stood a little way back and watched closely as Mietek squared up to Adolf. This was more about defiance than preparing to fight. Mietek didn't get too close, but he soon let us know he was within breath-smelling distance: 'Christ Almighty, you stink like a distillery.'

That did little to improve Adolf's mood or demeanour. Fourteen-year-old Mietek was several inches shorter than Adolf and, again as we later learned, three years younger. I suppose Mietek calculated his greater agility and the fact that he was not drunk meant he would be able to stay out of the clutches of the inebriated half-wit. There was still no sign of Mietek wanting to take on Adolf, but, equally, despite our urging Mietek to walk away, it was obvious Mietek was livid at this outrageous bullying and destruction, not to mention the abominable bigotry. Mietek had the bit between his teeth. He could not be persuaded to vacate the danger zone.

'Call yourself a Christian? Call yourself a Catholic? You're no bloody Christian of any type I know. You're as bad as Hitler and his goons. Piss off back to the hellhole you came from and leave us alone. It's not me who should be going to confession, it's you.'

Adolf took a swing at Mietek, who ducked. Adolf lost his balance and, with a sound of tearing cloth, fell over face first while somehow the apron flopped over his head and torso. For a brief moment, all anyone could see was a pair of legs flailing about with an arm brandishing a chisel.

Everybody laughed, including Adolf's friends. Adolf picked himself up with hatred burning even more fiercely in his eyes. At this point, Mietek was off like a shot, sensing that the peril was far too close and large for comfort. That chisel had to be avoided at all costs. We all heaved a sigh of relief as we followed

Mietek departing the scene of Adolf's humiliation and our ruined game.

The remaining footballers scattered, and the drunks carried on, dancing and jigging in the middle of the pitch like the imbeciles they were, revelling in their easy victory. But as the footballers were vanishing in all directions, Adolf called out to Mietek and warned him he would pay for spoiling his clothes and trying to make him look a fool. His parting words were, 'I know who you are and where you live. You even live with fucking Jews. We'll meet again soon.'

As we made our way back to Zagajnikowa, we paid no attention to Adolf's threats. It was the booze talking. I suppose we assumed that when he and his mates sobered up, we would hear no more about it. On that we were completely wrong.

Calamity arrived two days later. Mietek was sent on an errand to the shops by his mum. It was 9.30 in the morning. Adolf was waiting outside on the street. He was alone and focused. Calculating. He was too ignorant to be familiar with the phrase about revenge being a dish best served cold, but that's what this was about. No doubt about it. Others who were on the street at the time later reported that as soon as Mietek stepped out of the house, Adolf abandoned his slouch against the wall of one of the houses on the other side of the street, springing to life and shouting at Mietek about hanging around with 'filthy Jews'. I was upstairs and heard the commotion so decided to go down and see what was going on. For that reason, I didn't see the blow being struck, but nearing the front door I heard the scream.

As I stepped out on to the pavement, I saw Mietek lying on the floor. Blood was gushing out of his neck or chest. It was hard to tell which. Even as I stood and stared in frozen, horrified disbelief, the force of the spurting stream began visibly to diminish. I had never seen a dead body before, but seconds later I knew I was looking at something that would shortly be one, if it wasn't already. And he was my friend. My footballing friend and neighbour, my best friend's big brother. I didn't know it at the time, but in a few years I was destined to become involved in a similar scene, although it would be me wielding the instrument of death, causing someone's life to drain away.

Mietek was soon quite still. A pool of thick red liquid was gathering beneath and around him. A woman from the neighbourhood who had been passing by was screaming, pointing and crying: 'The boy did nothing. He just came out of the house and that man stepped up and stabbed him. Oh Jesus, bless us and save us.'

She was directing our attention down the road to where I saw two men in soldiers' uniforms holding someone on the floor. It transpired the soldiers had been driving by on a motorbike and they too had seen the whole thing, whereupon they had pulled over and gone after the attacker.

As I saw the soldiers dragging someone back towards us and I began to understand what had happened, tears of rage and fear welled up in my eyes. It was Adolf. I immediately realised what had just happened. I remembered Adolf's parting words. He had not been joking or making idle threats. He had killed Mietek. It was premeditated murder, at least it was as far as I was concerned. Eventually, the Polish courts would take a different view.

Without thinking, I ran at Adolf screaming every obscenity my young ears had absorbed and committed to memory. When

I reached him, I kicked and punched as much as I could, until someone grabbed me from behind and pulled me away.

Where moments ago there was a jinking-passing-body-swerving-laughing-joking-football star and buddy, there was now an inert and bloody mess. It's a wonder Adolf was not dragged off and lynched. If it hadn't been for the soldiers holding him, now defending him, perhaps he would have been, and there is no doubt at all it would have been an inter-communal lynching. Everyone on the street was gathering, shocked, speechless with rage. Jew and Christian.

There had been fights and violence before. That was nothing new. But this? I had never seen anything like this. Something foul, evil and completely alien had found its way into our lives.

One of the ladies who lived across the street came out with a bucket of water. Maybe she thought Mietek had merely been knocked unconscious. She shouted his name and threw the water over him. Obviously, it had no effect, other than to spread a diluted pool of blood across the pavement and further into the street.

Then Mietek's mum arrived. As she came through the door of the house, it was obvious from the puzzled look on her face that she had no idea what had happened or what all the fuss was about. Close behind her were Cesek and my mum. The wailing and grief that then overtook and overwhelmed Mrs Karbowski and my mum ripped at my heart. Parents should never have to bury their children, and they should most certainly never have to gaze upon their bloodied, recently murdered, lifeless bodies lying on the pavement on the street where they live.

The lady with the bucket of water had obviously still not cottoned on to what had happened. She reappeared with another bucket and started to approach Mietek intent on throwing its contents over him once more. We all started to shout at her to stay away with the water. We didn't need water; we needed a miracle.

The woman with the water added to the sense of surreal chaos. As the truth about what had happened dawned on her, she put the bucket put down and went back indoors, returning with rosary beads in hand. She kneeled on the pavement, made the sign of the cross and started to pray for Mietek's soul, and for Jesus to bring comfort and consolation to his distraught family.

Before the day was out, the incident was being blamed on the Jews. The Jewish boys had provoked Adolf, a fine Catholic patriot, and Mietek had had the misfortune to get in the middle of it. Adolf was, of course, not trying to kill or injure anyone. He was provoked by the anti-Catholic sentiments being expressed by the Yids who lived in the house that was owned by a Yid, these killers of Christ. Adolf momentarily lost it and waved his carpenter's chisel in defence of Jesus, the Pope and all the saints in heaven. It was an accident. A tragic accident that would never have happened if the bloody Jews hadn't got involved.

If the two Polish soldiers had not been passing by and witnessed the whole thing, I am sure someone would have stepped forward and swore that Mietek had run on to the chisel because he wasn't looking where he was going or, worse, that I had done it, or if not me, some other hapless Jew who had been walking by or in the neighbourhood at the time. Any Jew would do.

The Lodz newspapers gave various accounts of the incident, but none of them reported the whole truth. To paint Catholic

Mietek's death as the result of, or being in any way linked to anti-Semitism, would have been too strong a dose of honesty. Not even the Jewish media made a big deal of it. As far as I was concerned, nothing that was said in the newspapers mattered. I knew what my eyes had seen on the football field and on the pavement. I had heard what the soldiers had said as Adolf was being dragged back to the scene of his crime. I had heard the first-hand account of the lady who had seen the whole thing. Mietek was dead. Nothing was going to bring him back. A raging, anti-Semitic bigot had killed him.

The Herszman and the Lewkowicz families, en masse, left town for four days until matters had settled down and more of the facts about what had actually happened that day gradually filtered through the neighbourhood and wider city.

We went to stay in the weekend and summer house of Szjandla Lewkowicz, Heniek and Yehuda's grandmother. The Russian word for such an abode was '*dacha*', and it was still in common usage in Poland. Her *dacha* was about fifteen kilometres outside Lodz, deep in some woods with lots of pine trees and lakes. I had been there before, but Heniek and Yehuda were regular visitors and knew the lie of the land quite well. The memory of those few days in that house became deeply imprinted in my memory. Every rustle of leaves in the night potentially heralded a bloodthirsty mob, or their agents, by which I mean the Polish police. They never came, but the belief that they might spoke volumes about how little faith many Jews by then had in the Polish state and some of its institutions.

Adolf eventually appeared in court and was found guilty of unintentional killing. In other jurisdictions, this is known as manslaughter. Somehow the court accepted he had not meant to kill Mietek. Hard to credit. When someone pulls out a chisel and waves it in front of someone's chest, indeed sticks it into them, how could their actions be viewed in such a generous light? Adolf went to jail for a paltry three years. Mietek was a Catholic not a Jew, but he lived among Jews and was a friend of Jews. The Jews of Lodz knew if a Catholic had been killed by a Jew in similar circumstances, things would have turned out very differently.

IV

As a kid, aside from the usual day-to-day family stuff, my life seemed to revolve around football, school and avoiding trouble on the streets. Mietek's death served as a reminder of where things could end up.

I can honestly say in those days I never initiated or directed any violence, gratuitous or vengeful, towards anyone, not least because, being so small and skinny, I knew I would probably end up at the wrong end of it. Even picking on smaller kids didn't make any sense, if only because they might have a big brother, a dad or an uncle who would come looking for me. Essentially, I was a pacific person by virtue of my strong instinct for self-preservation. Maybe virtue is not the right word there? Non-violent by dint of cowardice is probably closer to the mark.

I realised early on that while trouble could express itself in all kinds of shapes, sizes and forms, at root there were really only three distinct types. The first, the one with which I tended to be most familiar, was the kind you brought on yourself. For example, if Mrs Jawinski's son caught me stealing from his mother's orchard, as had happened a few times, I would get thumped. I never felt Mrs Jawinski herself had her heart in me being walloped. She just didn't actively object. Whenever I saw her out and about on the street, Mrs Jawinski always smiled or gave me a big wave. Being a cherubic, blue-eyed blond had many upsides. She knew I was a Jew but never showed any sign of caring. Nope, being cherubic seemed to be enough for Mrs Jawinski. Then there were the buses and trams that shuffled around the city. Finding ways to cling on to them from the outside and hitch a ride could result in your backside being reddened by the sharp end of a policeman's boot or bruises acquired following an unplanned collision with terra firma or a lamppost. Nathan was a world champion at this kind of public-transport freeloading.

Anyway, the orchard kind of trouble I could easily avoid by just not going there. This had the miserable consequence of me eating fewer apples, pears and plums, but you can't have everything. Same with buses and trams. We could walk. It just took longer.

Then there were two kinds of trouble over which one had limited or absolutely no control. One you might call bad luck, happenstance or carelessness. Wrong place, wrong time; for example, when on your own straying into an unfamiliar neighbourhood and being trapped by a gang of street hoodlums intent on violence, robbery or both.

The third type of trouble could confront even the most cautious, prudent and alert individuals, even a hermit, like one of those stylites I had read about. Following the death of Marshal Pilsudksi in 1935, anti-Semitism among Poles became more blatant, public and frequent. It didn't seem to matter what was said by the relatively few Catholic leaders and even fewer German community leaders who spoke out against it. It was so much hot air for the Polish and German anti-Semites of Lodz.

Anti-Semitic attitudes and behaviour were by no means uniformly shared by all Germans or by all Poles. There were a great many decent people in both communities. They refused to change their deeply ingrained habits of courteousness, respect, and acceptance of differences.

What was going on next door in Germany, where the guy whose birthday I shared was in charge, seemed to be going from bad to worse to terrifying. The increasing number of Jews coming back to Lodz from Germany was testimony to that. Many had lived and worked there for decades. Some even brought back German wives, Jewish and otherwise. They told stories of Jews constantly being abused and assaulted on the streets, even killed. Jewish businesses were boycotted or destroyed, learned professors removed from universities, work denied them and much more. This all had increasingly loud echoes on the streets of Lodz.

After the Anschluss with Austria in March 1938, and in particular after Kristallnacht in Germany in November 1938, everything moved up a notch. A speech in Berlin led to violence on Piotrkowska, our main street. Germans in Lodz started to strut their stuff a little more boldly. This incensed the Poles almost as much as the Jews. Hitler's remarks about Slavs in general and Poles in particular meant the Poles had no great love for their neighbours. Gratifyingly, most of the German football regulars remained with us right up to the outbreak of the war, although it did not go unnoticed that one or two started to stay away. That was unforgivable. The whole of the rest of the squad were all agreed about that.

The increasingly worrying events in Germany under Hitler's leadership made me hate the fact I shared a birthday with him even more.

In later years, I would look back and smile when I thought about the lengths to which I would go to address something that maybe I should have ignored or regarded as a minor and inconsequential irritant. Yet when you're a kid, the last thing you want, and definitely the last thing I wanted, was to stand out, to be different, at least in a way that allowed others to poke fun at me or make me an object of scorn or pity. It was bad enough that I looked so different from most of my community. The birthday nonsense made it feel worse.

Many of my Jewish friends who knew about the 20 April connection simply could not resist calling me 'Yoisel the Nazi'. 'The Blond of Berlin' and 'Adolf' were also favourites. 'Heil Chaim' had a certain rhythmic quality that went down extremely well with the German kids. They would roar with laughter, even after the hundredth time. In Polish, the cadences were also OK, but it didn't really matter because everyone understood the 'Heil' bit and started falling about, particularly when the insult was accompanied by the stiff-arm Nazi salute.

Obviously, there was nothing I could do to hide, suppress or change the truth about my birthday with people from school, my family or large parts of the neighbourhood. They were already acquainted with this cruel intersection of biological fact and chronological circumstance. I would just have to learn to live with their slings and arrows. I knew it was the combination of the birthday, the looks and the religion that made me a gift for wise guys everywhere, but I was keen not to allow it to expand beyond its present confines.

I did a little maths. There were about three million Jews in Poland. That was more than there then were in New York, so this was the largest concentration of Jews anywhere in the world. Assuming Jewish births were randomly distributed across the 365 days of the year, that meant there must have been more than 8,000 Jews in Poland cursed as I had been cursed. Since Lodz had a population of about 200,000 Jews, that meant there were probably about 550 Jews in my own town who could have formed or joined the 'Society of Polish Jews Who Share Hitler's Birthday'. I wondered what the membership card might look like. A cake with candles and a swastika on one side, the Star of David on the other, the Polish flag superimposed but clearly visible? That would offend just about everybody. Naturally, I liked the idea.

But how come I didn't know or had never even heard of any of these potential members of this recondite brotherhood? Maybe all the other 20 April Jews had emigrated to avoid the shame or embarrassment? Or they had opted for deep, self-deceiving denial. Was there a generous rabbi somewhere who had found something in the holy books which said in extreme circumstances it's permitted to adopt a new date of birth?

Was I the last or only Jew in Poland to think like this? Why wasn't there something like a support group for Jews who had unfortunate birthdays? Maybe there weren't that many days that were damned in the way I felt 20 April was damned.

The brilliant idea I came up with in the end was not wholly original. I was going to tell a lie. I would invent a new story. Credible but false.

To be clear, when I was still in Lodz, I didn't meet many new people in circumstances where my date of birth would naturally crop up in conversation, but there were one or two, so I was able to rehearse my lines and buff them up.

After a little research, I discovered the Polish language's most famous poet – Adam Mickiewicz – was born on 24 December. Christmas Eve. In future, if the subject of my birthday ever came up with people or institutions who didn't already know me, that's the date I was going to give. It never did, but I was ready anyway. Choosing Christmas Day itself seemed too likely to be questioned or queried by someone who might think I was just being smart or sarcastic. A bit like saying 20 April to a Nazi. On the other hand, Christmas Eve was easy enough to remember. Rather comically, my own private joke, it also brought me into some sort of proximity with my namesake, the original and real Yoisel.

I had also observed that Christmas seemed to be of huge importance to the Christian two thirds of the city of Lodz. It seemed to make most of them feel happy and generous, particularly if they had had a drink or three. I even developed stories about how, for example, having a birthday so near Christmas was a misfortune because everybody only gave me one present rather than two. Earlier experiments in untruth had taught me one needed to marshal collateral or supporting minor lies if one's headline lies were to go unchallenged or remain substantially unexamined.

Then there was the little matter of my name. If someone ever took the trouble to construct a listing of unambiguously Jewish names, I'm willing to bet Chaim Herszman would be right up there. Herszman could have been a German name. There were non-Jewish Germans called Hirschmann, so, as spoken, Herszman as a family name did not instantly or reliably tell you anything about the owner's religious beliefs or the condition of his penis, assuming the person had one. However, once you stuck Chaim in front, it was like waving a banner with a twenty-foot menorah in the middle.

Sometimes, as I got a little older, during the school holidays if I wasn't out with the cart helping Dad with his business or playing football, I might try to find casual work with a shop-keeper or a market stallholder, sweeping up or carrying boxes. I'd get paid in small change or with something to eat or take home – maybe a cabbage for dinner. This would be a big prize that would win me many brownie points with Mum and Dad, but scornful looks and digs from my siblings. Nathan and I developed a little friendly rivalry around being a provider of food for the family table, but it was always done in good spirits, with Mum and Dad both seeming pleased at our self-reliance and ingenuity.

With Jewish stallholders, obviously, my name was never going to be a problem, but if they didn't already know me, they would take one look, assume I was a *goy* and tell me to clear off. Frequently, it might be a bit less polite than that, particularly if it was said in Yiddish, which they assumed I couldn't understand.

I might let it go and move on, but if there were slim pickings elsewhere, I might argue back in Yiddish. This would normally evoke one of two responses. They would either just get angry, try to kick me, presumably in disbelief or mortification, or they would go through a process of first looking shocked, then shamefaced or intrigued. Sometimes they would end up giving me some work, by way of an apology, sometimes not. My mum said I had a winning smile.

With Polish or German shopkeepers or stallholders, it tended to be more straightforward. If I spoke to them in their own language, they seemed naturally to assume I was one of them. But if the question of my name did eventually crop up, I soon learned if I said Chaim Herszman matters might instantly, though not always, take an unhelpful turn. My employment could end abruptly and unpaid. This got me thinking. Having made the leap with a false birthday, a false name seemed like the logical next step.

It was clear that I needed a name that was neutral, suggesting nothing that would cause anyone automatically to get antsy one way or another. Obviously, as with the birthday, it wouldn't work with family, at school or where I was already known. There was nothing I could do about that. I was thinking more about the whole other and larger world I knew was heading in my direction, not just the market and street stallholders of Lodz.

I shared my thinking with Cesek. He thought choosing to be born on Christmas Eve was a tad unnecessary, but on the matter of my name, we were at one. Cesek had a material interest, because when I went looking for casual work, he would sometimes be with me. Several jobs were easier to do if there were two pairs of hands. However, if anything went wrong for me, it would almost invariably go wrong for Cesek as well. If we were sacked because there was a Chaim in the house, we'd both end up not getting paid or kicked up the backside, or both, and in Cesek's case often with an extra admonition about associating with Jews.

We decided I would be Cesek's cousin. If questioned, I would say I was visiting Lodz but normally I lived on a farm outside Zakopane, the furthest away and most remote part of Poland we knew anything about. Checking up would proba- bly be a lot of hassle in relation to any of the relatively trivial misdemeanours likely to engage us. Cesek had been down there recently visiting relatives. He told me what he remem- bered about the place. We were both sure I could blag my way around any superficial enquiry about Zakopane and its environs.

This was how Henryk Karbowksi was born, Henryk being the closest approximation to Chaim that I could think of at the time.

Of course, it was unlikely anyone in Lodz would ever bother to ask for a check to be carried out down in Zakopane. There were Karbowskis in Lodz who could be spoken to if anything came up. Cesek's parents. That ought to be good enough, so all we needed to do was square it with them. Cesek and I explained the whole thing to his mum. Mrs Karbowski got it straight away: 'You never know when that might come in handy.'

Mrs Karbowski's prescience was something I would reflect upon more than once.

So now I had a Catholic name, an alias that would soon become a *nom de guerre*. Which brings me back to football. For most football-loving Catholic boys in the eight to thirteen- or fourteen-year-old age range living in our neighbourhood, and that meant most boys, the footballing action was focused on the football pitches on Saturdays. These were close to the church and might have been owned by them. Either way, the church ran several teams. Some of the teams were highly organised, graded by age and ability. They played against other teams from other parts of the city and surrounding area in properly defined competitions and leagues. Team selection for some of the non-competitive games was a bit more haphazard. It depended on who turned up. A bit like our games. However, the point was they always played with real leather balls.

For me and Cesek, the leather balls, flat grass pitches and goals with posts and nets were a major attraction. We were determined to be in a team together. It has to be said that we might have been motivated as much by devilment as we were a love of the beautiful game. Stealing the footballs was off the agenda. Now the challenge was to get a Jew and his best friend on to a football team run by the Catholic Church. Who would ever imagine a Jew would want to play football on a Saturday, let alone play as a Catholic? A member of the Holy Trinity, that's who. A Jew who was frequently mistaken for a *goy*, who loved football to distraction and had tasted Catholic doughnuts.

A pathway soon showed itself to us. According to Cesek, the slightly myopic Father Nawrat, the priest in charge of these things, only seemed to need to have vaguely seen or been aware of you around the church for your participation in a game to go unquestioned, at least in the informal, kick-about matches that he put together. Sometimes he also refereed them, often with strange consequences given his short-sightedness. These were the games Cesek and I agreed were within our reach, at least to begin with. We'd see how it went. Maybe we could progress further. Suck it and see. Actually, the whole thing went remarkably well. For a short while.

The first challenge was how I was going to imprint my face on the priest's memory. We agreed I needed to embrace Catholicism. Becoming an altar boy, an acolyte, seemed the obvious route. We couldn't think of a better way to get close enough to be seen and remembered by the cleric.

I'd had the Christmas carols experience. This had given me an inkling of the strangeness of Catholicism. I had a crucifix and the looks. All I needed to do now was take a few more steps towards Rome and we would have a clear run. The idea of me helping serve a Catholic Mass as an altar boy was completely insane at many different levels, but the more we thought and talked about it, the more determined we became and the more certain we were that we could pull it off. I talked to Nathan. I don't think he really believed we were serious. He laughed out loud but didn't stop us.

Cesek had by then been an altar boy for a couple of years, having first been on some kind of training course. Midweek there was a rota. He often served a morning Mass at 6 a.m. or a bit later. There were normally supposed to be two acolytes helping at these everyday Masses, but if one of them didn't turn up, the other would go it alone. Either way, midweek Masses were ruled out. Organising for me to step in as a last-minute substitute so I could join Cesek on his shift was just too difficult. The risk of exposure was unacceptably high.

High Masses at weekends and on Sundays and Holy Days of Obligation were a bit different. Yes, there was still a rota for the main servers, but Cesek told me there would always be a much larger crew, and the arrangements for getting kitted up and going on were a bit more haphazard, if not chaotic.

There were a small number of Latin responses which all the altar boys had to know. Cesek assured me they weren't hard to learn and repeat. I reminded him I was a gifted linguist. All I had to do was memorise and regurgitate them when everybody else did. As part of my preparations, I snuck in at the back of Mass the following two Sundays to make myself more familiar with the set-up. It didn't seem too complicated, and I loved the smell of incense.

Cesek explained the process of getting up to the altar, for which read, getting noticed by Father Nawrat. It was quite straightforward. On the day, you simply walked into the vestry through a side door in the church and picked up a surplice and a cassock that looked like they would fit then follow the priest up to the altar, where proceedings would begin more or less immediately. For a High Mass, as long as there were enough cassocks and surplices, and as long as the line proceeded to the altar in an orderly manner and everybody could fit on the seats, all was well. There would be no one with a tally stick checking people off.

Timing was everything. To avoid getting drawn into a conversation with any of the other altar boys who would be in the vestry, we would delay entering until a couple of minutes before everything was due to begin. Then we would just go with the flow. Like a dancing girl in the chorus at the Folies Bergère, you could lose yourself in the press, hide in plain sight, although no acrobatic kicks were required here. I just had to move my lips and chant when everybody else did.

We waited until we knew Father Nawrat was going to be saying a High Mass alone. The plan worked brilliantly. Smooth as silk. Cesek and I walked into the vestry laughing and joking, like we owned the place. Cesek said hello to a few boys he knew while shielding me from full view. We grabbed the gowns and went to the back, away from the milling throng. I copied every move Cesek made. The other altar boys who saw me with Cesek just assumed I didn't go to their school but to another one in the area, and the fact that I looked how I looked, was with Cesek, crucifix perhaps rather ostentatiously visible, meant no questions were asked. What did they care? They had no reason to suppose or imagine any sort of perfidy was afoot.

Actually, one of the other altar boys did know me and did know I was a Jew, but he appeared to be completely dumb-struck. We winked at each other. He said nothing, and later we brought him in on the joke. Or we thought we had.

When the responses to the Latin prayers, incantations or whatever they were, came up during the service, I was able to pitch in with the rest of them. Cesek had been a good teacher. I heard the first few syllables and was able to deliver the remainder *con brio*.

And so it was that over a period of several weeks, and in the name of football, I familiarised myself with sufficient Catholic Latin liturgy and rituals, as well as a few common hymns and prayers, to pass muster as a follower of Jesus of the Roman persuasion. In the end, I was, of course, found out. But I had a good run. Over a period of four weeks, I was able to play football with a real leather ball with Cesek by my side. Oh joy. Mission accomplished.

I might have preferred for this phase of my relationship with Rome to come to a conclusion in a different way, but there you go. Unexpectedly, a new priest came to say Mass on one of the days I was acting out the part of an altar boy; Father Nawrat had been taken ill rather suddenly. Before we began our procession to the altar, the new priest spoke to all the boys waiting in line in the vestry and asked them which schools they attended. I hesitated, then one thing led to another, the boy who knew the truth spilled the beans and there was instant uproar. Cesek and I were sent on our way.

There was hell to pay for both of us. We acquired the sort of transient fame Nathan had predicted we would have if we had been caught stealing Catholic footballs. Everyone at my school and Cesek's knew what we had done. Our footballing friends seemed to split evenly between those who thought the escapade was a hoot and those who thought we were mad, bad or both. The adult world, on the other hand, remained absolutely united. They were all furious. At times speechless with rage or disbelief. The two generally went hand in hand.

A procession of angry big hitters – teachers, rabbis and priests – paid visits to Zagajnikowa. They all purported to be deeply shocked, and at least some of them probably were. Much later, long after the fuss had died down, one of the angry visitors, a football lover who held some minor post at our synagogue, did give me a nod and a sly smile. I was greatly encouraged but right then, in the immediate aftermath, the teachers, rabbis and priests who visited our house let loose an avalanche of damning invective.

And that was how I learned two of the great religions of the world were agreed that inter-communal football leads to no good. If they had nothing else in common, here at least there was unanimity. Praise be.

V

The physical fabric of number 15 Zagajnikowa was in a bad way and deteriorating rapidly. The street door-frame was moving steadily sideways, leaving the previously adjoining wall behind. Closing the door required a degree of dexterity to get it to slide into and remain within its now angled architrave. Wind would rattle in through several visible and enlarging gaps. In the winter, we would stuff the holes with rags and paper to keep out the snow and icy blasts. Slamming windows or internal doors too hard made the walls wobble and a number of the floorboards in the hallways, stairs and landings sagged alarmingly. A disgruntled recent ex-tenant, someone who had been paying rent, reported the property to the municipality. He wasn't the first. Local authority officials came to visit and gave Beelzebubska a long list of things that needed to be put right, ranking them by what they considered to be the degree of urgency.

According to Beelzebubska, she didn't have enough money to fix even the first item on the list, and everything else was a pipe dream. The municipal authorities in the end informed everyone the property could no longer be considered safe or habitable. We all had to leave, though the recycling businesses were allowed to carry on. We still had use of the backyard and the storage sheds housed there.

In early 1939, we moved to Baluty, the main Jewish area in Lodz. Correction, the main area where poor Jews lived. We got a place on Wawelska, a few kilometres from Zagajnikowa. Heniek's family and the Karbowskis moved close by. The Holy Trinity continued, and my friendship with Cesek was maintained but not for very much longer.

As the year progressed, talk of war got louder and louder, more and more insistent, scarier and scarier. It was on everyone's lips. Young and old, Jew and Gentile, Pole and German, although in the latter case generally from a somewhat different perspective. Having said that, it became increasingly apparent that not all members of the German minority in Lodz were Nazi sympathisers. Some were positively and openly hostile to them – socialists, communists, deeply religious people or those who just liked things the way they were and most decidedly did not favour the sort of major upheavals and danger which was part and parcel of war.

Barely a day went by without rumours, some called it 'news', of a rich Jewish family getting out to somewhere or other, generally abroad, leaving behind only their servants to look after whatever of value they couldn't take with them or hadn't already shipped. I didn't think we had that many rich Jews in Lodz, but there certainly were some. The Jews left behind, the majority, felt, they were being stranded on a sinking ship as the well-fed rats deserted. Yet, at least as far as my mum was concerned, in our heart of hearts nobody could truly blame anybody for doing what we would all have done in a heartbeat, without giving it a second thought. The impulse to protect one's kith and kin is strong. Those who were getting out, by hook, by crook or by banknote, weren't rats at all, or if they were, they were the kind of rats we all aspired to be. These

Jews were only protecting their loved ones, probably uprooting themselves from everything that was familiar and held dear, maybe impoverishing themselves in the process. But who wouldn't do the same given a quarter of a chance, never mind half of one?

We learned of the pact between Hitler and Stalin, officially known as the Molotov–Ribbentrop Pact, the non-aggression treaty between Germany and the Soviet Union, on 23 August 1939. A few weeks later, Poland would be carved up, again. What's that old line from Karl Marx about history repeating itself, first as tragedy, second as farce? He definitely got that wrong in Poland's case. This was no farce.

The pact sealed Poland's fate. It also sealed the fate not just of the Jews in Poland, but Jews in large parts of Europe. War was inevitable, and only the blindest of blind optimists, or self-deluding idiots, could continue to believe the Germans wouldn't be heading our way soon.

That very same night, the entire Blumowicz family network, blind optimists and self-deluding idiots included, went back to Zagajnikowa to Beelzebubska's place. As the talk got going, by which I really mean as the shouting and arguing got going, about what we should do now the imminent arrival of the Germans was pretty much guaranteed, it was obvious the different branches of the clan had arrived with fairly well worked out positions that could not have materialised just that day.

Before the discussion got fully underway, all the adults said how much they regretted – oh how they regretted – not having acted upon Nachman Blumowicz's invitation to join him on his kibbutz in Palestine back in 1934. But it was no use crying over spilled milk. That was then. This was now. We all needed to focus.

Beelzebubska was an increasingly frail sixty-nine years old. She made it clear she was going nowhere, pleading old age and creeping infirmity. Indeed, exactly one year and one day later she would be dead. But tonight, in full flood she declared, 'I can see why you're all worried. You have yourselves and your children to think about, but the Germans won't be bothered about single old women like me. Anyway, what will happen to my properties if I'm not here? The rest of you must make your own decisions. Have no fear. I'll find someone else to help me collect the rents. Don't concern yourselves about that or delay doing what you think is best for you. When you get established somewhere else, if these old bones let me, I'll come and visit when things settle down.'

From the very beginning, the Levinson branch, volubly led by Uncle Aron, although Aunt Ruchia and their children showed no signs of dissent, assured us the Hitler–Stalin pact did not necessarily mean Germany would invade Poland. Here was a self-deluding idiot speaking. Uncle Aron thought Poland and the Poles were being conned by German propaganda designed to ensure the country's swift submission with minimum or no casualties, at least on their side. Look what happened with Austria and the Sudetenland! Not a shot fired. Sure, we all knew the Nazis had expansionist ambitions, he argued, but 'We'll give them some land. Who cares about Danzig anyway? We've lived with Germans in our midst for hundreds of years, haven't we? We could get used to a few more being around. And sure, the Nazis don't like Jews. Who does like the Jews, besides other Jews? Sometimes even that's not the case. This will pass. It always has before. The Jews will find a way to adapt and survive.'

Uncle Aron also thought that if France and Britain made clear an invasion of Polish territory definitely meant war, the

Germans would see sense. They'd back off and dial it down. This was all high politics and drama to win concessions on territory, which would be resolved through diplomatic channels. The Germans knew they couldn't win a war going against such large and well-equipped western armies. If he, a bookkeeper from Lodz knew that, Hitler must know it as well. 'It's all a big political game of bluff and double bluff,' he said.

'And supposing they did invade? We were all foolish getting so worked up and planning this or plotting that.' Aron reminded everyone of the propaganda put out about Germans during the last world war. 'Most of it turned out to be complete baloney.' Beelzebubska nodded vigorously at that point. 'Lots of Jews fought in the German Army at that time, and most of the German officers and soldiers whom people from Lodz met during the German occupation were perfectly decent and civilised.' We all needed to calm down. That was the burden of his message.

'It's all bullshit' summed up Uncle Aron's views. There spoke the idiot again. Come what may, the Levinsons were staying put. They didn't want to hear about, talk about, much less take part in any 'silly nonsense'.

'We should all hide somewhere? Don't be childish. Fight the Germans? With what? Escape plans? Ridiculous! Where would we go? Who would give us visas? Even the Brits and Americans have refused. Everybody knows that. But let's say visas suddenly started falling from the sky. Who has the money to get to these mythical places? If the Jews of Lodz are rats trapped in a cage, we need to think of ways to make the cage work for us.'

The Lewkowiczs were equally firm, but on a different tack. They were heading for Warsaw. They would walk if necessary; in fact, they were pretty sure that would be the only way to get there, judging by the volumes of people already on the move.

Uncle Moishe was convinced our proud capital would be well defended, and with help from the British and French air forces we would be able to resist long enough for the allies to land troops on the Baltic coast to join with Polish forces in a land war which would have only one outcome. Defeat for the Germans, and quickly.

Of course, Uncle Moishe was not going to Warsaw to volunteer to fight; he just believed it would be safer there, safer than Lodz, which had the misfortune to be that much closer to Germany. If he was wrong and Warsaw did look threatened, there would be more escape options available in the capital, maybe even to foreign countries who would accept refugees without visas if there was a war going on. Uncle Moishe was sure visas wouldn't come into it.

Dad looked more crushed and defeated than I had ever seen him. He said he was glad the Lewkowiczs thought they might be able to get to Warsaw, then, if necessary, out of Poland, but they had more money than the Herszmans, and they did not have very young babies to worry about. On the Herszman side, Golda was still only two and Czypa was a fragile seven. Walking to Warsaw wasn't an option for us. The Herszmans were staying put. We had no choice. Uncle Moishe and Aunt Liba-Sura assured us they would find a way to get us all out, even the Levinsons when they finally realised what fools they had been. I'm not sure who really believed this would ever happen, but we all appeared to appreciate the sentiment.

Everyone, including the Levinsons, then chipped in with suggestions about hideouts in Lodz or the nearby villages. They were all put on a list to be checked out as soon as possible. We discussed building refuges in the woods, tree houses, maybe finding a deserted *dacha*, ideally one owned by a prosperous citizen of Lodz who was known to have already fled abroad. Nothing came of any of this. Everything happened a great deal faster than we thought possible. Uncle Aron had spoken of rats trapped in a cage, but, really, we were rabbits frozen in the headlights, dazzled and paralysed by the crushing momentum of overwhelming and rapidly approaching adversity.

On 26 August, the Lodz City Council at last started to consider what they might do to avoid or minimise any damage to the city or its inhabitants in the event of war breaking out. Suddenly, it all felt intensely, urgently imminent. Mayor Kwapinski appealed for volunteers to go to police stations and sign up to help construct defences of various kinds. It was said that more than 50,000 people responded. Not bad in a city of 600,000, which included a substantial German minority.

Devout Jews and assimilated Jews set to work side by side with their Polish neighbours and the small number of Germans who were brave enough to step up. Nathan, my big sister Chana, Srulek and I went with Dad several times. I saw Heniek and the Lewkowiczs, even the Levinsons were out there doing their bit. It was heroic but also pathetic. We dug ditches, and prepared barricades and gun emplacements, more as an act of defiance, or maybe as a kind of pagan prayer in what turned out to be an unheeded attempt to propitiate the gods of war. This puny effort did not last long. Less than a week. The Polish Army commanders finally asked the City Council and the police to stop the voluntary efforts because the civilians were getting in their way. Instead of going out to dig, the Holy Trinity went out to watch an army preparing for battle. Not an everyday sight.

On 1 September, the German Army made its move across the Polish frontier at several points. Two days later, Britain and

France declared war. The Second World War had started. The rest is history, as they say. However, this particular bit of history, my bit, had yet to be written.

What had previously been a trickle, then a stream, now became a huge flood of refugees, all pouring out of Lodz, with most heading northeast, presumed destination Warsaw. A great many were Jews, and a great many were Poles, but there were also Germans who presumably wanted to get out of the way of any fighting, or perhaps just get out of the way of the Nazis. I imagine they kept quiet about their identities in among the moving masses. I saw some of my German footballing companions in the straggling lines. We waved. Blond to blond. It was all we could do.

On 6 September, as promised, the Lewkowiczs became part of the northeast migration, setting off on foot. Before they left, Heniek came to see me and whispered, 'The Holy Trinity is not over. Temporarily, we have to suspend operations pending the outcome of hostilities. We'll be back for you guys. I'll make sure my parents keep their promise.'

Heniek was right about the Holy Trinity not being over, and he was right about his parents coming back to Lodz, but probably not in exactly the way any of us could then have envisaged, and definitely not as soon.

That day, 6 September, it became clear the Polish authorities in Lodz, including the police, were joining the exodus. I heard various Polish and Jewish adults say how disappointed they were. How they had hoped for something better from their elected leaders and their officials.

But it was absurd to suppose the Nazis would have paid any attention to an intermediary just because they had been elected or because they represented someone who had been elected.

Elections were a thing of the past in the Reich. Why would they care about anybody else's, particularly Poles'? The truth was, if you identified yourself as any kind of Polish leader, the chances are you would simply be shot or hung. The 'Master Race' doctrine held that Jews were the lowest of the low, but Poles were also *untermensch*, with barely a genetic millimetre between the two. Poland would become the only occupied territory where, for a range of offences, including a great many minor ones, a Polish citizen, Jew or Gentile, could be summarily shot. And they were, in very large numbers.

Anyone who could get out before the German Army arrived was right to go, but the fact that the last vestiges of established civic and political authority were disappearing, visibly and tangibly, added to the sense of panic and despair among those left behind. Which included us.

While many Jews from Lodz had, like the Lewkowicz family, decided to head for Warsaw, or alternatively had gone southeast, the largest number headed due east, towards Russia or some other part of the Soviet Union. True, the Hitler–Stalin pact had precipitated the war, but there was something phoney about it. Weren't there millions upon millions of Jews in the Soviet Union? Wasn't half the Soviet Communist Party Jewish? They would be sympathetic and let us in. Surely? And many of these Soviet Jews were by the border with Poland. Probably they had family in Lodz. We were a cosmopolitan lot, us Jews. There was no denying that.

Dad was always somewhat dismissive of the idea of the Soviets being any better for the Jews than the Germans. When he was born, his part of Poland was also part of the Tsarist Russian Empire. He had grown up with stories of pogroms and saw the Bolsheviks merely as a replacement for the Tsar, therefore unlikely to presage any change for the better, at least as far as the Jews were concerned.

Nevertheless, and allowing for that, on 6 September the Soviet Union suddenly mattered to the Herszmans in a way it had never mattered before. That was the day Nathan bade us a tearful goodbye. His destination was Russia. It was a journey invested with great fear, great hope, great love and great desperation.

Dad hadn't declared that we had been working on this plan when the Blumowicz clan met the night the Hitler–Stalin pact was announced. When I asked him why, he simply said it was not directly relevant to the discussion about what the families as a whole were going to do. Nathan going east was only about what one member of the Herszman family was planning. Right up to the moment of departure, Nathan could have changed his mind, or he and Mum could have changed theirs and insisted on cancelling it. If that had happened, we would have looked stupid and indecisive. Nathan's journey was the Herszman back-up. If the Lewkowiczs did not come good on their plan to get us out, Nathan surely would. And, of course, if Nathan did get us out, we would do what the Lewkowiczs had said they would do and offer sanctuary to all our relatives.

Heading for the Soviet Union was the least-worst option. That was the limit of Dad's enthusiasm for the idea, whereas Mum positively endorsed and encouraged it – maybe she had been behind it. Saving one child was better than saving no child. Was that what was in her mind? Nathan would go east alone. I wanted to go with him, but I was overruled. Nathan and both my parents said I had to stay behind and help ensure everyone was safe. This was a responsibility, a command, that would weigh heavily on me.

The plan was for Nathan to join one of the groups of refugees making their way from Lodz towards the Soviet Union. Once he had established himself there, he would find a way to get us all to join him. Quite a responsibility for someone not yet seventeen. The Karbowskis had maps of Poland, and we had all gathered with them to chart a possible route, which Nathan had memorised, but we figured he was probably just going to follow a crowd of people with the same idea, becoming invisible within a larger group. There was likely to be safety in numbers. That was the hope.

Even within that first, fateful week of the war, Jews and Poles who had set off from Lodz on the road to Warsaw and other points on the compass had come back with terrible stories of what they had seen as they tried to escape. The slow progress made by the columns of refugees on the jammed-up main roads and many country lanes meant German fighter planes could and did strafe them at will, irrespective of whether there was any sign of the Polish Army nearby.

Nathan's bravery and determination therefore represented a sliver of hope, a positive, optimistic act dedicated to the preservation of the Herszman family. The actual moment of departure was incredibly emotional for all of us. As Mum and Dad stayed with Srulek and the younger kids, I walked down the street a bit with Nathan, telling everyone I was just going to wave goodbye but secretly hoping he would relent and take me with him. He wouldn't. He just kept reminding me of my responsibilities to 'be the tough guy' and how important it was for me to help Mum and Dad with whatever lay ahead. At the corner of the street, we cried again. We hugged once more. Nathan swore we would meet again soon. He would be back in a matter of weeks, a couple of months at most, like Moses, to lead us to a new and better life. He was depending on me to keep things together until then. Then with one more tearful hug he was gone. I shouted after him, 'Don't worry about us. We'll be fine. Just come back quickly and get us all away from here.' But the truth was I instantly felt the weight of the world on my shoulders. As Nathan disappeared from view a great and scary void instantly opened up in front of me. I had no idea if or when I would ever see him again, how I would fill his giant shoes or honour his injunction to keep all the Herszmans safe and together. It was a while before my tears finally stopped.

Nathan's plan was better than no plan at all, and we knew many other Jews were doing exactly the same thing. They couldn't all be wrong, could they? The Lewkowiczs' offer to get us out once they were safely settled had been noted and was appreciated, but not long after they left, they came back. The Herszman Plan B was now promoted to Herszman Plan A.

The Lewkowiczs had made it to Warsaw, on foot, but the devastation of the city and the general anarchic pandemonium there persuaded them they would be better off back in more familiar Lodz. They walked back. Their description of the congestion and dangers of travelling on major roads was a worry, but the Herszmans convinced themselves there had to be a way through for a resourceful single young man such as Nathan, a knapsack on his back, unencumbered by children or any heavy objects. And maybe the roads to the east weren't so bad. The Soviet Union wouldn't appeal to everyone. If it didn't work out, Nathan could always come back, like the Lewkowiczs had done. Couldn't he? He didn't.

In those first few days of September 1939, we got via the radio Polish, German and, from the BBC, English accounts of what was happening. Somehow listening to the BBC was considered to be important by everyone, because it was thought they were the people least likely to exaggerate or tell outright lies about how the hostilities were progressing. None of us could speak much English, but one of the people who lived in the same building as us could, and he came in to listen and translate for lots of families who huddled around.

Nevertheless, by 8 September it was all over for Lodz. In the previous days, we had heard the boom of guns, seen flashes of cannon fire in the evening. Soon enough, obviously defeated and demoralised Polish soldiers came into town, walking away from the fighting. There was to be no brave last stand or fierce resistance. No *Götterdämmerung*.

German cavalry enter Lodz

No pomp or drama accompanied the arrival of the Wehrmacht. It was all rather anticlimactic. In a rather matter-of-fact, almost casual, prosaic way, soldiers looking like they were out for an afternoon stroll, only in full combat gear, accompanied by horse-drawn trailers carrying supplies, started to appear, looking wary, watching for snipers or any sign of armed resistance. There was neither. Then came cavalry officers on horseback, followed by officers in staff cars speeding through the middle of their ranks. First, the soldiers stayed on the main thoroughfares, then they gradually made their way through the whole of the city. This is what being occupied by the enemy looked like. Along the pavements and sides of the main streets a great many children ran around excitedly, not remotely grasping the significance of what was happening, what they were witnessing. Neither did anyone else at the time, including me. Nonetheless, as a Jewish boy I felt nervous and did not share the excitement of some of my peers.

Red-and-black swastika flags were soon everywhere, including atop the main municipal building and every other major vantage point. The German Army General Staff set up their HQ in the Grand Hotel on Piotrkowska, the main street, soon to be renamed 'Adolf Hitler Strasse'. The Poles were humiliated. The Jews were in quiet dread, in the main staying indoors, although I didn't. I watched, probably more out of ghoulish curiosity than anything else but also testing whether my looks would continue to protect me. They did.

Vast numbers of a newly belligerent and triumphant German civilian population of Lodz started to pour out on to the streets in force, knowing the arrival of their armed protectors meant they would be safe. Wearing their swastika armbands, they were cheering, applauding and embracing their fellow countrymen. Conquering heroes. I spotted one of my regular football pals with Nazi insignia all over him. He at least had the good grace to be embarrassed and explained that while he thought it was all rubbish his parents said he had to do it. He hoped we could still play football together and have a game soon. That never happened.

A handful of idiotic Poles, perhaps hoping to ingratiate themselves with the new bosses, also hailed the arrival of the Wehrmacht as an act of deliverance from Jewish tyranny and their corrupt communist puppets in the government in Warsaw. They were scowled at and sternly rebuked by their fellow countrymen, not for their overt expressions of anti-Semitism, much less for anti-communism, but for their evident lack of patriotism or sense of proportionality. However bad the Jews or communists might be (they didn't want to argue that point), no sane, sensible Pole should be willing to accept Germans as the means of liberation or deliverance from, or improvement on, anything.

The new situation was not good. Within hours of the first German soldiers appearing in Lodz, some of the few Jews out on the street were killed or abused, and Jewish shops and homes were attacked, their goods stolen, premises vandalised, often making them completely unusable. Within days, many Jewish shopkeepers who had previously refused credit to German customers, or who were suspected of sleeping with a German wife, sister or daughter, or who had offended local Germans in some other way, were victims of revenge attacks. On 13 September, Hitler himself paid a visit to his victorious troops in Lodz. That seemed to spark another bout of uber brutality towards the Jews of the city.

A proclamation was issued banning all religious services on the holiest days in the Jewish calendar. Jews were banned from using public transport or from walking in the main streets. There was a rumour that all the schools were to be closed. This caused some initial confusion and consternation among the younger members of the Jewish community. Just how bad could the Germans be if one of the first things they did was ensure there was no more school? The answer was not long in coming, but it was a while before I realised that, at the age of thirteen, my formal education had ended. It evaporated as the jackboots arrived in Lodz. From now on I would have to learn everything on the fly and live by my wits. It brings tears to my eyes. Losing the chance of an education hurt, even if I only fully realised it many years later. They say childhood lasts a lifetime. There was no doubt this was true for me.

The following month, every synagogue in the city was torched, starting with the two largest and most beautiful ones that were renowned across the whole of Poland and far beyond. Our new lords and masters announced Lodz would become 'Litzmannstadt' after a German general who died nearby in a battle during the First World War. All the street names would also be 'Germanised' – Piotrkowska becoming 'Adolf Hitler Strasse' was just the first and most offensive. The Jews of Lodz all ignored the name changes as best they could, a small act of resistance, but what they could not ignore was the larger fact of Germanisation. That whole part of Poland became incorporated into the Reich itself. Polish law no longer applied. German law did. '*Lebensraum*' in action.

On 14 November, a decree was issued requiring all shops in Lodz to put up a sign indicating whether they were owned by Germans, Poles or Jews. Any Jewish-owned shops that had been missed by the mob in their initial burst of anti-Semitic destruction and theft were soon sorted out. A couple of days later, another decree required all Jews to wear a yellow star. Many non-Jewish shopkeepers wouldn't even let a Jew on their premises now. Fewer and fewer Jews by then would go any-where near the major shopping areas anyway. They would be taking their lives in their hands. Not only did they risk being set upon by locals, German soldiers or officials could, without any reason or explanation, drag them off for a week or more and force them to perform arduous, humiliating or pointless tasks, then, if they felt like it, instead of letting their slave go back home, they might just shoot or hang them. The unpre-dictability and randomness of these disappearances were another form of terror, an additional and extremely unsettling aspect of the lives of Jews in Lodz in the early days of the war.

I am not going to turn this story, my story, into a catalogue of Nazi horrors and atrocities directed at the Jews of Lodz. Goodness knows I saw plenty during this period. I also want to avoid giving the impression that it was only the Jews who had a hard time. Huge numbers of Poles were killed or muti-lated by acts of random violence, as were several famous anti-Nazi Germans. Oskar Seidler, leader of the German Socialist Party, was murdered in October 1939. Guido John and Robert Geyer, both factory owners, were killed. Dr Juliusz Bursche, bishop of the Evangelical Augsburg Church, was sent to Sachsenhausen, a concentration camp near Berlin, where he died in 1942. No opposition would be tolerated. Even from other Germans. Nobody was safe.

Astonishingly, at about this time a postcard arrived from Nathan. After a comparatively short interruption caused by the dislocations of war, a form of tranquillity returned, and the postal system resumed operations. On the postcard, Nathan told us he was well and in Radom, on his way to visit Aunt Deborah in Wlodawa. We had no relative called Deborah, and no family of any kind in Wlodawa, but the town was on the

Bug River at what had become the easternmost edge of German occupied Poland, where fascism and communism met and held hands.

Nathan's message was clear. This was where he was going to try to cross the frontier to complete the first part of his mission. The news from Nathan was thrilling and hugely encouraging for the whole Blumowicz family network. Amid the grinding, grim reality of our new daily lives, here was a flash of sunshine and hope. We told the Lewkowiczs and Levinsons what Nathan had in mind, what the Herszmans had plotted. The adults' scepticism about the possibility of its ultimate fulfilment was apparent, but for the rest of us it was a joyous moment. It was good to know Nathan was alive and a long way from Lodz. If this bit of the plan had worked, why not the rest? We all needed to believe it was possible.

The ghetto. X marks the Herszman household

VI

November 1939 brought the news that Lodz was to become the site of the first major ghetto in the new German hegemony. Forming the core of the ghetto, Baluty had a well-deserved reputation as being the least salubrious, most decrepit and dangerous, dark, ill-kept, unhygienic neighbourhood in the whole of the city. As the fences and walls began going up, the ghetto started to take sharper physical shape. We were like the famous frogs sitting in water that was gradually being heated. There was no immediate sense of panic among those of us already there. I was aware of a growing apprehensiveness at being hemmed in, but because the physical barriers which would eventually be the boundaries of our lives did not appear complete and finished overnight, it was more or less business as usual. For now.

Catholic Poles and ethnic Germans living in Baluty started to leave, the Karbowskis among them. On their last day as Baluty residents, Cesek came and found me to give me their new address in Lodz. We held back our tears in as manly a way as thirteen-year-old boys can then bade each other farewell, talking about the first game of football we would have as soon as all this mess had been sorted out. It had to be with a real leather ball. On that we were agreed. Did I think then that I wouldn't see him again? I'm not sure, though seeing Cesek disappear around a street corner felt like a definitive moment. At that point in my life, aside from Nathan, whom I assumed would be back for us soon, I had not really said goodbye to someone, and I felt the loss of my friend immediately. Of course, it was not the last loss I was to feel, but as the first it was particularly painful.

New Jewish residents started to pitch up in Baluty in ever larger numbers, clutching what few possessions they had been able to assemble and carry. Because in those early days most of the new Jews came from other parts of Lodz and the surrounding areas, they knew Baluty by reputation if not from first-hand experience. For those of us already settled in Baluty or coming in from other parts of Lodz, the realisation that there was to be a new and substantial limit to our geography was real and disturbing, but the feelings of those Jews who had been uprooted from further afield were markedly different. Most of them arrived expecting something horrible and were surprised at the extent to which they had underestimated just how bad it would be.

Lodz Ghetto. The sign reads: 'The residential
area of Jews. Do not enter.'

The sights, sounds, smells and overall strangeness of Baluty, its increasingly claustrophobic conditions, could have a particularly acute impact in the case of Jews from better-off backgrounds who suddenly found themselves in what for them was a strange and disgusting environment. This might as well have been another planet. *Schadenfreude* is one of the least noble human emotions, and appropriately enough it belongs to the oppressor's lexicon. Nevertheless, it is singularly apt to describe the highly uncharitable gales of laughter which could break out among the ghetto's hoi polloi as the head of a once comparatively wealthy Jewish family was being publicly berated by his wife or one or more family members for not having got them out of Poland while it was still possible, because now look where they had ended up. Here in Baluty. A litany of names of wider family members and friends who had got out of Poland would then be trotted out, noting their present whereabouts, typically great distances from anywhere the German Army was now or was likely to be. Whereas this poor unfortunate man, the world was informed, was 'the genius who told us the Germans would be reasonable. Don't listen to all the propaganda, he said. This is reasonable? Being in a ghetto? All my clothes are gone, and we don't have a bathroom or a maid. You were just too mean and frightened . . . Now, your brother . . . what a *mensch*. We should have listened to him and did what he did when he did it. He did the right thing. He won't be living in filth in Alexandria. Maybe by now he will even be sitting in the sunshine in Palestine.'

Plainly Aron Levinson had not been the only self-deluding optimistic idiot. As the ghetto's population grew, it became noticeable on the streets, in the shops and elsewhere that many more people seemed to be getting bad tempered or prone to arguing. It doesn't take much to provoke an argument among Jews at the best of times. These were not the best of times. The ghetto police were kept busy, as conciliators and counsellors as much as in enforcing the law, although that began to change as crime in the ghetto started to increase. Anywhere that food was being stored or processed was kept under constant surveillance. Take your eye off something for a second and it would be gone. All wood was valuable. It could be burned to keep warm or to cook food. Buildings not yet allocated a purpose would find that a whole staircase had been removed, and sometimes buildings that were inhabited and in constant use could similarly find doors, floorboards and other bits gone walkabout, taken by people frantic for fuel or for something to trade for food.

Dad was soon allocated a job by the Jewish administration. He was put in a pool of two-men teams that, every day, whatever the weather, hauled a wagon to the various communal latrines dotted around the place. His job? To shovel human excrement into a large container then remove it in time to allow for another day's usage.

Outside the ghetto, Dad believed that as a rag-and-bone man he had occupied the lowest rung of the occupational ladder. He frequently remarked that he never imagined it possible to sink any lower, but 'look how wrong I was'. Coarse puns about being at 'the bottom of the pile', even if obviously delivered as jokes intended to lighten the mood, rarely had the desired effect. Dad was the guy who hauled the 'honey wagon'. We were the children of the guy who hauled the honey wagon. I had a father who did a crappy job. Literally.

Chil Herszman, Chaim's father

That first winter was bitterly cold. As 1939 shaded into 1940, parts of Poland recorded their lowest temperatures ever. This did not make my dad's job of extracting the target substance any easier, as the excrement, along with everything else, would freeze solid. Dad's cart sported axes and crowbars, and these were not for the purposes of self-defence, neither were they leftovers from an earlier incarnation when the honey wagon had been a war chariot. They were essential tools of the trade if you needed to loosen and shovel shit in winter.

Life in the growing ghetto became completely dominated by concerns about food. I told the Holy Trinity we needed to act. I suggested we find a secluded spot to discuss an idea that was forming in my head: 'The rations are useless. They will barely keep a mouse alive, and things will get worse not better. We need to figure out a way to get more food for our families or to stockpile stuff we can barter later. It is obvious that means getting into the city to steal and bring back whatever we can. I suspect when they finally finish the ghetto fences and walls, getting in and out will get a lot harder. We need to do something now if we are to have any chance of making a difference.'

The rest you know. I killed a guard and had to run for it. Alone.

VII

Nothing about the way that day finally turned out had been anticipated. As I ran away from the ghetto fence, soaked in blood, carrying only the bag with the change of clothes in, a knife and wearing a crucifix, I did not know it was a forever moment. I had no idea I would never see my mum, dad, Srulek or any of my three sisters ever again. I had no pictures, indeed anything, to remember any of them by. Why would I? I had believed I would see them that evening, as I had done practically every day of my now nearly fourteen years of life.

I was in the grip of visceral fear. My first and overriding preoccupation was, I've got to get a long way from here as fast as possible, followed swiftly by, I'm a murderer. I'm a thirteen year old who has just killed a man. And not just any man. A member of the 'Master Race'. At least I assumed he was. He certainly spoke German, but maybe he wasn't a German at all. Perhaps he was a Pole who was an ethnic German. Had I just killed a fellow countryman? If he was a Pole, I didn't imagine he could have been conscripted, so he must have been a Nazi sympathiser, a volunteer auxiliary of some sort, but a Pole nevertheless. Damn him either way. He shouldn't have wanted to kill Srulek.

After the initial panic, I had two further thoughts as I ran: I had to change into my warmer clothes, throwing away or destroying the bloodstained ones I was still wearing, and get a little breathing space to work out a plan of action. What was I going to do next? Tonight? Tomorrow?

The only place I knew on the Polish side that was likely to be safe was the Karbowskis'. I had never been there, but thankfully Cesek had told me the address on his last day as a resident of Baluty. The street was close to another place we had played football. The look of horror on Mrs Karbowski's face when she saw me was another of those images that burned its way into my memory, never to be erased. As she opened the door, I half stumbled in without speaking a word. Maybe if she'd had a moment to think, if I hadn't been inside before she could consider the situation, she might have thought more deeply about the danger in which she was placing herself and her family, but she acted instinctively, instantly, compassionately and with love.

Mrs Karbowski told me to go and clean myself up, handing me a set of Cesek's clothes, saying I should change into them and leave mine behind as replacements. At that moment, I knew she had already decided I wouldn't be staying long, but this coincided entirely with my own feelings, so I did not dwell on the potential ramifications. I thought about telling Mrs Karbowski that I had a spare set of clothes in my bag, but I let that pass.

Having washed away all traces of blood from my hair and everywhere else, I got dressed in the fresh garments and went to chat with Mrs Karbowski. We talked about everything except what had brought me there.

A few hours later, Cesek and Mr Karbowski came home and were at once astonished and clearly a little dismayed to see me, but before the talk could take a dangerous turn, Mrs Karbowski stepped in to explain I had turned up at the door in a terrible state, covered in blood and very upset.

I decided it was best not to saddle the Karbowskis, including Cesek, with the full story of what had happened, and they did not press me, probably sensing that it couldn't be anything good. Nevertheless, I felt I had to say something, so I said the first thing that came into my head: 'I had to get out of Baluty. It's terrible in there, but some idiot, a boy who lives in the next flat, tried to stop me going to the wire, so I had to deal with him, and I got covered in his blood in the process. I'm sure he'll be fine, but his nose was well and truly broken.'

From the look on Mr Karbowski's face, I don't think he bought it. Keen to avoid further enquiries about what had brought me here, I jumped in and volunteered that I would be on my way the next morning. I only wanted to stay for the night. The curfew would be down soon. It was too dangerous for me to go back out. To reassure everyone, and make them think I had some sort of well-worked-out idea, I told them my intention was to head for Warsaw to see if any of my dad's relatives there could help me get over to the Soviet Union, where I believed Nathan was safely ensconced. We would sit out the war there along with a great many Polish Jews who had done exactly the same.

Mr Karbowski spoke up at this point: 'Chaim. It's great to see you. Really it is. But we're scared and worried for ourselves and for you. We could be shot for harbouring a runaway Jew. We don't want to know what really happened, and we definitely don't need to know what you're going to do next. In fact, the less we know about all of it, the better it is for everyone. I suggest we all just settle down for the evening as best we can and not talk about this any more.'

It wasn't easy getting to sleep that night. The adrenalin was still pumping, and once more, as when we went into hiding following the death of Mietek, every unfamiliar noise made me think I had been found out. Death would soon take me. Probably the Karbowskis as well.

As I tried to sleep, I recalled the discussions we had had in the Blumowicz clan meeting before the Nazis arrived. We had talked about possible means of escape, flight, hiding places and survival. But now I was on my own, it was obvious that what I had blurted out instinctively, unthinkingly, to the Karbowskis about finding Nathan had to be my plan. Leaving aside the Karbowskis themselves, and the relative in Palestine, Nathan was now the only person in the world whom I knew who wasn't in the Lodz Ghetto, where I had just killed someone. My destination had to be Wlodawa. That's where I would pick up Nathan's trail.

Having made that decision, going to Warsaw was the first logical step. The Soviet Union was due east of Lodz, and Warsaw was northeast, so sort of en route, and, as Uncle Moishe Lewkowicz had said that night we were gathered, the city was likely to offer many more possibilities to get transportation that would take me nearer to the frontier. I would walk to Russia if I had to, but I'd rather not.

I first had to get out of Lodz, and it made most sense to head for the nearest woods to the northeast of the city. In a rather messy way, the woods merged with the city's boundaries and then stretched onwards, right up to the Baltic Sea as far as I knew. Anyway, Warsaw was up there somewhere. I'd find it. More immediately, I knew that deep in those woods some of Lodz's wealthier inhabitants had their *dachas*. Maybe I could hide out in one. I was not certain I could find Heniek's grandmother's *dacha* again, and anyway it was probably too far away for me to try, so I would have to chance my arm on finding another. I figured several of these houses were probably deserted and might provide a ready source of supplies for my journey, or at least a resting place for a night or two while I gathered my thoughts. Maybe I could even lie low in one for an extended period?

In the morning, as soon as the curfew was over, I said a tearful but rapid farewell to the Karbowskis. It was another, then unknown, forever moment. I would never see Mr or Mrs Karbowski again, and it would be more than forty years before Cesek and I met once more.

Lodz under occupation

The tears continued as I walked along leaving the Karbowskis, head inclined, cap pulled down, crying, almost blinded by the salty flow and fear. Now it really began. Suddenly I felt truly alone in what I knew was an extremely hostile world. No money, no papers, no 'right' to be anywhere other than the ghetto, the place to which I could never return. Once the guard's body was discovered, probably it already had been, if it was ever linked to me, not only would I die, probably straight away, so would all my family. I had to ensure that never happened.

Part Three

Henryk

VIII

I reached the outskirts of Lodz and began to traverse a stretch of scrubland to get to the edge of the woods. It was then that I realised moving in open country while there is snow on the ground would make me a rather conspicuous target. Now I understood why Alpine soldiers I had seen on newsreels wore those distinctive white uniforms. I resolved to steal or somehow acquire a big bed sheet or something large and white I could wrap around me so as to minimise the chances of being spotted from a distance.

As I approached the woods and started to get in among the trees, I began to relax a little and feel less exposed. It was then that a very large realisation was dawning on me. I could no longer be a Jew. No more lapsing into Yiddish or using Yiddish expressions. I would now have to speak only German or Polish, and I would have to be careful who saw my dick.

Now that I was out and about on the Aryan side I knew I could be killed immediately if a German soldier, police officer or SS man got hold of me and had any reason at all to believe I was a Jew on the loose or a Polish fugitive from their justice. The truth was they didn't really need a reason. Nobody really cared about dead Jews or Poles howsoever they had ended up in that condition.

I had no idea if anyone in authority would make allowances for me being so obviously a child, but I didn't think I could count on that. Of course, if they learned or believed I was responsible for the death of one of their own at the perimeter of the Lodz Ghetto, they'd try to kill me twice and torture me as well, both before and after life had left me.

From now on, unless I was in the company of Jews I was certain I could trust, which probably meant until I got to Russia and found Nathan, I was Henryk Karbowksi, a good Catholic boy. Blond, blue eyes and wearing a crucifix. It had the ring and look of plausibility. It was a persona I had cultivated. I was going to be a Yoiseler for real. I knew my parents and other family members would be shocked and horrified but they were back in what I thought of as the comparative safety of the ghetto. They were not living on the edge of oblivion as I now was. I was sure they would forgive me if it meant I lived, particularly as, for me, living meant, somehow or other I would get them out. I would rescue them.

I had to hope this would work because it was all I'd got. I had faked it to get hot doughnuts, and I had faked it to get into a football team, but from here on in I would be faking it in a game of life or death. I knew I would need performances at least as convincing as the one I had improvised when talking to the German guard just before I'd killed him. How many times would I need to do it? No idea. Would it work? No idea. I would practise and rehearse some lines when I got the chance.

The best, simplest and most obvious thing would be to avoid any kind of contact with officialdom, but if it was inevitable, I had to make them think I was an ethnic German. If they believed I might be a German, say a *Volksdeutsche**, they would be more careful, even if I had no papers. I would work on a believable line about being separated from my parents and my papers still being in their possession. Or something like that. But that was for tomorrow.

Right now, my head, my thoughts and my actions were a jumble. I had not deliberately escaped from the ghetto following the execution of a carefully calculated plan. I was not prepared for what was happening to me at this very moment, let alone what could happen tomorrow or in the days, weeks, months or years ahead. All I knew was that I had to carry on, that if I wanted to live I had to move forward. On some level I hoped to find Nathan, to complete the mission of rescuing the family. And beyond that perhaps I wanted to fight against the forces that had so upended my life. But in that moment, I was motivated entirely by a desire to survive.

I thought again about trying to get to Grandma Lewkowicz's place, where we had gone after Mietek's murder, because I knew for sure its real owner was back in the ghetto, so it would very likely be empty. However, I quickly realised I couldn't be absolutely sure even of that. Suppose it had been requisitioned by a German officer or had just been occupied by a local Pole who knew its owner was indisposed thanks to Herr Hitler.

Mercifully, I soon reached an area where *dachas* started to be sprinkled thinly throughout the woods, typically off a short path leading from a wider track. Use of *dachas* in the winter months was not exactly common, but neither was it unheard

---

* These were people whose language and culture was German but they were not living in Germany. Before the war there may have been as many as ten million *Volksdeutschen* in eastern and central Europe.

of. It was midweek, though, so people were likely at home in Lodz or at work, and most of the *dachas* certainly looked empty.

The canopy of trees in the woods meant the ground was not fully carpeted with snow. It lay around in patches. I looked for a *dacha* that was fully or partially hidden by bushes or growth of some kind, one that wouldn't be over-looked by anyone in a neighbouring house or be easily spotted by someone who might be passing by on the track. I found one that had obviously not been used for weeks, if not months, judging by the way leaves and other woodland detritus had piled up along the bottom of the steps, on the steps themselves, in the porch and on the terrace, up against the doors and in among the louvred shutters of the windows. Neither were there any footprints in the snow anywhere near the house, although that was not conclusive proof no one was in there.

From the front and sides, I judged no one could see what might be happening in or on the property. The house sat on the prow of a small hill, which meant, at the back, it looked over what would probably be, in the spring and summer, a large ploughed field with more fields beyond stretching into the far distance. Being able to see a long way was reassuring.

I judged it to be a little before 10 a.m., so, not wanting to take any chances, I resolved to keep the house under observa-tion all day to confirm it was safe to attempt what I planned to do next: break in and see what I could find, first to eat, then to steal – ideally, I would also be able to rest a while.

I found a hidey-hole in among some sort of evergreen shrub. It afforded a view of the house and was quite near a small stream which had a fast-flowing section that was not frozen over. I could drink but that was it. There were no berries or indeed signs of anything that might be remotely edible. Hunger pains were nothing new to me.

I walked around in circles in order to keep warm before settling back to take up my observation post. My thoughts were all back in the ghetto. They must have found the body by now. What was going on? Had Heniek and Srulek made it back OK from the perimeter fence to the protection of the buildings and the streets? Had they got home and said nothing? How had they explained my absence? They must have at least said I had gone through the wire. But what else? The uncertainty was gnawing away at me.

Had the authorities assumed that whoever had killed the guard had gone back into the ghetto? Had there been a search for a culprit? Or perhaps they had concluded it was a smuggling operation gone wrong and the guard had come off worst? Maybe the guard had been in on it and had got himself murdered for attempting a double-cross? If anyone had seen a blond-haired boy running away from the ghetto perimeter into the city, that could be a plausible explanation, and one that might make the authorities want to hush up the whole thing. Of course, if anyone had seen what happened before the guard was killed, that wouldn't wash. As with many other things from this early part of my life, I was never going to know the answer. I never had any feelings of regret about killing the man – he was very obviously intent on ending my little brother's life, and I simply could not let that happen. But the instinctual and immediate violence that seized and took over, driving me to act, the sensation of his warm blood on my hands and face never really left me and years later could still produce an involuntary shudder as it evoked the envelope of fear in which I, the automaton, had mindlessly moved in a red mist.

During the day, I heard various sounds in the woods, but I stayed put. Likely they were coming from lonesome Poles chopping or collecting firewood, but no one came towards me, and I heard nothing which sounded like hot pursuit. I heard no German voices, just the occasional word called out in Polish.

As dusk approached and there was still no sign of life in or approaching the house, I broke in round the back using a fallen branch as a lever to remove a shutter. The noise was dreadful as it sheared away from the outer wall to reveal a pane of glass, which I smashed. I ran back to my observation point and waited another hour just to be sure no one had heard and been drawn to the spot where the sound of a murdering Jew breaking into someone's house had come from.

On my return, I was delighted to discover enough moonlight coming through the broken window to illuminate the greater part of its interior. The house was sparsely furnished, but there were a few blankets, a whitish sheet and, joy of joys, a horde of tinned foods, Kilner jars containing vegetables in brine, maps, a large knapsack, binoculars, a paraffin lamp and matches. There were also some walking boots in a box and lots of other things I knew were going to be useful. This was to be my first major piece of luck. Actually, my only piece of luck for a while. It seemed I had stumbled into what appeared to be the weekend retreat of one of the head honchos of the Lodz Ornithological Society, or some such similar nature-oriented club. There were stuffed birds in glass cases everywhere, along with pictures of birds, drawings of birds and books on birds. Up until now, this football-loving Jewish boy had never given much thought to ornithology, but I was certainly glad somebody else had.

I did not dare start a fire to heat the place up or cook. The smoke would have been too easy to spot in the moonlit woods. I disgorged the contents of a tin of peas and a tin of pork and wolfed the lot down cold. I had never cared about the prohibition on eating pork, but in the ghetto I had noticed the kosher rules and rituals had been set aside by almost everyone so as to address the new exigencies of surviving in the ghetto. As far as I was concerned, my entire existence had become one long continuous exigency.

When I thought about it, being Jewish was something you mainly did with boring old grown-ups, or it was some sort of branding that only mattered on the streets to crazy Poles and bad Germans. Yes, I was a Jew; yes, it was my culture, a warm and familiar comfort blanket. But now it had to be history, at least until I figured a way out of my current predicament. Could I grow back a foreskin for while? That would be handy. God? Who knew? As far as I could tell, at the very least he must be asleep at the wheel. If this was how he let his Chosen People be treated, what use was he to me? None at all.

I settled down for the night feeling snug and warm. Nervous, but snug and warm. The silence was deafening. The loneliness unnerving. I was again reminded of the time we spent in hiding following the murder of Mietek. The sound of leaves rustling in the wind or an animal moving in the bushes, in my paranoid state, signalled the arrival of the Gestapo. This was also, I realised, the first and only time in my life I had spent a night in a room on my own. I didn't like it one little bit, I longed to be back with people who knew me and loved me, would protect me, but I guessed ahead of me there would be a lot I had never experienced before and probably wouldn't like.

As I lay there, I began to think more carefully about my predicament and prospects. I knew the Polish countryside was going to be a dangerously exposed place for a solitary boy, even one who looked like me. Poland outside of the major urban settlements was really a network of small communities where everybody knew everybody and was likely as not related to most of them. Any kind of stranger would be bound to be noticed, and being noticed was often a prelude to being inter-rogated. That had to be avoided if at all possible.

I needed to get into towns, the bigger the better, places where I could lose myself in the anonymity of the masses, find deserted buildings, warm places or cellars in which to sleep and hide, places with shops and markets with food I could steal or work for.

I wondered about the owners of the place I was in. Had they just fled Lodz or got out of Poland? It seemed odd there were so many items of value here, waiting for organised gangs of looters or people like me to steal. The owners must still be around or else they were dead or trapped somewhere. Nobody would willingly leave behind or abandon all the things that were in this *dacha*. There was a lot I could carry away with me to consume, barter or sell later. Selling would be important. I knew I would need money in my pocket to buy food on the days I could not steal or obtain it through honest work. I imagined I would need money to buy train or bus tickets or pay for other types of rides as I headed east towards Nathan and a mini-family reunion.

When I wasn't wondering about the owners that evening, other darker thoughts began to encroach. They were to become my constant companion. I obviously had no idea when the body at the wire had been discovered, but I didn't imagine it would have been long after the deed was done. A vigilant passer-by could have spotted it within minutes and raised an alarm. Or maybe a supervising officer went to look when the guard didn't check in for some sort of roll call. If the Nazis concluded the killer came from within the ghetto, there could be no doubt they would want revenge. The victim had, after all, been going about the Führer's business. Even the ghetto administration would be mad, because they would be fearful of the example that had been set and the potential consequences for others. Had the Nazis selected people at random to shoot them as an act of retribution? A warning. I very much hoped not, but it didn't take much for them to do that kind of thing anyway, so if anyone was to be blamed for these hypothetical deaths, my share of it was somewhere between small and non-existent.

And suppose the guy I'd killed was a *Volksdeutsche*, a Polish national volunteer or auxiliary of some kind? There weren't then any Polish authorities to speak of, but later I would fret that when the war was over, assuming Poland became a state again, one of the guy's relatives might try to find out who was responsible for the death at the wire. A nightmare vision began to form during that first night on the run. It would repeat, fertilise and enrich itself in the years ahead.

I imagined, unbeknownst to us, we had been seen. Someone on either side of the wire had witnessed the whole thing and ratted on us. Srulek's club foot and gammy leg made him conspicuous. It would be relatively easy for the German or ghetto authorities to find him, find the wounds on his legs inflicted by the barbed wire and take that as confirmation of guilt. Had they shot only him, or had they also hanged or shot the rest of my family? Did they torture them first? Had I, leader of the Holy Trinity, been the cause of the painful death of nearly all of my nearest and dearest? And what would Nathan think? I was supposed to stay and make sure everyone was safe, but I had just deserted them all and in so doing had brought danger and the risk of death directly to their door. These were great, wearisome thoughts.

I would also often think about how things might have turned out had I not had the knife with me. Or what if I had been just a bit further away and could not have reached the guard in time? What if he had walked faster or run? What if he had taken the shot from further out and not even bothered to approach the wire? Srulek would have been dead for sure, and his death would have been entirely my responsibility. Just thinking about it made me shudder. With Srulek dead and me still outside the wire, would I have waited on the Polish side, looking for an opportunity to get back into the ghetto? I doubt it, not just because of the fear of my involvement in Srulek's death and the presumed attempt at smuggling, but also because I could not have faced my parents, my sisters and other relatives as the person who had engineered his younger brother's demise.

Or what if my talking to the guard hadn't engaged or fooled him and he'd worked out I was a co-conspirator or a party in some other way? Srulek and I would both be dead. Maybe even Heniek too if the guard had spotted him. That wasn't a happy thought either. For the rest of my life, what ifs plagued me. What I could never rid myself of, though, was the belief that we should have just said a flat 'no' to Srulek. Heniek and I should have told him he simply could not go through the wire, and, yes, worries about his dodgy leg were the reason.

I thought this without ever being completely clear that what happened at the wire had anything at all to do with Srulek's deformed limb. It seemed likely but not definite. I did, however, become convinced that if Heniek had attempted the wire and not Srulek, there would be no uniformed corpse lying by the wire, and we would have made the trip out and back just fine. I would definitely have stayed in the ghetto in Lodz and kept my promise to Nathan. Would I have been able to find a way to keep my mum and dad, Srulek and my sisters alive for the duration? I would never know, but the idea that I might have done, however absurd or irrational, never left me. I never wholly shook the feeling that me remaining in the ghetto could have made a crucial difference, perhaps *the* crucial difference.

These were, of course, insane thoughts and ideas, ludicrous, returning in the darkest sleepless nights but also in my waking hours. As the years went by, the flashbacks and morbid contemplations became less frequent, although they never wholly disappeared. This was to be my own personal and perpetual reservoir of familial guilt, a highly customised version of survivor syndrome. It became a form of tinnitus. A constant background buzz, a source of nagging, gnawing culpability, sinful neglect or cowardice, a wound which, without notice, could cause me pain at any time, never allowing me a sense of settled tranquillity, of being at peace with myself.

I woke at first light to begin preparing for my departure. Tempting as it was to stay longer, I was scared the owners of the property might appear at any moment, and who knew what might happen then? I couldn't take any chances. I had to go.

Warsaw was my first objective. In Warsaw there were Herszmans, family on Dad's side. I had visited a couple of times and believed, if I could reach them, I would be safe, at least for a while, until I worked out how to get over to Wlodawa. They might know a way. Maybe they would also have news from Lodz about the dead guy at the wire, although I guessed that was unlikely. It had only happened a couple of days ago, and against the larger backdrop of the war what I had done was microscopically small and insignificant.

Judging by the size of some of the clothes and boots in the house, the ornithologist, or maybe it was his wife or one of his children, was only a little bigger than me. Cesek's clothes were fine, still relatively clean and in good shape. Well mended. No holes. No reason to abandon them. I stuffed them in my knapsack as a spare set, because clothes in the house were better; ones that were obviously designed or intended to be worn when crawling through, over or around thorny bushes or rough terrain of various sorts, presumably in search of a better vantage point from which to observe a feathered friend.

First on were some long woollen socks. I couldn't remember the last time I had worn socks of any kind. Then I pulled on long trousers that looked and felt as if they were made of some sort of canvas or sailcloth. Rough but sturdy. Thank goodness for the underwear I had also found and put on. I had to roll up the trouser legs by a few centimetres so that I didn't trip over the bottoms, but otherwise they were fine. Stuffing bits of old newspapers into the toes helped ensure that the boots I proposed to steal stayed on without being too uncomfortable. The shirt, pullover and jacket were, like the trousers, a tad too big, but to see a boy wearing ill-fitting hand-me-downs was not unusual. There was a large mirror in the house. I took a look. The outfit and the way I carried it all seemed OK. Exceptionally ordinary and unremarkable. Just what it needed to be. I began to feel a glimmer of confidence that I could and would make this work.

From one of the maps of the area that littered the house and from my own knowledge, I knew there was a town not far away that had a market every Thursday – at any rate, it did before the Germans arrived. It was Thursday tomorrow. If I could reach that market, I might be able to persuade someone to give me a lift to Warsaw, which was over a hundred kilometres away. Or maybe I could sell something from this house and use the money to pay someone to take me to Warsaw.

I filled up my knapsack and pockets with as many things as I could carry without overburdening myself to the point where I couldn't cut and run if that became necessary. Among these things were a catechism and a missal, two commonplace items in any devout Catholic's religious paraphernalia. Carrying them while also wearing the crucifix would add to the credibility of my claim to be a Catholic should the need arise. This provided another boost to my self-confidence. If there was such a thing as a God after all, this was divine intervention working its magic.

Then there was a map of the whole of Poland and some binoculars. I hesitated before sticking those in my bag. To be caught with binoculars and a map might suggest I was a spy – a young one, but a spy nevertheless. That might cause deeper or more urgent enquiries to be made as to my real identity. On the other hand, if I also took and carried with me pictures and drawings of birds, maybe I could carry off being a young orni-thologist. Yes, there was a war on, but birds still flew. I felt a twinge of conscience about stealing these things from the unknown bird watcher. It was a twinge that lasted all of a second, maybe a bit less.

I ventured out of the house to get my precise bearings and to chart a course for the town. Thank goodness, once more, for my days in Hashomer-Hatzair, where map-reading was one of the skills we learned. I worked out a route and made it to the town in a couple of hours, keeping to woodland tracks and hedgerows, away from the roads where a lot of German military and police traffic was constantly on the move in both directions. I kept my ears pricked for the sound of anyone approaching and continually scanned the horizon looking for potential threats and places to hide should one appear. When I had to cross open ground with snow on it, I wrapped the sheet around me as best I could without making walking impossible.

I managed to avoid meeting anyone in the woods and fields bar an old man whom I almost stumbled upon as he sat there on a wheelbarrow talking to himself quietly, looking like he was just having a rest. The wheelbarrow contained small branches and twigs, suggesting he was one of the people I had heard yesterday, a peasant out foraging for firewood. I was furi-ous with myself for being so careless and not having seen or heard anything before I was almost on top of him.

I was also astonished when the man did not say, by way of greeting, 'Ah, so you're the little Jewish bastard who's on the run from Lodz after killing the German guard. Oh, and by the way, Hymie, all your family are dead. They raped your mother and two of your sisters, forcing your dad and Srulek to watch before shooting them along with a hundred other Jews who just happened to be near their house when the Germans' trucks went into the ghetto to get them. Of course, they picked up Heniek and the rest of Lewkowicz family, who are also all dead, along with the Levinsons. Too bad about the Karbowskis. They're dead too. I hope you feel real bad for all the death and trouble you've caused, you selfish little creep.'

No, instead of saying all that, he just said, 'Good morning. Lovely day.'

I agreed in what I hoped was not an excessively histrionic Polish Catholic sort of way: 'Yeah, lovely.' I resisted the temptation to add '*Dominus vobiscum*', just to underline how really Catholic I was. I figured a real Catholic would not feel the need to keep telling or reminding everyone he was a Catholic by making frequent allusions to aspects of the faith. On the contrary, that sort of thing might arouse suspicions, particularly in the present circumstances where sensitivities about religion, or at least one particular religion, were somewhat heightened.

Yes, I know, or thought I knew, a lot about Catholicism, but I had no idea how much I didn't know. I just had to hope there was no way of saying please and thank you that was *de rigueur* for Catholics when speaking to each other – something I had missed during extended chats and initiation with Cesek or in my other observations of the species. Was there a particular Catholic way of buying soap or cabbages in a shop as opposed to from a market stall? How did Catholics blow their noses or open a newspaper? Was there some small tell-tale detail which, if I failed to observe it, might give me away and lead to my early departure from the planet? I had to hope not, because now was surely too late to find out.

I had to put such thoughts and fears from my head. This Catholic thing was going to be easy. I just wished I could have had a bit more practise, got the feel of it a bit better, before having to deploy the subterfuge in very stressful circumstances.

I entered the town from a field, routing myself down a small track between the backyards of two houses. Coming out from the houses I found myself on a narrow path leading to a street that went through to the market square. The German presence was light, reflecting the comparative unimportance of the place, but not non-existent. My heart skipped several beats as I strolled past a German soldier or a policeman, trying for all the world to look as if I had a perfect right to be there, instead of being dead or back in the ghetto, or both.

The market was strangely silent, and half or more of the stalls I remembered from previous visits didn't seem to be there. It wasn't my imagination. Half or more of the stalls weren't there, and half the people who would normally be shopping were also missing, because the missing stallholders and shoppers were Jews. No Jews selling in the market, and no Jews buying. Poland was now another country, or it was on its way to becoming one.

There had been Jews in Poland for more than a thousand years, since King Jagiellon had invited them to come in 870 to help build his fledgling state. Every Jewish child in Poland knew that. Now Jews were gone or going, and even though I knew I was in part of Poland that had been incorporated into the Reich, that was only on paper. Important paper, but paper even so. It was still a Polish landscape, but a Polish landscape without Jews is like Switzerland without mountains, the Sahara without sand. In a few short months, *Judenrein* was becoming the new reality. It was a chilling thought and showed at once both the cruel impudence of the Germans' project and the vastness of their hateful vision.

Turning back to my plans to get to Warsaw, it dawned on me that I would need to tread carefully. How did you approach a complete stranger and convince them to give you a lift for a hundred kilometres or thereabouts? It might be a risky business identifying someone from the Warsaw area whom I could approach and ask for a ride or offer a trade in return for transportation. I wanted an old man, someone who might not be hard to escape from if he started to turn nasty or tried to rob me. Maybe an old man might just be glad of the company and not be bothered about trading with or cheating one so young as me.

The person who looked as if he was the oldest vendor in the square was shouting the odds from a dirty grey van which had an address in Warsaw written on the front door panel and had a windowed side which opened up to display an array of goods. Or rather an array of one single product, because today he only seemed to have medium-sized saucepans for sale.

When there were few people around, I asked him if he needed any help running his stall or packing things away. He didn't. I then just straight out asked him if he could give me a lift into or near Warsaw, offering a tin of pork as an inducement. That clinched it. Maybe he sensed desperation in my voice and pitied me.

I realised I couldn't trade lifts for food very often, as I would rapidly run out, never mind the risk of advertising myself as a target for robbers. Poland was said to be full of robbers or people willing to become robbers if it meant they could eat.

We agreed to meet at one o'clock as the market started to pack up. My sense of anxiety and worry about what I might be getting into soon evaporated as I realised the guy was mainly just glad of the company. Someone to talk to.

As I climbed into the passenger side of the van, my chauffeur announced, 'My name is Tadeusz. What's yours?'

'Henryk Karbowski,' I said without giving it a second thought but still hardly believing that I had in fact uttered those oft-rehearsed words to a stranger who had asked.

This was Henryk Karbowski's first public appearance, and it seemed to have worked. Aside from later that day when I reached my relatives' flat in Warsaw, it was going to be a long time before I would use my real name again, the name that illuminated my true origins, the name that spoke volumes about my history and that of my family. I was acutely conscious that were Chaim Herszman to emerge at the wrong moment, or were his name to be beaten out of me, it would not only imperil my own life, but it could also imperil the lives of any of my family if they traced it back to Lodz. Henryk Karbowski was here to stay.

The journey to Warsaw was uneventful. Tadeusz hadn't sold anything for hard cash, but various barters had been completed, which the guy was sure he could work to his advantage when he got back to the capital.

I soon discovered from Tadeusz that the wagon we were both now travelling in and all of its contents had belonged to a Jew who lived in Warsaw but who, under new Nazi laws, had been forbidden to carry on this trade. He was told he had to sell everything connected to the business within forty-eight hours or risk losing the lot. The Jew sold. Tadeusz bought.

'I got the whole kit and caboodle for a song. A steal, you might say. Still, if I hadn't bought it, someone else would, so why shouldn't it have been me?' This was a rationalisation which Henryk was to hear with sickening regularity. The old man wondered aloud about the fate of the Polish Jews. He told me the situation in Warsaw was bad and getting worse. There was talk of a Lodz-like ghetto being formed, but nothing official had been announced up until then.

While the old man was not the worst anti-Semite I had ever met, it was plain that for him anti-Semitism was simply part of the background music, the ambient noise of Polish life. Even with a common enemy, the Germans, very visibly in our midst and harming both communities, there were no feelings of solidarity or shared suffering with my co-religionists emanating from Tadeusz.

I practised a bit of routine, low-level anti-Semitic stuff to see how naturally I could get it to come out. Nothing too heady to start with: 'Well, they've only got themselves to blame, haven't they? Stupid bastards living apart like that. Dressing like they do. Who do they think they are? This is our country not theirs. They made themselves an easy target.' Judging by the nods from the old man, I was not doing anything too wrong. That was a relief.

The van reached the outskirts of Warsaw just as it was starting to get dark. Tadeusz told me the curfew started soon, but it transpired he was going quite close to the part of Warsaw where my relatives lived. He agreed to drop me off there, so I hoped I wouldn't be caught out.

Where the Warsaw Herszmans lived was part of a major Jewish area. I was a little uneasy about going in. Here's where my looks could be a handicap. Maybe people on the street would think me a *goy* and try to rob me. Maybe they'd ask no questions and just kill me or hurt me, take my knapsack and run. It felt a bit as if I was walking towards the sound of gunfire while all my instincts were to go in exactly the opposite direction. However, I knew no one else in the city. The Warsaw Herszmans were my only hope.

My luck was holding out. As the van drew to a halt, I saw my dad's cousin, whom I knew as Uncle Izaak. I remembered the street where he and his family lived, and he was walking towards it. I was filled with enormous sense of relief. This confirmed they were likely still there, in the same flat, not dead or disappeared.

IX

I hung back and waited until Izaak had vanished into the tenement building before heading for the gloom that was the entrance to his block. I remembered they lived on the ground floor behind a shiny red door with a large scruffy letter box. It couldn't have been much more than a minute before I banged the knocker. Almost immediately the door was opened, but not fully. Izaak peeked out with a quizzical stare. His face was weakly lit by a flickering light that must have been coming from a candle.

'Yes, who are you? What do you want?'

'I'm Chaim Herszman. Chil Herszman's son. From Lodz. Don't you remember me? We visited here before. I escaped from the ghetto, and I'm on the run.'

The quizzical stare turned into a look of utter dismay: 'Are you mad? You're on the run and you come here to us? Do you want to get us all shot? Go away! Now. And anyway, we don't have enough food even for ourselves. There is nothing we can give you or share with you. Just go. Quickly. I'm sorry. Leave now.'

I felt completely deflated. This was not the sort of welcome I had anticipated from a relative. I'm not sure exactly what kind of welcome I had expected, but it wasn't this. I panicked.

It was going to be dark soon. My knowledge of Warsaw was sketchy to say the least. If I was picked up for breaking the curfew and with no papers, I could be in big trouble.

'Please, you've got to let me in. If you send me out, I could get caught by the Germans and I'll be shot. I have no papers. I have no permission to travel. And they might trace me back to you. We have the same family name, so if they get me in this neighbourhood, you're going to be at risk anyway. I'm really sorry. Let me in and the danger will be nil. I will be on my way as soon as possible when daylight arrives. No one saw me coming here. I am certain of that. And I have food with me. I'm happy to give some to you.'

My mention of something to eat seemed to help. This was further confirmation that food was becoming a universal currency in wartime Poland, definitely for the mass of Jews, probably also for the Poles. If only I had brought more with me from the ornithologist's *dacha*.

The tension between me and Izaak didn't entirely evaporate. I was still outside, almost on the street, but our whispered commotion had finally attracted the attention of Izaak's wife. I later learned her name was Ruth. When she came and heard what was going on, she opened the door completely, obviously embarrassed at her husband's callousness, and urged him to 'let the boy in – he's only a child.'

Izaak stepped aside to make way. 'But only for tonight,' he said as I passed him. 'We don't want any trouble.'

I then repeated, 'I've got food. I am happy to share. The meat is pork, but it's wholesome, and I have vegetables as well. I'll be gone tomorrow.'

I was ushered into a spacious, high-ceilinged room made small by the presence of six souls of varying ages and sizes. I guessed these were other cousins or sundry Herszman relatives, but I didn't ask. I just waved and said, 'Hello, I'm Chaim Herszman from Lodz.'

There was a bit of a discussion about eating pork, but it was clear this family was not observant, and the pangs of hunger were strong. We opened a Kilner jar of vegetables and two of my tins of pork, to which I added the remnants of what I hadn't eaten from yesterday in the *dacha*. This was not exactly a feast fit for a king, or the nine poor Jews who were about to devour it, but from the looks on the faces in that room it was likely more food than any of them had seen for some time.

After we had eaten, I was regaled with news about the situation of the Jews in Warsaw. Things were every bit as bad as they had been in Lodz before the ghetto was formed. In Warsaw, there was no requirement to wear a yellow star that had to be sewn on to your clothes. Here the requirement was for Jews to wear a white armband showing a blue Star of David. Random killings and humiliations on the streets, being snatched and forced to perform stupid, menial, or disgusting tasks were still common. At least inside the ghetto in Lodz, if you stayed away from the perimeter, the chance of a German randomly shooting or abusing you was low. Maybe Rumkowski had a point. Could a self-governing Jewish ghetto be a form of protection for the Jews? Although that might sound stupid today, maybe it wasn't all that clear-cut for everyone then.

The life of a Jew in Warsaw was now a never-ending sequence of worries about what might be around the corner or coming up behind you or from the side, and how you would secure your next meal. If your children or other family members were out of sight, you worried for them as well. All this tore at the nerves in ways which could, and all too frequently did, bring on depression, madness and suicide, usually in that order.

Any lingering thoughts I might have entertained about maybe losing myself in Warsaw, among the largest concentration of Jews in Europe, were finally dispelled by this brief conversation. I understood why the Lewkowiczs had abandoned their sojourn in the city and returned to Lodz, but going back was not an option for me. I supposed I could try to hide in plain sight as an Aryan, but finding Nathan remained my primary goal. I had to press on to the east, to the Bug River. If I could reunite with Nathan, I would be safe and the plan to get everyone out of the Lodz ghetto would be but a short step away. Yet even as I thought that, dark clouds of doubt crowded in on me.

In the course of the evening, it also became clear that my relations were a rather dull and unenterprising lot, bar one of the children, Baruch, who was maybe a bit older than me. He was a live wire. As the evening wore on, Baruch began to talk about fighting back against the Germans. He argued this meant we had to make common cause with the Poles. He claimed he understood the risks of working with the Poles, simply asserting, 'However bad the Poles were, we rubbed along, and they never were anything like as bad as the Germans have been towards us. It's going to be worse in the future for both the Poles and us.' Then he added, 'Not all Poles are anti-Semites, but as far as I can tell practically every Pole hates the German occupiers, so we have something to work with there! An alliance built on shared hate could be extremely strong.'

Izaak said he wasn't so sure most Poles wouldn't prefer the Germans to the Jews, but anyway 'Jews don't fight. We negotiate. We compromise. We survive. We do a deal, or we run. That's how it has always been for us.'

Izaak brushed aside and dismissed Baruch's contrary protestations even as Baruch reminded him that the leader of the Red Army during the days of its most glorious victories against the forces of reaction in Russia was one Leon Trotsky, also known as Lev Bronstein. Jews had fought in the German and Austrian armies during the First World War, so where was all this ridiculous talk coming from about Jews not fighting?

Izaak would have none of it: 'The Germans are fighting a war. They're already short of manpower in Germany. Recruiting offices are springing up all over Poland to get Poles to go to Germany and work in their industries and on the land. Of course, they won't take Jews to Germany. They want the Reich to be free of Jews, but that's all politics! It'll change. Everything can change. You wait. Pragmatism will defeat the lunatic Nazi ideologues. Some kind of common sense will prevail. If the Germans see we're useful, they'll look after us. All this shooting in the streets, the abuse and so on, it is just a few hotheads, out-of-control zealots. We shouldn't provoke them. The German authorities will bring them into line. They'll have to. The Germans believe in order.'

It was quite a speech, and, once delivered, I was more certain than ever that I had to get away from this place as soon as possible. Uncle Izaak sounded just like Chaim Rumkowski back in Lodz. Put your faith in collaboration. Baruch was having none of it: 'You can't be best friends or live with a tiger. Things don't work like that.' Turns out Baruch was right. Rumkowski was wrong.

Most people in the room knew Nathan, having met him on visits he had made to Warsaw, but they had no idea he had left Lodz and headed east. They were astonished to hear about the postcard we had received but said they'd heard similar accounts of Jews heading for the Soviet Union.

Izaak confirmed there had been lots of stories about Jews getting across into Russia at the new border, the Bug River. Hundreds, maybe thousands, were said to be doing so every night under cover of darkness. There were even legal ways of doing it at official border crossings, but he was less clear on what those legal ways were and did not think they would be open to Jews anyway.

This sparked a brief discussion, or rather a series of expletive-laden declarations, about how shocked everyone was that Germany and the Soviet Union had entered into a pact. Hitler's whole project, and the way he rose to power in Germany, was based on a promise to deal with the Red Menace in the east, the Asiatic hordes who were but a plaything of a global Zionist conspiracy.

'Some conspiracy!' declared Baruch. 'We should be so lucky! Now these two monsters are helping each other out. Can you believe that?' Plainly everyone did. There was also a consensus that the unholy alliance between the Soviets and the Nazis couldn't last, but by the time it ended who knew where the Jews of Poland would be?

The Warsaw Herszmans' confident confirmation that many Jews had made it into the Soviet Union by crossing the Bug River was music to my ears. It was the first independent evidence that I was on the right lines. Lublin was the major city and transport hub in that part of Poland. It had to be my next objective. From there, I would make my way towards Wlodawa, or somewhere nearby, and work out how to get over the water. I could swim, but I imagined at this time of year the river would still be frozen and that ought to make it even easier. What could possibly go wrong?

I didn't mention Wlodawa to the assembled company. The question of my precise intentions in respect of a point of exit from Poland did not come up. Neither did I fill them in about what had happened at the perimeter fence in Lodz. It was unlikely anyone there would turn me in, if only because it might put themselves at risk by implicating them further. They would gain nothing of value by knowing they had a killer in their midst. When the war was over and we all met again in Palestine, that would be the time to reveal all.

One of the other adults, I think he was called Yitzak, poured a small amount of cold water on my plans when acknowledging that while it was true there were lots of stories about Jews making it across the Bug River, there were also quite a lot of stories of failed attempts. Since the Germans and the Soviets were partners in crime, the local German military commander occasionally protested to his counterpart about the laxness of Soviet border guards who did not take steps to stop refugees crossing. I said I thought the Germans were probably delighted to be getting rid of more Jews, but others countered by suggesting the Germans were really worried about allowing young Jewish men to get across because they would probably hope to come back as partisans to kill them.

Whatever the explanation, for a few days following a diplomatic protest by the Germans the Soviets would apparently get busy and difficult. If you happened to be trying to get across at such a moment, it could turn out badly. There were stories of Soviet troops on one side and Germans on the other simultaneously shooting at some poor unfortunates as they tried to cross. There was also one story of refugees stuck overnight on a bridge – in no-man's-land – with neither side willing to help. Everyone died from hypothermia. In their doubtless weakened state, it wouldn't have taken long.

'A lot of it is luck,' Yitzak said. 'If you're spotted by a guard on the Russian side who is a Jew, or maybe he has a woman with him so he's feeling content, he might just let you go through. If the guard hasn't eaten, has a hangover or is in a bad mood for some other reason, then you're as good as dead.' That was his last word on the subject.

Baruch was not aware of any organised way of getting out of Warsaw and over to the Russian border, but he'd heard that, once clear of the city, groups and individual refugees with the same idea were hooking up and banding together to help each other along the way. The groups tended to be defined by national or religious characteristics, but occasionally there were mixed groups of Jews, Poles and communists from a variety of places. Seemingly, there were considerable numbers of foreigners who'd got trapped behind the advancing German lines and whose countries were now at war with the Axis powers. If these people were caught, they would at best be interned or at worst be shot. They had therefore resolved to avoid both by getting out. Intending to comfort me Baruch added, 'But you needn't worry, Chaim. With your looks, if you play your cards right, you'll be able to pick and choose which convoy to join.'

That was exactly what I hoped. Chaim the chameleon. Emboldened by the comparative ease with which I had got to Warsaw from Lodz, I announced, 'I'm off to Russia tomorrow. I'm not a communist. I just want to find my brother in a country where they're not locking us up or shooting us just for being Jewish. I'll get across the river somehow. I'll find Nathan, and we'll get the rest of you out, maybe at the same time as we bring out the Herszmans and others from the Lodz Ghetto.'

Izaak exploded: 'Don't go talking like that in this house. It's criminal. I don't want any of the younger ones going out on to the street and repeating any of this. We'll all end up dead.'

Baruch, of course, wanted to go with me, but Izaak had heard his whispered request and uttered oaths and promises of retribution which hit their mark. Baruch backed off, saying that he might follow later. I wonder if he ever did.

When Izaak was way out of earshot, I explained that I wanted to know only two things. First, was there a market or another place where I might be able to connect with someone with transport heading east so I could hitch a ride? There was, and it wasn't too far away. Second, how could I contact a forger to get some ID papers? I didn't know how long I would be in Poland before I got to the Soviet Union, so getting hold of papers seemed like a smart idea. Warsaw had to be the best place to do that. I had no idea what these 'papers' were exactly. I just knew I needed some. Baruch said he didn't know what kind of papers a boy of my age might need, but he did know where a forger lived.

The word was fake IDs were not that hard to come by. They could be obtained by bribing German officials, but that was impossible if you didn't know any, which obviously I didn't. Catholic priests had also been known to be helpful by issuing phoney birth and baptismal certificates to Jews, but, again, I didn't know any priests in Warsaw. Neither did Baruch.

Baruch gave me the forger's address and said he'd take me a large part of the way there, but we agreed because he would be wearing a tell-tale armband and I wouldn't be, when we left the Jewish area we would walk on opposite sides of the street. Should anything go wrong for one, the other would not automatically be dragged into it, as there would be no sign we were connected in any way. Just before we left, he explained how to get to the market after coming out of the forger's place but then changed his mind and said he would hang about near the forger's so if my business with him was concluded reasonably swiftly, he could also take me there or close to it.

We set off with only a perfunctory nod to polite family goodbyes, although I'm pretty sure Ruth shed real tears. Izaak made clear I should never come back, and in a whisper I told him I certainly hoped I would never have to see him again. As we were walking out the door, I heard Izaak shouting that Baruch should stay at home, but Baruch ignored him.

I was amazed at how full of people the streets were so soon after the curfew had ended. I supposed they had a long day ahead securing food and other necessities. They needed to get as much as possible done while there was daylight.

As we walked, before we crossed to opposite sides of the street Baruch explained he didn't know how it worked with the forger, but by way of reassurance he said he had never heard anyone speak ill of him. I would just have to trust that my knapsack's contents would be sufficiently attractive to get him to prepare some documents for me.

Baruch walked me to the end of the street where the forger lived. It was in the fourth tenement block down on the left, the third flat on the first floor. He said he would wait ten minutes or thereabouts. It took less than that.

I knocked on the door of number 3 and said '*Shalom*' to the man who answered. Clearly disconcerted by the sight of this Aryan-looking boy, the '*Shalom*' greeting was not uttered in return. Instead, a surly 'Who are you and what do you want?' came snarling back at me in Polish.

It was starting to dawn on me that, with my looks, seeking out Jews to do business with, whatever kind of business, might put me in danger. If they didn't already know me, and no one outside of Lodz would know me, they would never immediately accept me as one of their own. Not at first sight, and usually first sight was all you ever got.

Maybe this guy thought '*Shalom*' was a smokescreen. Maybe he thought I really was a *goy* sent there to dupe or rob him, or more likely, given my size, I was merely confirming his presence so others could shortly pile in and rob him instead.

I slipped into Yiddish. His eyes widened, but he clearly remained sceptical. I told him I wanted papers and was here to find out how much they would cost, how the whole thing worked, how quickly I could get them. He expressed angry indignation and denied he had any knowledge of forging anything. He had no idea what had brought me there or who had told me he was a forger, but he would thank me to disabuse them of that. He was a God-fearing, law-abiding citizen of Poland and had no desire to get involved in any kind of illegal activity so could I please 'clear off, right now, before I go find a policeman'.

The whole exchange was over in less than a minute.

Why did I ever think it would be simple? Because I was a greenhorn kid. That's all there was to it. I would have to do more homework before putting myself at risk again. Baruch had been well-intentioned, but I was a fool for relying on him.

Baruch was still waiting outside. I explained what had just happened, gesturing that we needed to move away as quickly as possible. He apologised profusely while at the same time asserting there was no doubt the guy was a forger who dealt in identity papers. Maybe the circumstances of my arrival had scared him, coming unannounced and with no one to vouch for me. Blond hair and blue eyes could do that to a Jew. Even if he didn't think I was setting him up to be robbed, he might have been worried that I was a police agent or informer of some kind.

Getting out of Warsaw as fast as I could was all I had on my mind. Maybe this wasn't entirely rational, but Izaak's lack of a warm welcome and the business with the forger made me feel I shouldn't hang about. There were too many moving parts I didn't understand. On the opposite side of the street, Baruch walked me a few blocks then pointed me in the direction of the market. My last words to Baruch were, 'Nathan wrote to us in Lodz. I'll write to you in Warsaw. All the Herszmans will reunite when this mess is over, either in the Soviet Union, back in Poland or, better still, in Palestine.'

Walking away, I was aware the promise I had just made would never be fulfilled. I knew the name of the district the Herszman's place was in. I could recognise the street, the tenement and the door, but I never knew, much less wrote down or had cause to remember, the street address. In the intervening years, I thought several times about what became of Baruch – by which I suppose I mean how and when he died. As with most of the people you will meet in the course of me telling you my story, the encounters I describe were both the first and last. It couldn't be any other way but that did not mean I would not wonder what became of those, like Baruch, who helped me or were kind as well as those who would have killed me if they had even the vaguest notion of the truth.

X

The market was several times larger than the one where I had picked up a lift the previous day. Again, I didn't see any Jews selling anything, but there were lots of people with white armbands milling about. I wondered if that was legal.

And so it was, roughly seventy-two hours after getting out of the ghetto in Lodz, I found myself on the back of a truck full of wood that was heading to Lublin via Radom. Not exactly a straight line but not all that far off. Maybe the roads were better going this way. I liked the idea of going through Radom, knowing that this was where Nathan had been when he'd sent the card referring to the fictitious aunt in Wlodawa.

I had offered the driver a tin of pork – only one more left now. He'd laughed and accepted immediately, but I'd been relieved he hadn't asked any questions about me, my entitlement to travel, purpose of my journey or anything else. Was it my looks? The glimpse of the crucifix that I had carefully arranged? Or had he just been glad of the meat and this had chased all other thoughts from his mind?

Thankfully, because the driver was in the front of the truck in the cabin, and I was in the back, it meant I did not have to engage in any kind of lengthy chatter with him, but I was partially exposed to the elements under a tattered tarpaulin. I wrapped myself up in just about every bit of clothing I was carrying overlaid with the white sheet, which I gripped firmly to stop it blowing away.

I was beginning to get a deeper sense of the dangers of being thirteen, small and a vagrant in hostile territory. As I sat back, I started to feel extremely sorry for myself. My relations in Warsaw hadn't wanted me around. They'd seen me as a danger to them and hadn't strained themselves to help me, Baruch excepted. Even Baruch hadn't exactly come up trumps, though he'd had a good heart. Tears started to roll down my cheeks.

Warsaw to Radom was around a hundred kilometres. We got there mid afternoon. After stopping at a yard, I helped the driver unload nearly half the contents of the truck, then we were off again, destination Lublin. The guy said it might be near the time of the curfew when we got there, but I told him not to worry. I had family who lived near the centre of town – I didn't know the address, but I knew how to find it. He didn't seem too concerned.

As we neared Lublin, we stopped for a toilet break. Moving along the road in the fading light I had noticed *dachas* in among the trees, so I figured, rather than going all the way into the city, maybe a better idea would be for me to abscond now and do a repeat break-in. I knew nothing about Lublin and knew no one who lived there. It would soon be dark, and I might be caught out by the curfew. As the driver started undoing his flies, I told him I needed to have a crap and so would go further into the woods but wouldn't be long. As he was at the front of the vehicle preparing to take a leak, he did not see me drop my bag on the ground and walk off with it into the woods. I went quite a way in before leaving the well-trodden path to hide. I heard the driver shout, 'Kid! Where are you? Hurry up! I have to go.'

A little later, I heard him walking towards me still shouting but obviously sticking to the pathway. He soon gave up, went back to his truck, started it up and drove away. I suppose given the brief and transactional nature of our acquaintanceship I was not entitled to expect any more, but, even so, I was a little hurt by how slight and fleeting his concern had been for my welfare. First Uncle Izaak, then the forger, now him. I was going to have to toughen up, lower my expectations of how many people were likely to want to help me or be mindful of my best interests. I had to accept any help they did offer might not be much, would not be strongly rooted and was likely to require a quid pro quo.

I followed the same pattern and logic as before in terms of selecting a *dacha* to break into, but it was getting late, so I did not have the luxury of being able to size up somewhere then hang about to confirm it was completely safe to enter and stay the night. I again found one that was not immediately over-looked by a road or lane of any size and had lots of dead leaves and twigs on the steps and porch, suggesting no one had been there for a while. An additional piece of evidence in this case was the untidy carcass of an indeterminate creature that a woodland predator had obviously tired of and abandoned by the door.

Breaking in this time was a bit harder than before because of the design of the outer shutters, but I managed it without too much difficulty. Having gained the inside on this occasion, I found the place stripped absolutely bare. It had not been vandalised or ransacked. There were no signs of a hurried, forced or disorganised retreat or prior break-in. Apart from a few old empty hessian sacks, there was nothing at all in the house. No chairs, no food, nothing. I settled down to an uncomfortable night's sleep inside one of the largest hessian sacks with the others laid on top of me while keeping on all my clothes. I slept fitfully, waking several times as unfamiliar nocturnal noises once more penetrated my slumbers. I was an urban creature. I was reminded why I had to get out of this dangerous and inhospitable place called 'the countryside'. It was strictly for the peasants, and I was not one of those.

At first light the next day, I decided to give Lublin a miss, although I did go through some of what I imagined were the outskirts. I was trying to make a beeline for Wlodawa. This was something I had turned over in my mind the previous day as I'd lain in the back of the truck. Having looked at the map, I had written down a list of the names of the villages and small towns that lay between Lublin and Wlodawa – I figured I could not be constantly pulling out the map to get my bearings, so I had sketched out a route and memorised it. From the map, I had been able to identify a string of villages that led me to my goal: the Bug River and the border with the Soviet Union.

I reckoned it was going to be a little over eighty kilometres from where I was starting from, and this much further east the temperature was now well below zero. Maybe this helped me to get lifts. As I trudged along the minor roads, people stopped. Mainly they were driving horse-drawn trailers, but there were also a couple of trailers being pulled by tractors. No exchange, no barter or explanation needed. Over the day, I think I must have had lifts with six or seven different people, farm workers or others involved with food production or animal welfare in the area. Through a combination of short lifts and walking I made it to Wlodawa by the late afternoon. At no point did I or my temporary travelling companions encounter any German soldiers on patrol or any other branches of officialdom, but given we were on small country lanes and any fighting had long since ceased following Poland's surrender, this was not surprising. Frequently, I would see or hear heavy vehicles moving on the nearby major roads. There was a constant rumble of military thunder as tank carriers, artillery transports and soldiers went about doing whatever they routinely do in a border area.

Having been dropped in the outskirts of Wlodawa – a reasonable-sized small town by the standards of those times – I made my way towards the centre. The place had been severely damaged by German bombers and probably Soviet forces too at the beginning of hostilities, because the Polish Army had had substantial artillery regiments stationed there. Wlodawa had been a town where Jews were in the majority, a fact evidenced by what had clearly once been a large synagogue and several smaller ones. I found a deserted square where the market was likely held. There were shops on three sides and streets leading down to the river. The river that would set me free.

I bumped into a co-religionist, almost literally. Walking along a lane by a field, I heard the tramp of boots approaching from ahead. They were still out of sight, around a corner. I heard German being spoken. There was a ditch running parallel to the road, with a hedgerow that constituted the perimeter bank of the field. Brambles formed a sort of canopy stretching across the ditch. I decided it was probably best if 1 absented myself. There was a gap in the brambles which seemed to lead into the ditch just at a point where the hedgerow met the slightly raised edge of the adjoining field.

I threw myself into the gap and scrambled along, right into the back where I discovered a small, elderly man was already there. He simply signalled me to be silent, making it clear he was aware of the danger above. I obeyed as my mind raced, searching for possible explanations as to who this person might be and what he was doing there.

When the voices and the sound of marching boots had faded into the distance and silence had reigned for a minute or so, the elderly man indicated with hand gestures and a friendly twinkle in his eyes that I might now speak, but quietly. Having taken care to ensure the crucifix was no longer visible, I took a chance and spoke a few words in Yiddish, which made the guy visibly relax. I then introduced myself as Ruben Blumowicz. I had no idea where that name came from, but it was fine. He told me his name was Jakub, a baker who had lived in Wlodawa all his life. He didn't ask where I was from or what I was doing hiding in a ditch with him, but then I didn't ask him that question either. Why would two Jews be hiding from German soldiers in a ditch in Poland in 1940?

From Jakub's point of view, finding an unknown Jew of whatever age near a border which provided a route out of Nazi-occupied lands didn't really need a great deal of explanation or much by way of conjecture. He later told me all kinds of people were suddenly appearing all along the Bug River, and just as suddenly disappearing. Many were Jews, but a large proportion were not. The Nazis were giving lots of people a hard time. People of all races, religions, political beliefs and nationalities were wanting out.

If you saw anyone not wearing a German uniform whom you did not already know around the town, walking down a lane, in a field or wherever, it was a good bet they were going to try to get across the river. I learned that various enterprising individuals had trained themselves to spot such people and would approach them with an offer of help, in return for coin of the realm or something of tradeable value.

Jakub revealed he was not only a baker. He was, he said, *the* baker who had owned one of the main Jewish bakeries in Wlodawa. 'Had' was the operative word. Because he was a Jew, he no longer owned it. A Pole now had that honour, but because Jakub was popular and a renowned craftsman, the Pole had kept him on. A good proportion of the Jews of Wlodawa still brought their custom to the shop. The wages were miserable, but bakeries were usually warm, and being in the shop meant he met lots of people all the time, so he knew a great deal of what was going on in and around the district. After the initial chaos of the invasion, they had flour to make bread virtually every day, likely because they were also supplying local German troops and commanders. At least for now.

Jakub told me that when hostilities had begun, the Russians had arrived in Wlodawa first, just coming over from the other side of the river. They'd waited for their German comrades to arrive, at which point they'd retreated, making the river the border again. I told Jakub I thought my big brother had crossed the Bug River into the Soviet Union. Maybe he had done so while the Soviets were in charge on both sides. Regardless, I planned to go across and find him.

As we climbed out of the ditch, I simply followed Jakub, unbidden, and asked if he knew somewhere I might find shelter until I worked out how to get across. I asked if maybe I could work for him for a few days? I told him I was completely fluent in German and had excellent French. The latter was not quite true, but I didn't think it would be put to the test in

Wlodawa any time soon. I suggested with my looks I could probably move around the town more easily than many people of his acquaintance. That might be handy in all sorts of ways. Jakub seemed to grasp that fact and agreed I could stay in the bakery and run errands for two days, maybe three, adding, 'I'll have to check with my wife, Rena, but I'm sure she'll be OK with it. We have not been blessed with children of our own, so she is forever looking for waifs and strays to look after and fuss around, even if briefly.'

That night, in the warmth of the bakery, Jakub told me that in the early weeks of the war, after the Soviets had come over to the west bank of the river, gigantic numbers of all kinds of refugees, not just Jews, had gone across seeking sanctuary, but this number had reduced to close to zero after the Germans had arrived and taken over. He then had a whole series of horror stories about what had happened to refugees who were still trying to get into the Soviet Union illegally from Wlodawa or the surrounding area. Jakub confirmed what I had heard in Warsaw, about people dying of hypothermia in no-man's-land in full view of both German and Soviet guards who refused to intervene. When the temperatures were as low as they had been lately, death could come swiftly and quietly. I supposed that was a mercy.

Jakub went on to say that if an escapee was not shot by a German guard on the way out, they might still be shot or caught by a Soviet guard on the way in. If they were caught by the Soviets, rather than shot, it was unclear what became of them. Probably they were sent to Siberia to a work camp.

Escapees who made it across without being caught or shot might still not be free and clear. If locals on the other side spotted anyone moving across country away from the river, they would often conclude they were illegally fleeing the Nazis and were probably Jews, therefore laden with gold, diamonds and emeralds. They would catch, strip, rob and kill the men or catch, strip, rape and rob the women before killing them too. Death could come from a knife, a rifle butt or a big rock to the head. Bullets were too expensive and attracted unwanted attention. Usually, it was a rock.

Alternatively, if the river was flowing rather than frozen over as it was now, an unconscious body would simply be thrown in and left to its fate. Jakub told me how frequently the drowned or bullet-riddled bodies of strangers were brought into town, generally by the military, sometimes by riparian landowners. In the depths of winter, when the river was frozen over, bodies or parts of bodies could be visible for a day or more out on the ice, presumably where they'd fallen and frozen to death, or had been hit by a bullet or blown apart by a grenade or other explosive. Guards on either side were not minded to step on to the ice to retrieve them, so they had crafted extra-long sticks so that the bodies or body parts could eventually be punted across to the opposite bank, rather like a puck in an ice-hockey game, or dragged to their own side of the river if that was appreciably nearer. On both sides, they used grappling hooks on thin chains to catch hold of bodies and drag them up the riverbank if they could not manoeuvre them to a spot with a gentler slope.

Jakub didn't know what they did with the bodies on the Soviet side, but all the bodies that arrived on the German side seemed to end up outside or near what had been the main synagogue, even though it was impossible for all the deceased to have been Jews. Nobody ever bothered to explain how the strangers had ended up dead, but the wounds or evidence of distress generally provided enough of a clue. The Jewish authorities in the town then took it upon themselves to deal with the corpses.

Jakub reckoned the river was unlikely to thaw in the next week or so, and if I did try to cross soon, I would be fine. The ice would be able to hold the weight of an adult, even a great many adults. He told me there were bridges at various points on the river that people still used to cross the frontier in both directions. There was still some such legal traffic, generally undertaken by farmers. Sometimes a traveller would pitch up and try blagging or bribing their way across a bridge. There were rumours to suggest that this sometimes worked but you never knew what to believe about such things. Jakub didn't recommend it. I dismissed it from my mind immediately. It was illegal or nothing.

To me, the advantage of moving across a frozen river was obvious. If I could find the right place and the right conditions, I could walk to the Soviet Union and take it from there.

Jakub strongly suggested I try to go over as part of a group, a small group being better than a large one, he said. That came as a surprise to me as I had rather assumed I would go it alone. There was an underground network in Wlodawa that Jakub seemed to know about. He said he would find out when the next predominantly Jewish group of escapees was planning to make a move. Jakub was a *mensch*.

Now that the moment of truth was upon me, I started to think a bit more carefully about what might happen if I did reach the other side of the river. I didn't suppose I could just walk up to the first commissar or Soviet soldier and ask if they knew my brother. But what would I say or do? In the end, it never came to that. Events took a dramatic and unexpected turn.

Courtyard in the Jewish quarter of Wlodawa

In the late afternoon of my third day in Wlodawa, Jakub took me to meet Artur, a local Pole who, for money or tradeable goods, helped people to get across the river. Humanitarian or mercenary? A bit of both probably, but I assumed Artur was trustworthy simply by virtue of the fact Jakub had brought me to him. I told Artur I had no money. He took all the remaining food and various other things I had from the ornithologist's *dacha*, apart from the missal, telling me there was a small group I could join that was going over the following night. He didn't mind giving me a nearly free ride, saying, 'Don't thank me. You should be grateful to Jakub. He obviously likes you.'

Even though I told Artur I would go with that group, there then followed a short discussion in which Artur advised me there were two schools of thought on escaping across the Bug River. One held that whatever the weather, sunshine or ice, going solo was the only way. Some people – generally single young men and the occasional woman – refused even to consider throwing in their lot with anyone else, whether they already knew them or not. Others were equally clear that small convoys or columns had a better chance because there would be more of you to keep watch on both banks, but particularly on the far side where the murdering vigilante robber-peasants were a real threat.

Artur said he thought my decision to go with the small group was probably the right one, adding that when you were in the act of crossing in winter over ice you were only exposed to danger when you were visible on the ice, but the distance wasn't great, so that wasn't for very long. We didn't discuss what 'very long' meant. Artur was confident anyone who was quick and nimble could make the trip. He said I had nothing to worry about. Smart people, even those going across alone, could easily stage a diversion some distance away from their intended departure point, enough to distract the guards for the short time required to get from riverbank to riverbank. A big part of Artur's job was to arrange such a distraction. It was all part of the service.

We were to make our way individually to a rendezvous point a little way out of town. Artur told me there were lots of over-hanging evergreen trees and shrubs on the Nazi side, looking across to plenty of the same on the communist side. Neat symmetry. We had to be there by seven o'clock and make sure no one followed us.

The following evening, with mixed emotions after thanking Jakub and bidding him and his wife goodbye, I arrived at the place a little early. After about half an hour, there were eight adults gathered, plus me and two younger children, I'd guess about four and six years old, eleven souls in total. As we were waiting for the off, the chap I assumed was the ringleader of the refugees spoke directly to Artur, but from his poor Polish it was obvious he was a foreigner. In fact, he was French and a Christian. I realised I had met him before, in Jakub's shop, where we had chatted briefly. He had complimented me on my French. I was glad to be able to help translate for him in his dealings with Artur as Artur explained what was going to happen next. Maybe Jakub had known the leader of tonight's group was French and a translator might come in handy, which is why he'd so readily adopted me then introduced me to Artur.

The French guy was called Albert, originally from Paris and a Catholic but married to a Jewish woman from Lublin. She was by his side with their two children. By definition, these kids were also Jewish, so it was not hard to figure out why the whole family was standing where they were this evening.

Albert and his wife had been in Lublin when the war had broken out – her mother had been ill and had in fact soon died – but when France had declared war on Germany, they'd figured, at best, Albert would be interned, meaning his Jewish wife and children would be left on their own or worse, and Albert had wanted to avoid that at all costs. However, life on the run with two children had been incredibly hard, particularly in this awful winter weather. They had to get out. Albert had been around Wlodawa for a few days getting ready to go across and had somehow connected with Jakub, who, in turn, had connected him with Artur.

In the group was a Polish man also from nearby Lublin. He was in his mid twenties and evidently an enthusiastic communist, as he spoke of going to join his comrades to prepare for the war against Germany, which he was sure would come soon enough. Then there was a Polish couple in their fifties who refused to tell anyone their names, let alone where they came from in Poland. They kept repeating, 'We must get out of Poland. Take us with you, and you will be very well rewarded when we arrive safely on the other side. We have family over there. They are rich. They have a big house only a few kilometres from the river. They will help us all. Just get us over there and help us get to our family's home. You won't regret it.'

There was plenty of cloud, so the bright moons of the previous couple of nights were no longer lighting up the landscape. That was just as well, as I reckoned, whatever Artur said, it would be suicidal to try to cross an iced river lit by moonlight. If your luck was out, you would be spotted immediately and be dead soon afterwards.

The mother of the two children placed handkerchiefs in their mouths to stop them calling out. The kids did not seem in the least bit alarmed or concerned. The parents explained to the rest of us that they'd had to do something like this many times since they'd been on the run. After tonight, they would never have to do it again. They were right about that.

Artur beckoned us to move further along the bank until we reached a spot just before a bend in the river. This was the point where he thought we should cross. He gave us all a few last-minute instructions about keeping quiet and low but moving fast. Artur took the mother's hand and helped her to get close to the edge of the ice then bade us all goodbye and good luck before reminding us to wait for some loud sounds before setting foot on the ice. Turning away from the river, he walked briskly inland. A few minutes later, we heard a small commotion of some sort in the distance, which we imagined was the pre-arranged diversion Artur had spoken about. I remember thinking, I hope it is all going to work as planned.

Albert stepped in front of his wife, positioning himself at the head of the convoy. He looked straight at me and said I should stay at the back of the line so I could warn them if anyone was approaching from the German side. Albert had said German soldiers would not hesitate to shoot us in the back, firing across the river into Soviet territory if they saw anyone trying to escape from their side. I still had my knife from Lodz in my possession. I seriously doubted it would be much use if anything went wrong, but I didn't really feel in a position to argue. I just nodded my assent and went to the back.

Albert was the first to step on to the ice. He was clutching the elder child to his chest. The child's face was not really visible, because he was well wrapped up against the cold, but his eyes showed he was terrified. Who wouldn't be? Albert's wife went on to the ice right behind him, steadied herself then waited until he waved her forward in step with himself. She was carrying the other child similarly wrapped.

They hadn't gone more than four steps when the next member of the convoy stepping down from the bank lost their footing, fell hard and, just as Srulek had at the perimeter fence in Lodz, let out an involuntary roar, presumably of pain but maybe shock and anxiety. Almost immediately there were sounds on the other side of the river. Four Soviet soldiers appeared by the riverbank. They seemed to have some sort of portable searchlight with them. Whatever it was, it fully illuminated the entire fifty metres or so of ice between freedom and oppression. I was convinced we were all as good as dead, and I dived for cover behind a tree, but then I saw one of the soldiers wave, signalling the convoy to come over.

Was this to be one of those nights when luck was running with us? A collective sigh of relief went up from the little column, and the young communist instantly started to help the others down the bank towards the ice, calling quietly to the soldiers on the other side that we were comrades seeking refuge. I have no idea if they could hear him, but he obviously felt better now he was in communication with representatives of the people's champions. Albert took the lead again and continued his procession, now with everyone except me either on the ice and moving forward or preparing to step on to it.

Having now put our faith in the Soviet soldiers, and with no apparent threat on the German side, instead of going across the ice one at a time or in twos in a crocodile as we had previously discussed, the whole convoy, still except for me, was now on the ice, fully out in the open. As the front of the column got a little past halfway across, a cluster of small, roundish objects suddenly zipped into the air from roughly where the Russian soldiers had last been seen. It was immediately clear to me what the objects were: hand grenades. Within a second of them hitting and skidding across the ice towards the escapees, they exploded.

A plume of water shot up into the air with bits of humans and chunks of ice in it. There was a much louder explosion to the left, suggesting a mine further up the river had been detonated, weakening the structure of the ice. I heard someone briefly thrashing in the water. Rather bizarrely I found myself wondering if they would die from shrapnel from one of the grenades or the mine, or from a heart attack brought on by being suddenly catapulted into sub-zero water, or maybe from the shock of both. Or perhaps they had died courtesy of one of the dozens of Russian bullets that were soon ploughing into the tangled mass of humanity lying still or writhing on the ice in front of me only yards from where I was still crouching in the bushes. One of the party, maybe the older Polish man, who had not been thrown into the water or killed instantly by a grenade tried to turn back, but the bullets got him. They were all dead. I knew that.

I saw the look of terror and shock on the faces of a couple of people who were twisted and thrown back towards the German side by the explosions. Maybe they were wondering if they had been betrayed or were screaming with silent rage at the injustice of how they were about to die, so close to achieving their goal of escaping the Nazis. As I started to retreat up the riverbank through the foliage, the Soviet searchlight illuminated the carnage. I got only a fleeting glimpse. I was looking forward, not back. There was nothing I could do. I ran off into the night.

XI

German soldiers would be all around that section of the river-bank within minutes. I had to get out of there. No dawdling, no thinking or reflecting on the horror of what had happened. It was over, and if I did not get out of there, I would be the next and last victim.

Flashing across my mind almost immediately was the thought that the plan to get across to the Soviet Union and find Nathan, a plan that had given meaning and coherence to my life – if only briefly – no longer existed. I had no idea what would replace it. Getting across to the Soviet Union suddenly felt impossible. My attempt had not been a mistake, but it had been in vain.

I needed time to think and come up with another scheme, another vision or strategy, and collect together new resources to help me achieve it. The only place I knew where I might have a hope of doing any of that was back at the bakery. It wouldn't be safe to try to get there this instant. If I was spotted going into or approaching the shop after dark, it might bring trouble both to me and to Jakub. The Germans might well be putting extra patrols into the town to remind people that messing about at the river was deadly.

For what felt like hours, I walked around, ducking and diving like a hunted animal. I could hear a major din coming from the river, a lot of shouting in German as soldiers looked for survivors or accomplices. Eventually, I hoisted myself up into a tree that I judged would be able to support me and provide a vantage point to survey the near horizon, although the noise from the river was fading fast. I think they must have concluded that no one had gotten away alive. Everyone was dead on the ice. Their work was done. They were giving up and going somewhere warm. I didn't sleep a wink for fear of falling out of the tree, then, at around what I judged to be midmorning the following day, I walked, as casually as I could, back into Jakub's shop.

Jakub's face was a study. Without giving anything away to any of the people present, he just nodded towards the back, and I vanished in the direction of the welcoming glow of the oven. I stayed in that room, nibbling on scraps of bread and crumbs, trying to collect my thoughts, until Jakub closed up and called me out.

After I told him what had happened, he said he'd guessed it had been something along those lines. Everyone in Wlodawa and Warsaw had heard the large explosion and the gunfire. Then, this morning, eight frozen dead bodies had been brought up from the river to be dumped outside the shell of the main synagogue. Jakub had gone to look. From his description, Albert, his wife and children were among them, buried within layers of frosted ice. None of the other lumps of ice he saw were configured in such a way as to suggest I was similarly entombed, so Jakub had assumed I had perished beneath the ice or made it to the other side. It had never occurred to him I might still be on the German side. Apparently, the German soldiers who brought the bodies to town told everyone this was not their doing. 'Ivan' was to blame. They weren't apologising or expressing any sorrow or regret. Just stating bald facts.

Jakub was happy I was not dead but less than delighted I had come back to his shop. He said Artur had been in to say he was going to visit a distant relative, and he did not know when he would be back. Jakub thought this meant Artur was frightened and would be suspending river-crossing activities for an indefinite period. I had the terrible idea that I could be stranded in Wlodawa for eternity. That must not happen!

I waited for Jakub to tell me I had to leave, but he held back, and later that day, when I made clear I did not want to stay in Wlodawa but merely needed some time and space to come up with another idea, he looked relieved and said he would help. I could stay for the time being, but I was not to leave the shop at all. In fact, I had to stay in the back completely out of sight at all times. Days drifted into weeks, and the subject of when I might go was mentioned less and less. I think if it had been left to Rena, with whom I was getting along famously, the matter would never have been talked about again. I could feel myself sometimes slipping into a reverie in which I sat out the war in this warm and welcoming place but that's all it was. A momentary lapse, a daydream. Eventually, Jakub needed an errand running. Rena had had to visit a relative and was therefore not available. Jakub asked me to do it. My task was successfully completed, and thereafter, gradually and with Jakub and Rena's blessing, I began to move around the town more and more.

In April 1940, I had my fourteenth birthday in Wlodawa. In fact, I stayed at the bakery until a week or so after it, by which time spring was underway, the ice gone and the weather decidedly better. Running errands about the town had helped keep me sane. Inevitably, there were odd contacts with German soldiers, but they were mainly ordinary stiffs in the Wehrmacht. My looks and street smarts kept me clear of serious trouble and encouraged me to believe I could make it. Unfortunately, and frustratingly, precisely what 'it' was continued to elude me.

I was absolutely determined not to stay in Wlodawa. If I could not hook up with Nathan and hatch a plan to get our family out of the Lodz Ghetto, I had to do something else towards the same end. I was champing at the bit. All the time I was out and about, I was gathering intelligence about what was happening in the wider world, by which I really mean elsewhere in Poland and sometimes beyond. I caught occasional glimpses of German newspapers, not that I regarded them as being reliable, but to the extent they corroborated other things I heard, they had some value. Foreign radio stations were continuing to broadcast in Polish, and even though the penalty for being found in possession of a radio set was death, people in and around the town were clearly listening because there was plenty of talk about how the war was progressing, and the information was frequently quite vivid.

As the weather improved, swimming across the Bug River or going over in small boats seemed to become the favoured modes, but guards on both sides of the river seemed to have stepped up their patrols, so more and more dead bodies were arriving outside the synagogue. Apparently, there had now been repeated Soviet protests about laxness on the German side. Thank you, Uncle Joe. On top of that, there were whispered reports that any Jews who did make it across would be sent to Siberia, which was generally regarded as being a death sentence. I hoped that had not been Nathan's fate.

I agonised over the decision I had to take and talked it through with Jakub and Rena. Although I had by now accepted that I was not going to try to get into the Soviet Union, they told me they had always thought, deep down, it was a heroically noble idea but also a foolish one. They didn't think it was their place to say anything, as I seemed so determined to find my brother. However, they pointed out that if Nathan had made it over – a big if – the chances were he was either dead or in Siberia, where he soon would be dead or unfindable, likely both. I could never accept that Nathan was dead, but I did understand their point about the probable difficulty of my finding him, even if I did make it over to the other side.

I briefly considered trying to go back to Lodz. The pull of home is always strong, but there were too many obvious risks. Would I break back into the ghetto? Or just show up at a gate and apologise for the fact I had wandered out by mistake and tell whoever was on duty: 'I would now like to return to the bosom of my family, if it's not too much trouble, thank you very much.' Probably not.

Another idea started to form in my mind, but it was far from complete. My hatred of the Nazis had deepened, intensely. Unless they were defeated, I did not see how I would ever find Nathan, dead or alive, or be reunited with my mum and dad, Srulek and my sisters. To help bring about that defeat, I had to either hook up with partisans or get out of Poland altogether and connect with whatever was left of the Polish Army. OK, I was only fourteen, but I could lie about my age – I was getting good at lying – or else I would just have to wait until I was legally old enough to fight assuming that war was still going on which, in a perverse way I hoped it would be just so I could be part of bringing down Hitler.

Jakub strongly counselled against trying to join the partisans. There were always rumours about partisan activity, but as far as

Jakub could tell, they achieved very little, and not all partisan groups would welcome a Jew, even a Jew who looked like me. That squared with comments I had heard other Jews make. I crossed that off my list.

That left joining up with units of the Polish Army who were still fighting, and on that score the reports were consistent if, geographically speaking, all over the place. A large part of the army had laid down their weapons and gone into captivity when Poland had surrendered on 27 September 1939, but some had escaped into the Soviet Union. However, according to Jakub, for as long as Germany and the Soviet Union remained allies, it seemed unlikely the Russians would allow Polish formations to remain battle-ready. He was therefore sure any Polish soldiers who were over there who were not communists would already have been interned, and he wasn't so sure what the Soviets would do even with those Polish soldiers who did profess to be communists. Stalin was not famous for his love of the Poles, irrespective of their professed brand of politics.

Heading north towards the Baltic with a view to getting out of Poland into Denmark, Norway or Sweden was one possible way of escaping and joining the fight-back. A few days before my birthday, that option looked closed off. The Germans marched into Denmark and occupied the south of Norway. Jakub thought that meant Sweden would be next. Who was I to argue?

Heading south seemed filled with uncertainty. Apparently, a good number of Polish soldiers and citizens had ended up in Romania and Hungary, but their fate was unknown. The key, and in the end determining, fact was that the Polish government had fled to France, where they had established themselves in Paris. All Polish military personnel in and around western Europe and any other Polish citizens who were inclined to carry on the fight were encouraged to find their way to France as best and as quickly as they could to join the Polish forces being assembled there. There was already a well-established and large Polish émigré community in France consisting of Jews and Catholics. There were schools, synagogues, food shops. The works. My dad's relative Dinah lived there, although I had no idea where, or even what her married surname was.

According to the reports I heard on the Wlodawa grapevine, large numbers of young Poles, including Polish Jews, were making the attempt to get to France going via the Balkans before crossing over to northern Italy then moving towards the French border near Monte Carlo. That sounded good to me.

But leaving aside for the moment the small matter of how I would get across Germany, wouldn't the French–German border be an active war zone with lots of shooting and bombing? Jakub thought not. There had been no serious reports of fighting along or near the frontier. Technically, it was true France had declared war on Germany back in September, but there had been no serious hostilities on land, and there was some speculation about whether or not there ever would be. A lot of posturing and posing. Jakub said he thought the Brits and the French had declared war on Germany after they invaded Poland only because they felt formally obliged. Really, they were not at all keen to get involved in another land war evoking memories of the Somme and the fields of Flanders.

Anyway, France had great defences, and the French Army was huge and well equipped. The Germans would think twice before starting that up again. *Lebensraum* was mainly about moving east, not west, although Alsace and Lorraine needed to watch out. Seemingly, Albert had told Jakub that even if the Germans went to France and defeated the French Army, France was such a big country they could only really hope to hold the larger towns and cities, not the great empty spaces in-between, with thousands upon thousands of small villages and *hameaux* covering every type of terrain and climate. There would always be an abundance of food, and, according to Albert, other than around the Alps, Pyrenees and northeast, snow and ice were comparatively rare or lasted only a short while. The implication was that French soil was likely to be safe soil. I spoke the language well enough to get by and could definitely improve. France became the obvious destination.

But how the hell would I get across Poland and Germany? Maybe I could walk and get lifts? The distance was more than 1,200 kilometres, so that was out of the question. Trains were the obvious answer. I had been on a train once, going from Lodz to Warsaw, so that was twice if you counted the return journey. I'd been with my dad and Nathan, but Dad had bought the tickets, and I had no idea if all he'd had to do was hand over the money. Did he also have to show some kind of ID? Get permission? Papers? And that was before the war. Jakub had never been on a train, ever, so he did not know for sure how these things were handled before or under the German occupation. However, I remembered from that one trip and from adventure stories I had read that there were lots of places on trains that were potential hidey-holes. People were always getting away with making trips on trains without paying and without being found out. Someone of my size should have no problem.

I assumed trains heading into Germany, into the devil's maw from the occupied territories, would not have the highest level of security, because who would try a stunt like that? Me, that's who. I would hide in among goods being transported in box cars or in the van. That was the plan. I wasn't entirely sure how I could check out any of this in advance, but I assured Jakub that was what I would do before climbing on board, and if I couldn't find anywhere to hide straight away, I would jump off and wait for another train heading west. It wasn't as if I had an exact destination in mind as I headed for the great big empty spaces of France. When I got there, I would find where the Polish Army was stationed and make a beeline for it.

I'm not sure how much confidence Jakub and Rena had in my plan, but they could see I was determined. I think Jakub thought I needed to leave anyway. Despite Rena's protestations, I did represent a continuing risk to this lovely couple, and I was an additional mouth to feed. Maybe this plan, my plan, was as good as any we could devise between us. Then I announced I intended to leave in three days. Jakub sighed but did not try to dissuade me. My course of action, the next phase of my life was set. Getting to France to join the fight against the Nazis had replaced finding Nathan as my mission.

In the next seventy-two hours, I set about gathering as much food as I could. I stole a bottle for water, checked the knife and other contents of my knapsack were still in good shape, and sold the missal, although I retained and kept on wearing the crucifix. I sensed from here on in I might have to present myself in an alternative, non-Polish persona, at least until I reached France, and maybe even then.

Where to catch a train? I believed Radom was a major rail-way interchange where there would be lots of opportunities to find one, but it was about 200 kilometres away. I decided Lublin would be a better bet. It was a bigger city so likely to be an even larger transport interchange, with a greater number of trains moving in and out. Crucially, Lublin was also much nearer to Wlodawa, so even if I had to walk all the way, it was not inconceivable that I could do it. I also knew there was always lots of traffic from Wlodawa and surrounding villages heading for Lublin, the regional metropolis. I felt confident I could either sort out a lift in Wlodawa itself before I set off or that out on the road something would come along. I mentioned my plan to Jakub. He approved and said if I waited an extra day, he could definitely arrange for me to join a crew that took a lorry to Lublin every week to pick up various supplies from merchants in the city for delivery either to shops and businesses in Wlodawa or to villages dotted around the surrounding countryside. Jakub said he would ensure the driver dropped me somewhere near the railway station in the centre of Lublin. And that is exactly what happened. My gratitude to Jakub and Rena knew no bounds. They had taken me to their hearts. I had taken them to mine. But needs must where the devil drives and I was driven, tremulously stepping out again, alone again, filled with even greater apprehension about what lay ahead.

In Lublin, I found a spot overlooking the marshalling yards a little way down the track from the main station. There were German guards around the perimeter but not many, and they didn't seem engaged in any kind of active surveillance. I watched trains and rolling stock being manoeuvred around the sidings, but because they had no visible markings on them – or at least none that I could intelligently decipher – I realised I had no real way of knowing what their ultimate destinations might be as they pulled out of the sidings and headed for the platforms in the station. It was unlikely, but not impossible, they were going east, but they could just as easily be heading north or south, and that was no good to me.

On the second day of my observations of the yards, a young boy who looked several years my junior, maybe he was ten, turned up with an older man who left him to his own devices as he went off to shunt carriages and assorted railway hardware. Father and son, I guessed. The boy wandered off to a section of the yard where damaged vehicles were waiting to be mended or perhaps scrapped. He stayed there alone for the hour or so that I watched.

The next day, the same thing happened. This time, when his dad climbed on board a shunter, I made my way towards the boy. He was on his own, kicking a can around. I introduced myself as Henryk Karbowski and asked if I could join in his game of football. When we stopped for a few minutes, I explained to the boy I was an ethnic German who had grown up in the east of Poland, which is why I could speak Polish to him, but my parents had been murdered by filthy communist partisans, so I was now an orphan, trying, without money or papers, to get to the western side of Germany where I had family around Baden-Baden.

After the attack in which my parents were killed, because I was not dead like the rest of my family, the German authorities at first suspected me of being involved in some way. I explained I had come back from town to find communist slogans daubed on the house, with the bodies of my parents and two brothers and a sister lying dead in the vegetable garden. They took me into custody, and I was put in a cell in a local police station. They said they believed my story, but it might take a while to sort out a place for me with a local German family who could maybe use some help on their farm pending my assignment to some more permanent arrangement. I didn't like the sound of any of this, so, lovely though the German family were that came and picked me up and took me to their house, I ran away the very next morning. If I handed myself in to the authorities now, who knows what would happen, so this was me taking matters into my own hands.

It was slightly mad me explaining all this to the boy, but at least it helped me to sort it all out in my head. I might need to use this line again. The boy nodded and accepted this as unquestioningly as one would the news that rain was wet. He was only a kid. I asked him if he knew which trains were heading west. He said he didn't but would try to find out. The key thing, I impressed on him, was for me to know where the trains would be laid up the night before so I could get on and hide.

The following day, the boy greeted me with the news that while no one was ever really sure when civilian trains would actually leave Lublin station for points west, the great majority of those that did left from the main two platforms and were therefore generally stacked up the night before in a part of the yard that he then pointed towards. He added the important caveat that westbound trains generally terminated in a German city, so a young Polish boy, albeit an ethnic German, might quickly find himself in a great deal of trouble if he was caught there without papers. I'm guessing he had told his dad about me and what I wanted, and that his dad had passed this on. I acknowledged the force of the boy's point but reminded him I had no choice for the reasons I had given earlier, and, actually, he shouldn't think of me as being Polish at all. I was a German who had been living in Poland, so once I got to the Fatherland everything would be sorted out. That was that. He turned away looking for something that would make do as a football.

The boy's information about the direction of the train I finally chose to board the night before was absolutely correct. I ended up on a westbound train. What the boy could not have known is exactly who the passengers were going to be or to which part of Germany they were headed. I was about to find out.

On what was to be my last night in Poland for several years, I went to the part of the marshalling yard the boy had pointed me towards. There was only one train there, and it had what looked like twenty or so empty coaches attached.

The seats were deep benches with luggage racks above. At the edge of the seat by the aisle next to the door, there was a recess that I guess fitted around the contours of the toilet that was adjacent. I squeezed in there and just about managed to fit with my bag at my feet. Exhausted, I fell asleep curled up like a hedgehog. There were advantages to being small and skinny.

I awoke when I felt the train move off. It stopped moments later. I had no clear vision of anything that was not straight in front of my eyes at floor level, but it wasn't difficult to deduce that we had moved from the marshalling yards into the station. Very soon, I heard doors opening and saw and heard lots of people with big boots getting into the carriage, putting bags on the floor and heard them arguing as they struggled to put things in the luggage rack. I couldn't see anything other than people's feet, but it was obvious they were all German men. Judging by the huge amount of bad language, and by the colour of those bits of garments I could see, these were soldiers. My heart sank as my mind raced. It didn't take long for me to realise I was in a troop carrier heading for Berlin. Worse and worse, not long after the train pulled out, one of the soldiers dropped a packet of cigarettes on the floor, which then got kicked under the bench, coming to rest on the point of my nose. When he bent down to retrieve his tobacco, he spotted me straight away.

On seeing me, the soldier let out a huge roar of laughter and shouted, 'Come on out, little shrimp. Out of there – your journey's over.'

I crawled out, genuinely terrified, crying my eyes out. A huge man lifted me clean off the floor as every soldier in the carriage turned and started laughing at the spectacle. In a blind panic, I implemented Plan B, a slight variation on the story I had told the Polish boy in the marshalling yard.

In floods of tears, I made my pitch to the carriage full of soldiers: 'Help me, comrades. I am Henryk Karbowski, a *Volksdeutsche* whose family was slaughtered by filthy communist partisans only a few weeks ago. I have family in Germany, near Baden-Baden, but the local police wanted to send me to an orphanage. I want to go to Germany. I am not a child any more. I can help with the war against the Slav scum and those damned communists.'

The soldiers seemed to have no difficulty believing my story, although I noticed one of them dragging out my bag and inspecting its contents. Finding only the knife, he seemed unconcerned, and checking my person the crucifix was fleetingly exposed. He just nodded.

While the soldiers clearly had some difficulty believing I was old enough or big enough to fight for Germany, they clearly liked my style and my spirit. 'A small boy but with the heart of a lion. A true Aryan,' one of them shouted, and this met with widespread agreement.

I sensed maybe some of the older men had sons my age, or wished they had. Perhaps I had softened their hearts. The younger soldiers took their lead from them. No one suggested I might be a spy or a Jew on the run. A debate followed about what they should do with me when we reached Berlin. My heart froze once more as the final destination was confirmed. It was the first and only scheduled stop. Everybody was clear that if they turned me in, I would be in deep shit. One of the older soldiers said he would sort it out and then, basically, most of the rest of them lost interest. A senior officer approached, and I was shoved back under the seat. Nobody turned me in. The lower ranks had bonded to fool an officer. I began to believe I might actually live to see midnight.

As the journey wore on, it emerged that most of the soldiers were going back to Germany for their first trip home, indeed their first leave of any kind, since they had formed part of the victorious advancing army the previous September. The soldier who said he would sort things out told me his name was Walther and that he was a native of Berlin, where his wife and three daughters lived. He had an older son away in the war. He asked me if I wanted to go and meet his family. They didn't know he was coming home that day, so they were in for a big surprise. That would now be even bigger when I was introduced to them!

By the time the train arrived in Berlin, I had become the cherished mascot of the coach, and everyone was more or less engaged in the challenge of getting me out of the station so Walther could take me home without being stopped and asked tiresome questions. In the end, one of soldiers simply wrapped me in his greatcoat and, courtesy of a fireman's lift, threw me over his shoulder. The others crowded around and were generally as boisterous as any group of soldiers coming home on leave might be expected to be. The station authorities were glad to see them through as quickly as they could.

I witnessed the touching scene of Walther being reunited with his wife Jutta and his children, three little girls, the oldest of whom might have been about my age. They readily agreed to help this brave German orphan boy.

In the evening, we all sat down to dinner, and I was given clothes that the oldest daughter had hurriedly adjusted from a set of her older brother's cast-offs. It emerged, from the tone of his remarks about what he had witnessed in Poland, that while Walther was a patriotic German, he did not approve of the way the Nazis were behaving or the things they were asking the army to do: 'I did not join the army to terrorise women and children, much less shoot them just because they're Jews or Poles. Leave that to the SS. Don't ask us to do it.'

I was amazed to hear such sentiments being expressed by a German. Obviously, I knew from Lodz that not every German was a Nazi supporter, but it had never occurred to me that anyone wearing a German military uniform might not be 100 per cent behind the Führer. I wondered if Walther wasn't deliberately trying to entice me into some sort of confession or an indiscretion, but I rapidly dismissed this as it became obvious his anti-Nazi sentiments ran deep and were shared by his whole family.

XII

Walther was on leave for a week, so I assumed I would have to work out a plan for what to do and where to go next before the seven days were up. I also assumed I would depart his hearth and home at the same time as him. However, in the first few days, the timing of my departure was not mentioned, and neither was I asked what my plans might be for the future. On the contrary, Walther's only concern seemed to be that I was happy in my new surroundings, which without doubt I was. Whatever anxieties Walther might have entertained about the precariousness of his current situation, he kept them to himself, or at any rate did not share them with me. He encouraged me to engage with and get to know his daughters, and he watched closely when I was with them, as if to satisfy himself that they also liked me, which indeed appeared to be the case.

During this time, I discovered something very important about Walther and Jutta. They were deeply committed Protestants, who, while obviously disapproving of it, were not so foolhardy as to oppose Hitler's regime outright, much less attempt openly to defy the Nazi hegemony by advertising their continued adherence to Christianity. Walther had already made clear how he felt about the things he had witnessed as a soldier in Poland, and maybe his and Jutta's decision to help me was them moving from silent and passive protest or resistance to something a bit more real, a bit more substantial. I doubt they could have suspected the truth about my real religious or racial history, because that would have meant they were willingly accepting a huge risk to themselves and their children. I didn't enquire. I was just hugely grateful.

Back in Lodz, I had been in and out of the Karbowksi household all the time, and I had visited other Christian homes, meaning Catholic homes, from time-to-time, but here, for the first time, I had the opportunity to observe at close quarters the way a family very different from my own lived. There was obviously a lot of love in this house in Berlin. No shouting or major domestic rows. Neither parent ever struck any of their children or even raised their voice. I never knew home life could be like that.

Walther was clear that whatever I might decide to do next, I had to get some kind of papers. He thought it was astonishing I had survived as long as I had without any. He understood that if I just walked into a police station and told my story, things would be unlikely to turn out well for me. But then he winked and suggested he knew someone who could probably help: 'People are buying and selling fake papers all the time, usually for good reasons.'

The day before he was due to return to his regiment, Walther told me the person who could help with the false papers was his sister. He said her name was Elsa, and we were going to see her right now in a part of Berlin I had never visited. She worked in one of the documentation-issuing offices for Berliners. Walther told me to put on a cap with a wide brim and a Hitler Youth jacket. He also said I should try not to look at the names of any streets en route and definitely not try to remember the location of his sister's office. He didn't need to spell out his reasons.

When we got to the office, we went through a back door. There was no chat and no fuss. Elsa, if that was her real name, had been briefed. I was led into a room, where Elsa took a photograph and my fingerprints plus a few details about me. Obviously, I could speak German and Polish, but I also added and exaggerated my ability to speak French. At that she smiled and nodded. I couldn't have been in the building for more than three minutes in total. The next day, Walther came home waving a *Kennkarte*, the standard German identity document for civilians. I asked no questions. I just took it and expressed my gratitude.

The *Kennkarte* included a date of birth that made me sixteen rather than fourteen, and it gave my place of birth as some obscure town in eastern Poland that I had never heard of before. It was on the other side of Lublin from Wlodawa. However, what the *Kennkarte* did not show was the name Henryk Karbowski. Walther explained that while there were lots of *Volksdeutschen* with Polish-sounding names, as we were engaged in subterfuge it was just as well to go a little bit further and adopt a name that was unambiguously Germanic. A name that would sit easily with my obviously pure Aryan looks. Hearing that made me wince, but Walther assured me that as long as I stayed out of any serious trouble no one was ever going to check the authenticity of my papers, particularly if they saw the name of a one-horse town in the east. Karl-Heinz Reitzenstein made his appearance in my life. That was the name on my forged documents.

I later learned Walther had suggested this name to his sister because he had a vague memory that there was a famous family of that name from down Baden-Baden way, and I'd told him I had connections there. I wondered, again, if Walther ever suspected that my underlying story was fiction, plausible fiction but fiction nonetheless, and therefore, in for a penny in for a pound, he was going to use his best endeavours to help me get away with it.

Walther acknowledged I would want to be getting along at some point, but he told me his wife and children would be happy for me to stay for as long as I liked, and now I had a *Kennkarte* they or Elsa could help find me work, so I would not be a drain on the household's resources. He later took me on one side to tell me having a 'man about the house' made him feel a lot more comfortable. Neither he nor his wife had any family in Berlin or anywhere nearby, and while his neighbours were OK, knowing that a resourceful person, someone like me, was in his house would be a great comfort to him. He said he hoped I would still be there when he next came home on leave, but he had no idea when that might be, so he assured me that whenever I was ready to go Jutta would not stand in my way.

This was great news. I had no intention of staying in Berlin or Germany for a moment longer than was absolutely necessary. I still wanted to get to France as soon as I could, to join up with Polish armed forces. Walther and his family were nice; they almost certainly saved my life, and it was fascinating observing the ways and rhythms of their family life. They were nevertheless living under an umbrella of evil that was destroying Poland and harming Jews on an unprecedented scale. More than anything, I wanted to bring that system down so I could

180

find Nathan, get my family back and go somewhere safe, ideally Palestine.

Walther went back to his regiment. The following month, in May 1940, France fell. Everywhere in Berlin people were jubilant. I was astonished to discover that, more than the British and the Americans, the Germans held France responsible for the national humiliation they had suffered at the end of the First World War. When Hitler insisted the Armistice with France be signed at Compiègne, in the very same train wagon the German surrender had been made in 1918, the population of the capital seemed to go completely loopy. Obviously, there was such a thing as a good German, a German who was not a Nazi supporter and did not appear to hate Jews. Walther and Jutta fitted into that category, and I had known others in Lodz. But there was absolutely no getting away from it: at that moment, at least in Berlin, Hitler and the Nazis enjoyed overwhelming support from the German people.

I learned that under the terms of the Armistice, Hitler allowed the French to retain control over substantial parts of their country, particularly in the south and west. The northeast and the Atlantic coast would be under German control. A new French government was installed in Vichy on the edge of the Massif Central. The Polish government in exile did not hang about. They relocated to London. London and the UK became the new rallying points for Poles who wanted to hurt the Nazis, so that was where I guessed I needed to go. But I put that from my mind so I could concentrate on surviving in Berlin.

It seemed that wearing a Hitler Youth jacket meant no one appeared to take much notice of me as I walked about the streets, but I knew in my bones it was ridiculous to imagine Berlin could be a safe place. I had so far managed to avoid going along to any meetings held by the Hitler Youth, but I had noticed other similarly attired youngsters in Walther and Jutta's neighbourhood eying me up as I walked about the streets – a stranger in a Hitler Youth jacket whom they never saw at any local Hitler Youth events. That made me feel very nervous. I wasn't sure how much longer that would last or what would happen if I was cornered and interrogated about my membership of the group. In anticipation of being press-ganged, I worked out a line about how, as a *Volksdeutsche* from the rural east of Poland only recently arrived in Berlin, I had never actually attended a meeting, because before the war there had been no branch or cell in my area. I hoped everyone would excuse me for my lack of familiarity with whatever the hell one was supposed to do there. Fortunately, I never had to go to a Hitler Youth rally, or any other kind of meeting held or organised by them.

Not long after Walther had gone, Elsa came round to say that my ability to speak Polish and French, as well as German, meant I should have no difficulty getting a job, but I might have to leave Berlin and go somewhere else in the expanding Reich. I assured her I was perfectly happy with that. Until something suitable popped up, she had found me a labouring job in a metal-working factory not too far from Walther and Jutta's house. As a completely unskilled person, all I would have to do was sweep the floors around the machinery, shift boxes and do other low-level tasks. The truly important things, though, were that I would earn money and I was in the system. Every day I stayed at the factory seemed to me to be a day that added to the strength of my fake identity. But after a few months, the strain caused by my situation and the tedium of the work were getting to me. I asked Jutta if I could go and see Elsa. Jutta said she would arrange for Elsa to come and see me, which she did at the weekend.

It was late November and winter was upon us again. Elsa explained she had been looking out for me and there was a job in Lorraine, which, like Lodz and much of western Poland, had by then been incorporated into the Reich. In both Lorraine and neighbouring Alsace, which had also become part of Germany, a great many of the local people had been expelled and new families were being brought in to settle. Both territories were being systematically 'Germanised'. I knew what that meant from what had happened in Lodz. In the meantime, this dislocation had created immediate and major labour shortages across every type of industry, particularly in the all-important agricultural sector. Elsa told me there was an opening for someone to work on a big farm, and this is where my ability to speak French, Polish and German had come up trumps. French was no longer an official language in Lorraine, but, naturally, it continued to be widely spoken. On the farm to which I was being sent, there would be a substantial contingent of Poles, and, as far as I understood it, I was to act as some kind of liaison between them and the farm's manager, whom she assumed would be a German. I had no real idea what Elsa was talking about but I felt sure that, whatever it was, if I could brazen it out in Berlin living at close quarters with a German family and wearing a Hitler Youth jacket, I could do just about anything. So, thanks to the Third Reich, I was going to France. They were arranging it.

Monhofen (Moncourt) i. Lothr.

Postcard of Monhofen during the German occupation

The farm I was allocated to was near the French town of Moncourt, south of Metz. Its German name was Monhofen. Elsa gave me precise instructions about how to get there, producing a train ticket to take me to Nancy, which was not too far to the west, and the fare for a bus for the onward journey. Once I got to Monhofen, I was to ask for directions and walk the remainder of the way, which is exactly what I did. Jutta and the three girls came with me to the railway station to see me off safely. This was my next major wrench. Following heartfelt goodbyes, once more with many tears, I was on the move.

A farm in winter in northern Europe can be a bleak and unwelcoming place. This one was no exception. As I walked up a track from the main road, without speaking or asking my business, a farmhand directed me, in French, towards the farmhouse. There I was greeted by the farm manager Claude, who said he had been expecting me. Claude was obviously not

German. He told me he preferred to be known as 'Chef' and pointed to a little alcove in the kitchen which he said was the office. If ever I needed to find him, that was his base. If he wasn't there when I came calling, he'd be back at his station if I sat and waited long enough.

Chef could manage reasonably well in German, but he preferred French. He and I agreed to communicate in French. I was going to be on a steep learning curve picking up French agricultural terms, but Claude was OK with that. He explained he was also the owner of the farm. His family had owned it and run it for more than a hundred years: 'We have been hosts to visiting Germans more than once.'

I quickly learned that there were a little over twenty Polish workers on the farm at that time, all men, but as the weather improved more *Zwangsarbeiter* and volunteers would apparently be joining us.

I was billeted in a hut with three old men, by which I mean they were in their late thirties and early forties. They hadn't been at the farm very long and didn't know each other beforehand. In effect, the four of us were to be Chef's management team. We were his production supervisors. Our job was to make sure all the workers knew what was expected of them by relaying instructions to the gang leaders of each team. A second and equally vital part of our role was to watch for and report any infringements of the rules, of which observing the curfew was key. The German authorities wanted to be sure the foreign workers were all tucked up safely in bed at night, and they were particularly concerned that the bed in question was their own. Any Pole found having sex with a German woman would be summarily executed, and in the course of the war several thousand were. The German women were disgraced, but they weren't killed. I never found out what penalty, if any, attached to a Polish man having sex with a French woman or indeed a woman of any other nationality. I soon learned there was a lot of that going on too. However, while the Germans cared about racial purity, for these purposes only their own race really mattered.

The way things worked out, the older guys were going to be more engaged in the day-to-day supervision of the farm workers than I was. Two were Germans from the south of Germany. They didn't speak any Polish or French, so I was not sure what use they would be supervising predominantly non-German-speaking Polish field hands on a farm in France. The other man was Pavel, a Czech. I was never clear how he came to be there. He spoke good German, so I imagined he was a volunteer, maybe a Nazi sympathiser, which would mean he was none too popular with his own people back home. Pavel spoke no French but claimed he could get by in Polish. In fact, his Polish was all but non-existent. Given enough time, he could come up with sentences, but in any kind of ordinary conversation he was quickly lost. I doubt he understood more than about ten per cent of what was being said in Polish.

Chef brought the four of us together and, using me as an interpreter, told us that the farm was engaged in the production and processing of vegetables, and their despatch to various parts of the Reich, but particularly to the military. Knowing that I might be helping feed the German Army did little to improve my mood.

As the youngest, most energetic and only genuinely multi-lingual person on the team, I was made the Chef's principal assistant, a kind of liaison officer, which is exactly what Elsa had said I would be doing. None of the other three argued with that. In fact, they looked quite relieved. I was careful not to behave or suggest I was in any way their superior and Chef more than once insisted no special privileges were formally attached to my role. Day-to-day it meant I visited the farm house office in the kitchen more frequently than the others. It provided me with opportunities to shelter from bad weather, steal or be given food, or glean intelligence about what was happening outside the confines of the farm. This was a time when I learned more about the limitations of my command of French, but it was good enough and getting better all the time as I used and heard it spoken more.

Other than his sly reference to his family being used to hosting visiting Germans, never once did I hear Chef make any adverse remarks about his lords and masters, but neither did he light up with joy whenever they were mentioned or were around. He made us aware that there were SS units in the area and reminded us about the omnipresent Gestapo. The regular police visited about once a week, so, all in all, 'be careful and watch your tongue' was the message.

The farmhands typically worked in gangs varying in size from five to eight workers, depending on what needed doing that day. If there were any individuals who were surplus to requirements on any particular day, they could be set tasks nearer the main house, which Chef would personally keep an eye on. The composition of each gang would stay roughly the same from day-to-day. The day's tasks were handed out to the chargehands every morning at breakfast by the other three guys after being transmitted to them by me. I was on hand to explain in Polish if anything was unclear.

Thereafter, the gangs would set off for whatever part of the farm estate their work took them, after which my main business was reporting on progress. I relayed messages and reported back if there were any difficulties that needed addressing. Maybe some equipment had broken or there were blockages that needed a team of horses to be brought over to tow away an obstacle. In addition, and this was the bit I enjoyed most, there were errands and dealings of various kinds with other farms in the area or in the town, for which I was provided with a bicycle. I was also taught to drive a car and a truck because a few journeys I was required to make were either too far to be practical on a bicycle or they involved fetching and carrying things which wouldn't fit in the pannier or little dog cart.

As the weather improved, life on the farm became reasonably comfortable. We even put together a football team with a neighbouring farm that played occasional games against similar teams in the area. There were a couple of odd moments when we were all shipped off on buses to take part in communal events with Nazi flags everywhere. When everyone else cheered, I cheered, but I never gave the Nazi salute, even on the occasion when we were taken to Metz to form part of an adoring rabble for some visiting Nazi bigwig from Berlin. I climbed up a lamppost to get a better view, and while everybody else was '*Sieg Heil*-ing', I excused myself by hanging on to a bracket.

It was also while I was in Monhofen that romance appeared in my life. I was sent on an errand to one of the more remote farms in the district. I had been there several times before and knew the farmer and his wife to be kind and considerate people. I walked up to the farmhouse door and knocked. When there was no reply, I shouted. Still nothing, so I lifted the latch and stuck my head around the corner.

A tin bath was in front of the fire, with no one in it, but some wet footprints were leading away from it, going into the kitchen. These plainly did not belong to either of the adults who lived in the house, a fact more or less instantly confirmed when madame came running in a couple of seconds later, fully clothed, fully shod in clogs and looking terrified.

Moments later, the monsieur arrived. I had seen him in the field as I approached the house, and he had clearly seen me. Rather jauntily and lightly I said the obvious, 'Ah, you've got a visitor. I'm sorry if I interrupted them having a bath. I'll be on my way.'

With this, madame immediately burst into floods of tears. All was clearly not well. They were scared about something. But about what?

They explained that their children were all grown up, living far away now, and no one else was registered as staying with them. They had not yet had an opportunity to inform the authorities that Martha was with them.

'So, what's the big deal? Just go to the town hall or the police station and let them know.'

Here is where the floods of tears started again. I stood there, puzzled. After a quick exchange, they obviously decided to take a chance. They called out to Martha to come in from the kitchen. As she walked through the door, I felt like I'd been hit by a mighty hammer. Into the room, modestly covered by a large towel, came such a vision of loveliness that I had to remember to breathe, otherwise I think I could have died – died happily, anchored to that spot, asphyxiated by love in the presence of what could only have been a goddess.

The farmer's wife explained that a little while earlier, a few weeks ago, she had found Martha in their barn. She was badly emaciated and in a deep sleep, obviously suffering from severe exhaustion and hunger. They knew straight away they should have reported her, but the farmer's wife insisted that until the child awoke and was able to tell them her story, they should do nothing at all.

When Martha regained her strength sufficiently to sit up and talk, in heavily accented French she told the farmer and his wife, 'I am Roma. My family normally lived and moved around Switzerland and parts of eastern France. I have no papers. If you hand me over, they'll rape me, like they did my mother and big sister, and then probably kill me, like they did the rest of my family, including my mother and big sister. I watched them do it. I'm on the run. I have been for weeks. I am worn out and frightened. My life is now in your hands.'

It was an appeal that they found impossible to resist. They had thereby put themselves at great risk, but in return they had acquired some help with the housework, some companionship and the virtuous knowledge that by wilfully and deliberately disobeying German law, they were striking a small blow against the enemy and saving someone's life. It helped them feel better about growing and supplying food which they knew went to feed soldiers, who, in turn, killed Frenchmen. This farmer and his wife were a French version of Walter and Jutta.

I knew immediately what I found so appealing about Martha. I could have been looking at any number of olive-skinned Jewish girls whom I had seen and mixed with all my life back in Lodz. The whites of her eyes looked so sharply white, clean and large against the darkness of her skin. I was truly smitten. Martha provoked a hitherto largely absent sense of homesickness and ethnic longing. Who knew such feelings could guide Cupid's arrow so surely?

I blurted out what I was thinking: 'Are you sure you're not Jewish? You look Jewish.'

Martha replied straight away, 'As far as the Germans are concerned, Roma and Jews are as bad as each other.'

I inwardly screamed with laughter, and later outwardly, at this outlandish grouping: the elderly French farmers who thought of themselves as resistance fighters, a young Jew and a Roma. Herr Hitler would not like this assembly one little bit.

At every opportunity, I would go back to the farm to see Martha. They had constructed a hideaway for her in the barn where she was first found. The barn shared a wall with the house but had been built on rising land. There was therefore an entrance to the barn through the ceiling in a room of the farmhouse at the back that was on a level with the floor of the barn. There was also an entrance to the barn from the back which led further up the hill straight into a nearby wood, where there was a second hideaway in a small cave, a second home for Martha. Depending on the weather and on how many visitors they had, Martha would alternate between her two homes. In common with many farmhouses in the area, the main dwelling was on raised land, with a view stretching into the far distance. At any sign of Germans or officialdom approaching, Martha went to her second home immediately. Visits by German officials were rare. Their main connection with any kind of officialdom was through Chef. In effect, they were a satellite of the place where I worked.

Martha and I never had sex, but there was a lot of passionate hand holding, kissing and furtive fumbling. I counted her as my first love. My feelings for Martha were in no way the same as those I had felt for my parents or any of my siblings, but when I was with her I was aware of a comforting warmth which generated a deep sense of a life affirming human connection.

The Polish workers did not accept me as one of their own. They believed what the farm manager and I told them about my status as a *Volksdeutsche*. I made sure they caught sight of the crucifix several times, but otherwise I was glad they were not keen to bring me into their circle. Even so, when the Polish workers were taking their breaks or at mealtimes in the large shed that doubled as a kind of canteen and club house, I would often be there. There was the usual banter about the appalling state of the world and the equally appalling lack of alcohol, tobacco and sex or the eye-watering cost of each when they were available. Nothing unusual about any of that, but there were two guys in particular, Jan and Gabriel, from the same village in Poland, who, on almost every occasion, no matter what issue was being debated, would find a way of blaming the Jews. They went way beyond everyday banter. I had heard similar vicious anti-Semitic views in Lodz but not often.

'I hate what the Germans are doing to Poland, but at least they are going to sort out the fucking Jews and put them in their place. We've been too soft on them.'

That was probably their most frequent comment. Then there were remarks about how venereal diseases originated with Jews. For good measure, they said they thought a small number of ultra-rich Jewish bankers had deliberately engineered the war so that they could profit from the sale of arms, not caring what happened to their fellow Jews as a result. All the important suppliers to the black markets were Jews; the brothels were run by Jews. The blood libel was in there – the one about Jews stealing Christian children and killing them to use their blood in various rituals. It was all utterly nauseating. Most of the rest of the Poles laughed and joined in more or less enthusiastically, even if I sensed their hearts were not in it to the same extent as Jan and Gabriel's, but these two kept it going. They were top of an anti-Semitic class of their own. I did not dare argue the toss, but I felt very bad having to sit there silently, and occasionally laughing, because some bits of their diatribes could be quite witty.

Nevertheless, I was getting absolutely sick of this gruesome duo's poisonous ranting. I may not have been a passionate or committed Jew in any religious sense, but they were my people. These arseholes were being horrible about my parents, my family and practically everyone whom I'd ever loved. What finally made me decide to do something was when they started boasting about a Jew they had 'strung up' in their village back home.

They happily told the whole room that one day an SS unit had come to their village. The two of them had been mooching about in the main square when the squad had arrived. It hadn't been obvious why they'd come, but the soldiers had sat around in their vehicles smoking and chatting, doing nothing at all. Maybe waiting for new orders.

There weren't many Jewish families in the village, but a very obviously Jewish young man had come into the square and, according to Jan and Gabriel, they'd just grabbed him, kicked him and spat at him, shouting over to the SS guys one of the few words of German they knew: *Juden*. That got their attention. The SS guys cheered and gave thumbs-up signs, making it plain that they had no intention of stepping in to stop the sport. They were enjoying the spectacle, lapping it up.

Jan and Gabriel said they'd dragged the poor Jewish boy along to a tree at the edge of the square, where a third guy, a friend of theirs, had suddenly appeared with a rope, which he'd proceeded to fashion into some sort of noose as the soldiers cheered again. The friend had thrown the rope over a low-hanging branch and secured it to the trunk then handed the noose to Jan and Gabriel, who were holding the Jew, preventing him from getting away. They'd put the noose around the poor Jewish guy's neck then the three of them had hoisted him up, holding on to the rope until he'd stopped wriggling. All the time, the SS unit had just looked on and done nothing; or, rather, they'd laughed and cheered ever more loudly and raucously.

Not content with this, the next day, having been admonished by someone in the village for leaving a corpse so indecorously hanging from a tree in the main square, they'd gone and cut down the poor unfortunate, dragging his body off to a rubbish dump, where they'd cut the head off and briefly kicked it about as a football. They said they'd been surprised how heavy and lumpy a head was, so it had proved useless as a football. They'd thrown it next to the torso.

I decided to engineer some sort of punishment for these bastards. The Germans were always apprehensive about the vast numbers of foreign workers they were importing into their midst. Perhaps some would be spies who had crept in under the radar. Maybe they were already in touch or soon would be with local partisans or resistance people. They were worried that one day, if all these foreign workers simply got their act together to protest about their harsh working conditions, they could disrupt the war effort in a major way. It was made clear to me that part of my job, as a liaison person with language skills, was to pass on anything I heard which sounded like more than the usual low-level grumbling, anything that had a hint of subversion or conspiracy.

In my short time on the farm, up until then, I had only reported someone once, and that was a Czech worker who had come back to the farm after curfew, drunk to the point of staggering. He'd knocked over a couple of large glass jars that had broken, so I'd thought I had no choice but to report him, if only to avoid suspicion falling on me being responsible for the damage. I'd followed standard procedure and told Chef. He later told me that he'd passed on the information to the German authorities, who would tell him whether or not they were interested. To the Germans, breaking the curfew was not a minor matter, although I don't think they cared about the broken jars.

A few days after I'd reported the Czech guy, two Germans in uniform and with weapons had turned up and taken him away. We'd been told that he was going to be kept in solitary confinement for two days as a punishment for breaking the curfew, and if he did it again, he could be sent away to a camp where hard labour was required. On the morning of the third day, the Czech had been brought back to the farm, looking no worse for wear. I'd been greatly relieved. At no point after his return had the Czech guy said anything to me about what had happened, so I guess he never knew I was the one who had squealed on him.

My plan was simple. I told Chef that Jan and Gabriel were ringleaders within one of the groups of Polish workers, always stirring them up about something and frequently saying terrible things about Germans, the Nazis and Hitler in particular. I told Chef they usually spoke like that when they thought I wasn't around, but just because I was out of their line of vision it did not mean I could not hear what they were saying. They were careless or stupid, probably both. Chef shook his head. I guess he knew this was serious. Something he could not ignore.

Later the same day, Chef came with me to where Jan and Gabriel were working so I could point them out to him without them realising. A week's solitary confinement was what I imagined they would get. Two weeks' maximum.

Four days later, having come back from a job that had taken me to the furthest edges of the farm for most of the day there, on a scaffold near to the canteen I saw Jan and Gabriel had been hanged. There was a handwritten notice in German and poor Polish, saying that this was the punishment everyone could expect if they broke German law and sought to undermine the war effort. Word was out that they had been killed for expressing anti-German and anti-Hitler sentiments.

The remaining Polish workers were seething with rage and convinced a great injustice had been done, as truly it had. At first, they wondered if this was just a random act of terror intended only to remind everyone that their new masters could do whatever they liked, whenever they felt like it, particularly with Poles. Most of them had witnessed random executions during and in the aftermath of the invasion of Poland the previous year. They acknowledged Jan and Gabriel had made the odd crack at Germans and the Reich but nothing they thought would warrant the guys being killed. Nothing that could be considered seriously treasonous. They were, of course, right.

I was upset. If I had had any idea that the guys would be killed, I would have thought of some other way of getting at them. That option was no longer open to me. Worse still, Jan and Gabriel's friends soon became convinced that I must have been responsible for their fate. They told me outright I was the informant and that I had lied or embroidered a story which had but a kernel of truth in it.

Maybe Chef had let it slip; maybe I had been seen pointing them out that day. The Polish workers could simply have worked it out for themselves. It hardly mattered. I was in peril once more. A knife in the back or a terrible 'accident' would be the end of me.

A few days after the hanging, Chef took me on one side and said he would arrange for me to be moved to another farm or another job not in the immediate vicinity and, meanwhile, I should stay out of sight as much as possible, particularly after dark. That is what I did, except for one last trip to bid farewell to the farmer and his wife and, above all, to say goodbye to Martha. I felt almost overpowered by a sense of longing and belonging, and the grief that went with knowing it was all about to end. Someone else I had grown close to was being ripped away by the unfeeling fortunes of war. By then, I knew my next move, my next job placement, was not going to take me many kilometres away from Martha's farm, but I did not know exactly where I would be, what I would be doing or what my situation would be like when I got there. I pledged that once settled I would get word back, and somehow Martha and I would meet again. It never happened.

XIII

Not long after the Jan and Gabriel incident, in that summer of 1941, I sensed things were getting a little bit edgier with the local German military units. Then word finally reached us that the Reich had broken their pact with the Soviet Union and invaded their now ex-ally's territory. My thoughts immediately went to Nathan. I hoped he was not caught up in the fierce fighting that would be taking place. I hoped that wherever he was was a long way from the border area or the advancing troops. I thought also about the people I had gotten to know in Wlodawa. It had already been substantially damaged in September 1939. I wondered what it looked like today. I crossed my fingers for Jakub and Rena, and Artur, if he had returned to Wlodawa by then.

Through the labour office, Chef arranged for me to be taken to my next posting, about eighty kilometres north of Monhofen, just outside Metz, in a place called Woippy, now known by its German name, Wappingen. There was a large factory there that made barbed wire and nails. I was going to work in a smaller establishment that was somehow associated with it and other businesses making agricultural equipment.

This time, I was billeted with a French family headed by Monsieur Mazeau, who, I was told, was the boss at my new

workplace. To begin with, Madame Mazeau was not excessively friendly, but neither was she completely cold or indiffer-
ent. It took a while for her to thaw, but she did. Monsieur
Mazeau was rather similar. He said I should call him Monsieur
Mazeau, and from then on I always did. Mazeau was engaged
in making a range of wooden parts that were to become inte-
gral pieces of the agricultural machinery being produced in
the town. There was a network of such small enterprises. We
were but one supplier, although Mazeau proudly said, 'We are
the best and I intend to keep it that way.'

Mazeau was clearly an enterprising man. He had trained as
a carpenter and had managed to set up on his own and expand,
keeping going even through the Depression. When I told him
I had learned a little carpentry in Poland, his eyes lit up, and he
said he would teach me more. For several weeks, merging into
months, at weekends Monsieur Mazeau and I could be found
in his workshop, where he showed me how to make various
types of joints and how to construct fairly simple tables and
chairs, even the frame for a large sofa or chaise longue.

My stay in Wappingen was not going to be a prolonged one.
In mid September 1941, I was stricken with a very high
temperature and an extremely painful sore throat. Because I
was on assignment to Monsieur Mazeau's place through the
German system for allocating labour, Madame Mazeau took
me along to the nearest office, where I was sent to a doctor.
The long and the short of it was I had a bad case of tonsillitis.
I was referred to the nearest hospital because the doctor thought
the simplest thing would be to have my tonsils removed.

The nearest hospital turned out to be an establishment in
Metz. I remember going into the hospital and seeing someone
who confirmed that removing my tonsils was the best option.

I stayed overnight, then the next morning I was laid on a trolley and taken to an operating theatre, where a nurse put a mask or something over my face and I lost consciousness. When I woke up, I simultaneously became aware of two things. My mouth and throat felt awful. I couldn't swallow and the taste and smell of blood, my blood, filled all my senses. The second thing was a man was peering at me very intently. He had a grave look on his face, and I knew whatever he was about to say was unlikely to add to the sum total of my personal happiness. Indeed, it did not. He was the surgeon who had performed the operation, but I could see under his white coat he was wearing a Wehrmacht uniform. He told me not to be alarmed at the uniform. Military medics often helped out in civilian hospitals as a way of keeping their hand in, and I was lucky that today he had been on duty: 'Not many people in my position would do what I am about to do.'

He then proceeded to tell me that after the operation, as I was lying semi-conscious on a trolley in the recovery area, I had started to talk openly and loudly. Some of the nurses and orderlies had concluded that since I was a Polish-born *Volksdeutsche* likely some of what I had been saying or shouting was Polish. But then there'd been some other stuff which had sounded a bit like German but had not always or exactly matched the German several people in the recovery area spoke. They'd called for the surgeon to come back, in case I was having some sort of post-operative reaction. He might understand the situation better than they did. He would know what to do. He was, after all, a German officer. They'd wanted his opinion, because the orderlies and nurses had already formed theirs and nobody wanted to take responsibility or have on their conscience what would be likely to happen next.

Apparently, as soon as someone had reached the conclusion and announced that I was speaking Yiddish, one of the orderlies had impulsively lifted my robe and seen that I sported a penis which had been circumcised, and there we have it. I'd been outed as a Jew. I gathered the surgeon had arrived and listened to my ravings. He'd also looked at my penis, then told the assembled company to 'leave this with me'.

They'd all departed. The room I was now in was empty but for me and the soldier–surgeon. He told me there was little doubt I was a Jew, therefore the identity papers I had in my possession were either forgeries or had been illegally obtained. His responsibility was clear. He had to inform the authorities. However, the soldier–surgeon also acknowledged that once he turned me in, if I wasn't taken out and shot in the hospital grounds, I would probably be shot or hanged within a few hundred metres of there: 'I don't want any part of that. I am a doctor after all. Aiding and abetting death is no part of my professional calling, particularly where the victim is plainly so young and therefore likely to be innocent of any serious crimes.'

The surgeon said he would arrange for my things to be brought to me. I would be put in a bed for the night, but at 9 a.m. the next morning he would file a report, and it would be as well if by then I had already vanished: 'You're essentially a strong healthy boy. You'll feel weak and woozy for a day or so, but you should have no trouble recovering from the operation. Even so, you should rest and lie low for a few days. The weather is fine. Find somewhere dry and warm, drink lots of water, and eat soft fruit or soft foods until your throat is in good shape again.'

During the night, a French nurse came into my room. Unsurprisingly, I was awake, quaking with fear, trying to collect my thoughts and form a plan. She looked at me solemnly and explained I was 'in grave danger. Everyone in the hospital knows about you and what the surgeon did. The promise he made. I trust him, but I do not trust everyone else who works here. You have to get away or you will probably be dead before lunchtime tomorrow. I finish my shift at 5.30 a.m. I will come to this room. Please be dressed and ready to leave.'

And then she yanked the crucifix from my neck: 'A Jew should not be wearing one of those. May God forgive you for that.'

I slept only in bursts, but I was dressed and ready when the nurse reappeared and beckoned me to follow her. In the corridor was a wheelchair. She nodded me towards it. I got in, and she wrapped a blanket around me, partially covering my head. What more natural sight could there be in a hospital than a nurse pushing someone in a wheelchair? We reached the outside of the hospital without let or hindrance, and she wheeled me a few hundred metres along the pavement before turning into the entrance to a courtyard, where she said, 'The next bit is going to be hard for you in your weakened state, but it is doable. I am going to leave you here. Don't worry about the wheelchair. Someone will take it back to the hospital. I am going to go back on the street and turn right. You should count up to ninety then you do the same. Stay on this side of the road and walk to the end. You will see me. As soon as I see you, I will walk across the street into a courtyard similar to this. Count to ninety again then follow me into the same courtyard. Go up one flight of stairs. I live at number 7. I will be waiting for you.'

Getting dressed on my own in the hospital had convinced me that, while I was definitely weak, I was far from completely incapacitated. I wasn't going to collapse in a heap immediately. I could follow her instructions. No problem.

The door to number 7 was partially open. The good nurse was waiting. She ushered me in to what I suppose was a guest or spare bedroom. I stayed there three days and was fed on a diet of homemade soups of various flavours. She told me a bit more about what had happened in the hospital recovery area after my operation and about the hue and cry as they'd tried to find me.

Soon enough, I was able to swallow again and felt strong enough to move on. The nurse was not exactly keen for me to go, but I knew I needed to get going as soon as possible. I had resolved I had to reach neutral French territory. The border with Vichy France was not that far away.

As I had been wheeled out by the nurse, I had noticed not far from the hospital there was a sizeable car park with all kinds of vehicles in it, including several that looked rather like the one I had learned to drive in Monhofen. As I lay in bed, or wandered about the nurse's flat, I resolved to go back there and see if l could steal one. I had often had to crank start my truck in Monhofen. The crank was clipped under a flap so was always accessible if it was needed when ordinary starting with a key didn't work because the battery was flat, usually following a spell of cold weather.

The previous afternoon, before she'd gone to work, I'd told the nurse I would leave the next day. I'd thought I'd detected a slight look of relief. She'd said she would leave me a glass bottle with some soup in it, plus a few apples and some bread. She'd hoped these would help me on my way but did not ask where I was going or what my plans were, and I hadn't told her, because I didn't have any plans that were worthy of the name.

I waited until she returned from her night shift, bade her farewell and expressed my heartfelt thanks. I remarked that she had never told me her name or asked me mine. A smile was all I got in return but it was a smile which once again reminded me I had benefited from the kindness of strangers. All humans were not the same. There were pockets of goodness left even in the presence of overwhelming evil.

I made my way to the car park and located a vehicle. It had a tailgate but no payload in the back and was slightly battered but not excessively so. I got it going easily and jumped behind the steering wheel. There was a workman's cap on the front seat. I put it on, hoping it would conceal my boyish looks and distinctive hair. I wanted to be as invisible as possible. After nearly four days, I doubted the hunt for a missing Jewish boy would still be in full flood, so I reckoned I must have a good chance of making substantial progress towards Vichy France. I understood that at that time the border between occupied and unoccupied France was still something of a moveable feast, but it seemed to be the case that Vichy began somewhere south of Dole and north of Lyon, about 300 kilometres away. I had no real idea what Vichy France would be like, but it could not be any worse than occupied France. The thought of being closer to the warmth of the Mediterranean was massively appealing.

I had ruled out the possibility of first going back to the Mazeaus' to retrieve the knapsack which had somehow managed to stay with me up until then. I therefore also parted company with the knife I had used to kill the man at the ghetto perimeter. Nonetheless, I still had my fake Karl-Heinz ID and a few Reichsmarks, which I had accumulated or stolen over the months.

The vehicle's petrol tank was nearly full. I believed there was a good chance I could put some serious distance between myself and the hospital before the vehicle was reported as missing. I knew I was riding my luck, but I had no alternative. This was how it had to be.

I drove south as fast as I dared, past Nancy, at times veering towards the Swiss border but then coming back west, onwards towards the border with Vichy France. I had heard it was impossible to leave the occupied zone without some kind of special permission or papers. I consequently knew that at some stage I would have to dump the vehicle and try to get across on foot or by hiding inside another vehicle that was making the journey but carrying the correct documentation.

Miraculously, by late afternoon I was still on the road. The needle on the fuel gauge was racing towards empty. I guessed I was somewhere around Dole and the border could not be far away, as more and more military and police vehicles were scooting about the place. I drove up to the top of a hill and pulled over. Looking down, I saw queues of vehicles and what looked like a short stretch in-between that was clear. That had to be the border, the clear stretch being no-man's-land, so this was where I would have to abandon the truck and figure out a way to get over. There was no ice-bound river this time, but there were lots of soldiers with guns.

I headed down the hill, cutting through a small wooded area. As I was coming out of the other side of the woods on to a small country road, a German military police car was driving by. Seeing me ambling along, they pulled up and called me across. They spoke French. I answered in German. Was that a mistake? Probably, but I doubt they would have been significantly more sympathetic if I had replied in French. They smiled but nevertheless still asked for my papers. These showed that I should have been in Wappingen, so they jumped to the conclusion I was a traitor trying to escape to help the enemies of the Reich or avoid my duties to the Fatherland. They told me I was under arrest and bundled me into the back of their car, taking care to handcuff my wrist to the fixed door handle. I was stuck. It hurt even to move my wrist. No possibility of escape. Aside from the moment at the ghetto perimeter, this was the worst fix I had been in. OK, it had been bad at the Bug River as well, but I had got away with no injuries. I had never felt I was in such danger as now. Looking at my clamped wrist, I had no idea what I would do.

Half an hour later, I was under lock and key in the basement of a nearby civilian police station. My life was flashing before my eyes. I was certain they would find the truck and discover it had been stolen, perhaps connecting it with the Jew who had escaped from the hospital, which would be curtains for me. I would be put up against a wall somewhere near this police station, perhaps round the back and it would be all over. My only hope was that they wouldn't do an even fuller investigation and trace me back to the nurse who had helped me. If they did, I guessed the doctor's complicity would become apparent, but how far back would they go? Walther, Elsa and Jutta in Berlin, Martha, the farmer and his wife near Monhofen, Jakub in Wlodawa or my family back in Poland? I had no idea, but in my terrified, paranoid state I could believe or imagine any number of horrible outcomes. Apart from my own life, so many other lives would be at risk if the Nazis had finally gotten their hands on me. This feeling of responsibility for others weighed almost as heavily with me as my screaming anxiety about my own position.

JOHN CARR

When a policeman came down a few hours later, he told me they had found what appeared to be an abandoned farm vehicle not far from where I had been picked up. They suspected I might be linked to it, and they were no longer satisfied my papers were in order anyway. They doubted I was the age declared and told me I would be taken to a 'holding centre' for onward transportation, maybe up to Dijon or back to Berlin, where everything would be investigated and resolved. Knowing I wasn't going to die immediately brought a slight sense of relief, but it was only slight.

The next morning, I was brought up from the cells, put in the back of another and more substantial police vehicle, and once again handcuffed to the door handle. I had heard that the Germans had these things called concentration camps and wondered if that was where I was really heading. 'Holding centre' was only a euphemism for some kind of hellhole.

There was no armed guard, only a single, portly and elderly police officer who also drove the vehicle. I suppose a handcuffed child didn't warrant the full, dangerous-enemy-of-the-state treatment. En route, I learned from my chatty companion Hans that the place I was going to was only for Germans and other Aryans, so it wouldn't be too bad. I shouldn't worry: 'We don't shoot Germans as easily as we shoot others, and looking at you who could doubt you were a German?'

If Hans was trying to humour or comfort me, it wasn't working. He assured me the mess and confusion would soon be cleared up. If it hadn't been for finding an abandoned truck, they might not have bothered to detain me at all: 'I don't believe a youngster like you could have driven that truck even a single kilometre. Your feet would hardly touch the pedals. But they don't listen to me. As soon as that is cleared up, I am sure everything will be OK, although you will need to explain what you were doing so near the border and so far from Wappingen.'

We were waved through the heavy gates that formed the entrance of the holding centre, not stopping for even the most minimal formalities. Hans nodded and the armed guards at the gate did likewise. By this time, I was feeling deeply depressed. Once inside the main square, the car pulled up at the side of a single-storey building, which I took to be the main office block or where the camp boss hung out. My handcuffs were unlocked, and I was handed over to another avuncular guard whom Hans obviously knew. They both made jokey comments about me looking like 'a mean desperado'.

My chauffeur then referred to me as a kid and assured the guard this was all just a mix up so I wouldn't be there long. He was dead right about that. Hans said he needed to use the toilet and maybe grab a quick drink in the staff canteen before setting off.

The guard said he would join Hans for a drink in a minute. He just had to leave me in the waiting room. This was next to the commandant's office, and he explained that, because I was so young and apparently an ethnic German, I would have to be taken through the admission procedures by the commandant personally. He wasn't around right then, so I would have to wait. I was led into the waiting room and pointed towards a chair. The guard went out, closing the door but not locking it.

The interior spaces of a holding centre, or a camp or what-ever this place really was, were evidently not the focus of major security concerns. The place was, after all, surrounded by high fences that were probably electrified, and it had watchtowers containing heavily armed men.

A light bulb went off in my head. In the car that had brought me here, I'd noticed the back seat was, essentially, a box, with the leather seat I sat on forming what was, in effect, the lid of the box. Maybe the interior cavity was used as storage, or perhaps it was just empty. After a couple of minutes, I opened the door of the waiting room, stuck my head out and, not seeing anyone who was looking this way, walked quickly back towards the car that had brought me here. I opened the back door, lifted up the seat and was relieved to find all that was in there were blankets. I jumped inside the opening and dragged the lid back over the top. I just had to hope that Hans didn't decide to say goodbye to me before beginning his return journey. If he did, maybe he and the guard, rather than signal a full security alert, which might expose their laxness, would simply initiate their own hunt and no doubt find me sooner or later, but right then I did not think I had much, if anything, to lose. With any luck, if they did find me, the two old guys would just think this was another example of my boyish exuberance or naturally enterprising character so in keeping with the warrior spirit of the new Germany. They would kick my backside or give me a clip around the ear and that would be that. Once more, I crossed my fingers.

Roughly fifteen minutes later, someone got into the driver's seat. I guessed it was Hans. I couldn't see. He started the engine, drove no more than a hundred yards then stopped again. I heard both back doors open, and two people got in and sat on the back seat. I held my breath. Two German posteriors were inches away from my head. My thoughts went back to the train out of Lublin.

The car started again, slowed as it approached what I assumed were the camp gates but did not stop. As with the inward journey, it was clear the vehicle had been waved through. I soon learned that the posteriors which were only a few inches away belonged to two German officers, probably of the military police. I deduced from the conversation that took place between them and the obviously slightly fed-up Hans that they were going across into France to pick up and escort back a German who had been arrested by French police for being drunk and violent. Likely as not, he was an army deserter from the war in the east. The French authorities had no desire to detain or deal with him, so they were just going to hand him over and be rid of him. Seemingly, this was not uncommon. The two guys on the back seat were plainly delighted at the thought of having a night off in authentic, French France. They were going to pick up the miscreant in the morning, and rather touchingly they apologised to Hans for this sudden change to his schedule, hoping it wouldn't inconvenience him too much. Judging by the very audible harrumph, it did.

About half an hour later, I heard Hans and the officers negotiate the border and explain at both sides what they were doing. Not long after that they pulled up, parked and everyone got out of the car.

I waited until it was dark before lifting the lid of the seat and scrabbling out on to the floor. I opened the door of the car. We were in a hotel car park. I walked away, at first nonchalantly. I may even have whistled, and when I reached the street, I stopped to look in a couple of shop windows.

But what now? I didn't stop to think. I was in the unoccupied zone of France. I did not know exactly where I was, but I was out of that part of Europe where Germans ruled and the German military machine held sway. This felt like an enormous relief. A gigantic weight was lifted from me. I did not imagine

I was out of any kind of danger. The Polish Government in exile might have gone to London but I knew large communities of Poles and Jews were dotted around and somewhere among them I would find sanctuary and help. It was not a homecoming but I did feel a strong sense of liberation. I turned a corner and ran as fast as my legs would carry me.

XIV

I was somewhere a little south of Dole. Karl-Heinz Reitzenstein
had left my life. I no longer had the *Kennkarte*. That was in the
hands of the Germans back at the holding centre in which I
had been incarcerated for around fifteen minutes. They did
have my photo, but I couldn't believe they would make a big
deal of trying to find me. If I stayed out of German hands, I felt
sure I could find a way through, although, in practical terms, I
was still not completely sure what 'finding a way through'
meant. I was in non-Nazi France, but the Polish government
and armed forces were in the United Kingdom, a country
about which I knew next to nothing.

Through a series of barters, casual work, petty and not so
petty thefts of clothes, food and money, and a combination of
lifts and bus rides, I managed to make my way to Grenoble. At
this point, if I was asked my name, Henryk Karbowksi, a Polish
Catholic, would reappear. I stole another crucifix. I guess if
you're a believing Catholic, stealing a crucifix is pretty low,
self-defeating behaviour. But I wasn't. This was completely
transactional religiosity.

Grenoble had seemed like the obvious place to go. I had
heard there was a demilitarised zone a little way to the east of
the city, and the Italian Army had responsibility for policing it,

but Grenoble itself was in the unoccupied zone and had become a focal point for all kinds of refugees and fugitives hoping to make their way to neutral Switzerland or points south and west.

Making my way towards Grenoble, I had encountered quite a few Poles walking along or talking to each other on the roadside. They'd had various stories about how they'd come to be in that part of the world. Some had been heading to relatives who lived in Vichy France. They'd been hoping they could stay with them until the war was over. Other Poles had just been drifters who'd seemed to have no plan at all, or if they'd had one, they had not told anyone what it was. However, the great majority of the younger ones, men and women, had said they were heading for Spain and a place called Gibraltar, a British colony at the far end of the Iberian peninsula.

As a major ally of the Brits, the Polish government and military had been allowed to establish a mission there to receive refugees and recruit combatants who were already trained soldiers, sailors or airmen from one or other unit of the dispersed Polish military, or were civilians ready to sign up to join the Free Polish armed forces. The Brits arranged for transportation to the UK, usually by sea. This had confirmed what I had heard before. A Polish fighting machine was establishing itself in Britain. I wanted to be part of it. My destination was now clear. I was heading for Britain via Gibraltar.

When I finally arrived in Grenoble, I was desperate to find somewhere to sleep, a base from which I could plan the next steps, but sleep was my immediate priority. Thanks to some successful thievery en route, I had enough cash to check in to a hotel. I looked first at a couple of slightly seedy, cheaper places but decided I might be taking my life in my hands if I stayed there. In the end, I settled on the Hotel Terminus, opposite the railway station, and asked for a room for two nights. The man behind the desk muttered something about ID documents, at which point I conjured up synthetic distress and let loose a stream of Polish. Reverting to French, I shrugged my shoulders and said, '*Pas compris, Polonais.*' (I don't understand. I'm Polish).

The receptionist replied, '*Un autre refugie Polonais, mais si jeune.*' (another Polish refugee but so young). I showed him the cash, he took my money and gave me a key. I slept for what must have been the best part of twenty-four hours.

Towards the end of the second day at the Hotel Terminus, I asked if I could stay a little bit longer. They seemed unsurprised that my spoken French had miraculously improved compared with when I arrived. I explained that I had an aunt who lived in the Auvergne. She was coming to get me, but I was not sure when. I had written to tell her where I was staying. Whether they believed me or not I have no idea. I suggested a further three days, and this was agreed as long as I could pay in advance, but I could not stay much longer without producing an ID, otherwise they might end up in trouble with the police. It was only because I was so young that they felt they could show some flexibility. It was also explained to me that in these turbulent times, with so many transient people, the hotel had been cheated too often. I said I understood and also indicated I would be able to pay the following morning.

I had become adept at pickpocketing and stealing women's handbags. I did feel bad about that, but in the grand scheme of things it was no more wrong than anything that had already happened to me and what would almost certainly happen to me if I ever found my way back into German hands. And I was heading to join in the fight against the Nazis. How does the moral arithmetic work here? If an otherwise devout Jew can disregard the kosher laws to survive in the ghetto, I thought a little bit of thieving would barely raise a rabbinical eyebrow.

I reckoned I might have to make more than one hit to obtain the resources I was likely to need, but that day I managed to get enough to pay for one further night at the Terminus, and I promised I would get more money to pay for the additional two nights. The manager and the receptionist looked a little sceptical but agreed nevertheless.

The next day, I chose well and hit lucky. There was an alleyway between a large building and a small park near the main shopping area. I climbed on to the alleyway's boundary wall and discovered it had a ledge on the other side, the park side. This meant I could stand on the ledge on the park side, the bit that would be invisible from the alleyway, and flatten myself along the top of the wall to observe who was coming into the alley from the main street. With my peripheral vision I could also make out if anyone was coming in from the other side. My idea was to wait for someone smaller than me who looked well off – such people did exist – or for someone who looked well off but was very much older. The ideal victim would combine both qualities. I would jump down behind them as they passed, grab something and run, probably after climbing back up the wall and making my way through the park. I had checked it out. I had a cap pulled down over my head covering my distinctive blond hair and, if required, a scarf which I could quickly hoist up to form a mask to cover my face.

Sundry Grenoble citizens paraded before me, but eventually a rather stout elderly lady came into view. She certainly looked prosperous and was carrying a large handbag. Here was my victim. A quick look in both directions confirmed there was no one else around. Then I had a brainwave. Using my feet to grip the far side of the ledge to ensure I did not fall over or off, rather than jumping down I could simply lean across and grab her handbag as the woman walked by me. I could be back up, drop into the park, stuff the handbag into a larger bag I had brought with me and hare off. Time taken for the swoop? Less than a second. Time to get away? Between three and five seconds in total. That's exactly what I did. It is unlikely the elderly lady really knew what had happened or saw anything other than a blur. It worked precisely as planned.

I walked casually out of the park, having removed my hat and scarf, and dumped them in the bag covering the handbag. It then occurred to me I had not heard the woman scream or shout or indeed do anything to draw attention to what had just happened. It didn't take long for me to develop a theory as to why that might be the case.

I went straight back to the hotel and up to my room. After I had calmed myself down and steadied my nerves, I opened the handbag. Aside from the usual stuff you would expect to see in a lady's handbag, there was her ID papers, a large envelope with an enormous number of bank notes, 100,000 francs (£1500 in today's money) in total, and a gun. A revolver of some kind. I could see bullets in the chamber. This was the first time in my life I had ever touched or handled a gun of any kind. If I didn't actually tremble with fear, I did something very close to it. Respectable and prosperous as she might have looked, this lady must have been linked to black-market racketeering or some other nefarious activity. Why else would she have been carrying so much cash and a gun? She must have done a swift calculation that screaming, drawing attention to herself and getting the police involved would land her in even greater trouble if she had to reveal the true contents of her bag or, if they caught me, they found out what I had stolen. At this point, any anxieties about moral arithmetic rapidly melted away. To steal from a criminal is not the same as stealing from someone who is wholly innocent. Naturally, I worried what might happen to me if the people who had given her the money to carry across town were ever to find me, but I didn't see how they could, and they didn't.

I hid the money in the room and went to the river and discreetly threw in the ID I had found in the woman's bag. Then I hid the gun, believing it might come in useful at some point. I went and paid for the additional two days in the hotel, as I had promised, and, to allay any possible suspicions, I asked the woman on duty at the reception desk if she knew anywhere I might be able to find casual work, because I was running out of money, and I did not know how long I would need to stay in Grenoble until my aunt got there. I told her I was happy to work in a kitchen, a garden, on a building site. Anything. Anywhere. She said she would ask around. Nothing came of it.

After two more nights at the Hotel Terminus, I told them it was too expensive and that I would come back and let them know where I was staying so they could inform my aunt when she got there. They said they would be happy to pass on the message, and we parted. I moved around frequently thereafter, particularly if anyone started getting unduly nosey about my circumstances. Some nights I didn't manage to find anywhere that would take me without an ID, so I slept rough, usually outside Grenoble itself. When I did find accommodation, I stuck with a line about being a Polish boy with relatives in

France. I had been separated from my parents in Germany, where they had been working, and was now here waiting for my aunt to collect me. Mostly people accepted that – or, rather, they didn't press for any more details. The older women, whom I saw only at breakfast in the different places I stayed, generally wanted to mother me rather than pry. I split the money up into different packages which I hid either in the place I was staying or about the town. Twice I walked right by the woman I had robbed. She didn't give me a second look. I was enormously comforted by that, as it confirmed she hadn't seen my face during my acrobatic felony.

As I stretched out the money I had amassed, I took elaborate precautions to ensure no one got an inkling of how much I had or where I kept it. When I went to a new hotel or *pension* or anywhere I was required to pay for something, I made sure nobody saw me holding much more than was needed then and there. I even faked going to work to make people think I was earning a living somehow. But mainly what I was doing was gathering information about how to get down to Gibraltar, what my next move should be to get me there or nearer to it. Staying in Grenoble for too long once again made me feel like I was tempting fate. I was sure the elderly lady would be connected to some kind of criminal network, and they would be trying to find me both to recover their loot and punish me or, if I was lucky, recruit me as a reward for my chutzpah.

Several times on my travels about Grenoble I heard people talking about a couple of places that sounded promising. One was a Polish school at Villard-de-Lans about thirty kilometres south. Apparently, it had relocated there from Paris after the German invasion. I also heard reports about some sort of hostel or shelter for Jews in a place called Voirons, about twenty-five kilometres north. Since heading north made no immediate sense, I headed first for Villard-de-Lans to see if Henryk Karbowski could find shelter, food and information. Crucially, during this period in Grenoble, I also connected with Poles who had been living there for many years, working in a variety of occupations. Some of these were linked with operations to help other Poles move south, either in the belief that the larger the distance between them and the Wehrmacht the safer they would be, or towards networks that would help them join Polish fighting units abroad. Critically, this network of Poles had connections with corrupt elements and patriotic elements within the French police who would happily assist in obtaining false identity papers which, as with the ones I had obtained in Berlin, were indistinguishable from the real thing, because they had emanated from a genuine source. Corruption and patriotism seemed to carry an identical price, 30,000 francs, and this was how Jan Szewczyk was created. He had been born in Paris, and my back story was that my family and I had left there in 1930 when I was four to go back to Poland before returning to France in early 1939. Great timing, but nevertheless wholly believable, and it explained my imperfect French. The French police never had cause to interrogate me in any depth, so I never found out how well this identity would have held up.

On arriving in Villard, it wasn't difficult to find the Polish school. There were lots of young Poles moving around, talking loudly in their native tongue. In fact, there were Poles of all ages everywhere, presumably attracted by the knowledge that there was a Polish community of sorts in a bit of Europe not occupied by Germans. The people of the town seemed to be quite used to new faces suddenly appearing, particularly Poles.

Crucifix once more highly visible and introducing myself as Jan Szewczyk, I was eventually directed to the school and a very polite and helpful senior teacher. I showed him my ID card and gave him the prepared story. He showed every sign of believing it or not caring that much, which was a relief, but I guess in those troubled times one never enquired too closely about such matters. If I had been a six-foot brute with scars, tattoos and teeth missing, maybe he would have taken more trouble to establish who I really was, but I wasn't, so he didn't. The teacher said that because of my age, and because I was alone, he was sure he could find me a bed in a dormitory for a few days until I got myself sorted out, but he didn't hold out any hope that I could become a pupil at the school. I thanked him very much but assured him that going back to school was the last thing on my mind. I explained that I wanted to get to England to strike back at the Nazis.

'I think you can say the same about a great many of the Poles you will meet here,' came his reply.

Villard was seething with sedition and talk about fighting back against the Germans. Groups of Poles were organising themselves into what they called operational units, although it was never very clear to me how, from within unoccupied France, they would actually engage the enemy. Other Poles were simply resting for a day or two, gathering their strength in the relative safety of a Polish enclave before they continued on their route to Gibraltar and then England. Ever since the fall of Warsaw, Polish soldiers and Polish citizens had been very active in developing escape routes to Spain then onwards to Gibraltar, initially by sea from along the Mediterranean coast west of Marseille. There were supposed to be boats from the Polish Navy or the Polish merchant fleet that were helping with this tide of human traffic. There were also land routes across the Pyrenees, where people tried to cross on their own or with the help of *passeurs*, French or Spanish versions of Artur, the man on the Bug River. They were either mercenary individuals with a good knowledge of the mountains or good-hearted souls who wanted to help people in trouble or were linked to anti-Nazi networks.

The people at the school in Villard were fine. I had a medical check-up and was pronounced fit and healthy. Inexplicably, the doctor did not examine my penis, although if he had done and had asked me any questions about its circumcised state, I had an answer good and ready. 'Trouble peeing when I was a kid.' I went to Mass a couple of times, joined one of the many football teams and was generally quite sociable, but I sensed I might be on the edge of outstaying my welcome, so after a week I decided to check out and head for Voirons. In Villard, there had been lots of references to Voirons as a place where there were many Jews, and while some of these references were accompanied by familiar anti-Semitic tropes, almost as many were neutral or positively warm, recognising that, Jew or not, they were still Poles who, like them, hated the Nazis and every-thing they represented. This was great to hear, as Jan and Gabriel's diatribes were still ringing in my ears. Villard reminded me of the Karbowskis and the huge numbers of Poles I had met and dealt with both back home in Poland and on the road who were decent and kind people who would normally be quite uninterested in someone else's religious beliefs.

I recognised that a major reason to go to Voirons was that I wanted to be among Jews again. Once there, I could drop the pretence of being a Catholic. I could shed, or at any rate temporarily hide, the crucifix. Without saying goodbye or telling anyone where I was headed or what my plans were, I just walked out of Villard and headed north.

Voirons, April 1942

I have very happy memories of my time in Voirons. I got there in April 1942. There was a Jewish orphanage, and various Christian and political groups in the area who were helping the transient communities in the town, including Jews. The local police were known to contain a cell of officers who were hostile to the government in Vichy, and, of course, to the German invaders to their north. One of the senior police officers was originally from Alsace, but he had refused to go back there because it had been 'Nazified'.

I spoke Polish and Yiddish most of my time in Voirons as I mingled with Jews from various parts of eastern Europe, including several who were originally from Lodz. The rest were Jews from Austria, Germany, Belgium, Holland and some from Romania. A truly cosmopolitan affair. There was one young man there, Pierre, who was a Jew from the French-speaking part of Canada. Who knew there was such a thing? Not me until then. I am not sure I had even heard of Canada, much less known that they had a French-speaking minority. I got to know Pierre particularly well and managed to explain the basics of football to him.

Pierre was only a couple of years older than me. His story was a sad one. His mother and father had been living near Bordeaux when the war had broken out. His father was an engineer who had been working at an oil refinery. The speed at which the French war effort had collapsed on the northeastern side of the country had astonished them, as it had the rest of the world. They'd realised that the Germans wanted to secure the whole of the Atlantic seaboard but, along with everyone else it seemed, had calculated that the war would be a little while getting down to their bit of the southwest. They would have enough time, enough notice, to be able to get their things together and drive down to Spain and then on to neutral Portugal well ahead of any nastiness. From Portugal they would take a boat across the Atlantic and make their way home.

Instead of weeks or months to get ahead of the German advance, they'd only had days. Instead of making it to Portugal, his parents were dead. Their car had got caught up in a column of soldiers fleeing south. The Luftwaffe had intervened, scoring a direct hit on their vehicle. Pierre had been out of the car when the car exploded, killing both parents instantly, just as they were trying to get out. A nun who was on the road had seen the whole episode. Aware that he was a Jew, she nevertheless took Pierre into her custody, bringing him back to Bordeaux with her. Through a network of convents and

Catholic religious establishments, Pierre was passed along until they finally handed him over to the Jewish orphanage in Voirons.

Pierre explained that while he was a French speaker, he was actually bilingual, because Canada as a whole was part of the British Commonwealth, and the majority of Canadians were English speakers. He helped me to improve my still limited knowledge of the English language. Pierre was planning to head for Spain in order to continue his parents' original plan to reach Lisbon then take a boat to New York or, ideally, somewhere further north. He hadn't yet worked out how he would get the necessary papers and permissions to make the journey, but that was a problem he would solve another day. In principle, it ought not to be a problem, because Spain and Portugal were both neutral. There should be no major difficulty about a Canadian entering or crossing their territory. He was waiting for a letter from Canada to confirm the main elements of his story so the orphanage could help secure the visa or whatever had to be presented when he got to the border. We both acknowledged such a possibility was closed to me. I was a Pole, possibly wanted for murder by the German authorities, and anyway my bit of Poland was now part of Germany. If I were to cross the Pyrenees, it would have to be illegally.

I told Pierre about my ambition to reach Gibraltar. He thoroughly approved but warned me that if I was caught in Spain, and if they managed to discover I was from a part of Poland that was now a bit of Germany, he wasn't sure what the Spanish authorities would do. 'Not sure' spelled danger to me. The government in Madrid was sympathetic to the Germans, and there had been all kinds of stories about them handing people

JOHN CARR

over at Hendaye on the French border, which now constituted the land border between occupied France and Spain.

As there was no question of me crossing into Spain legally, Pierre had just given me a great idea. If I was picked up, I would claim to be what he was: a French-Canadian child separated from his parents in France by the war, now trying to get to Lisbon to go home. I figured I would not mention Gibraltar, because it was a staging post for escapers and others seeking to avoid the attentions of the Germans. I just had to pray my French was good enough to sustain the pretence. I did not want them working out I was Polish. Pierre said not to worry. Everybody knew French Canadians spoke French with a slightly odd accent. If they cared at all about a young lad like me and picked up any hints of strangeness from my accent, they would put it down to that. But it was still better not to get caught or get involved with the Spanish authorities if at all possible.

Nothing I learned in Voirons persuaded me to deviate from my plan to head for Gibraltar, often otherwise referred to as 'The Rock'. On the contrary, as intelligence seeped through about what was happening to the Jews of Europe in general, and the Jews in Poland in particular, it made me even more determined to get there as soon as possible.

Perpignan was my next target, the next step on the way, but I stayed in Voirons for about five months, during which time Pierre continued to teach me English. We both knew it was going to be an important language for me quite soon. Pierre said if I made it to Gibraltar, it was certain I would be transported to the UK, where I could join the Free Polish Army. He was right.

I still did not have a clear timetable in my head, but, once again, Herr Hitler made the decision for me. On 11 November

1942, when I was still in Voirons, the man whose birthday I shared decided to join me. The German Army crossed the demarcation line established between themselves and Vichy France. Five young Jews in Voirons, me included, decided we were not going to sit around waiting to be picked up and transported. Now was the time to head for the western Mediterranean coast and the Pyrenees. Without ceremony or saying goodbye to Pierre or anyone else, we set off together. Pretty soon, however, we realised that travelling in a group would only draw attention to us. We split up. I was on my own. Again. I resigned myself to the familiar reality.

A week later, following an entirely uneventful passage I arrived in Perpignan around midday, I made my way towards the centre of town and started to check it out. I was looking for churches or other establishments with a sign suggesting they welcomed strangers, maybe in particular young strangers. Could I find the Quaker place I had heard about in Voirons? As a back-up, I was scouting potential nooks and crannies where I might be able to sleep rough if need be. The weather was deteriorating, but it was still not that bad. Simultaneously, as was now an ingrained habit, I kept a sharp eye out for things I might be able to steal easily, either to eat, drink, sell or wear.

In what I judged to be the old quarter of Perpignan, there were several little streets and squares with lots of cafés and restaurants. The weather was mild that day, so lots of people were sitting outside. As I walked by a couple of them, I heard Polish being spoken. Not loudly – German soldiers were now in the town – but it was unmistakeable.

I needed information about routes across the Pyrenees, hazards, patrols and so on but I knew it would be dangerous to attempt it alone. I had to hook up with a party going across, particularly as I had discovered that I should anticipate the journey taking up to four days, depending on weather conditions. This time it could not end like it had on the river at Wlodawa. Could it?

When you are on the run, first encounters with anyone are always fraught with danger. All my senses were on full alert as I approached what I judged to be the more youthful looking group of Poles. Whispering, I used a predictable opening, '*Dzięki Bogu w końcu mogę znowu mówić po polsku*' or 'Thank God. At last I can speak Polish again.'

It got a laugh and quizzical looks, but it had worked. Once more I thanked my youthful appearance and discreetly visible crucifix. One of the guys in the group was from Lodz, and he took me inside to a secluded back room where he interrogated me quite intensively about the geography of our hometown. I guess they had to consider the possibility that Nazi agents, even very young ones, could have infiltrated Polish and other organisations in order to close down escape routes for foreign airmen and the like who were making a 'home run', or to disrupt networks that were helping to channel new recruits to their enemies' armed forces.

Anyway, my interrogator could not fault me on my knowledge of the geography of Lodz. I also told him I had attended the same Catholic school as Cesek and that I had played football for one of the local church teams, casually dropping Father Nawrat's name into the conversation. That seemed to spark some sort of recognition and at the same time rather conveniently headed off any potentially deeper or further enquiries about my religious background. When he took me back to the group, they were only marginally interested in when and how I got out of Poland. Every refugee's story was an astonishing mixture of luck and courage driven by determination, desperation or patriotism, or usually some permutation of all three. When I puffed out my chest and declared my intention to get into Spain then over to Britain to join the Polish Army and fight the Germans, I got a big cheer, as they all said that was exactly what they were thinking.

I got a fair amount of ribbing about my age – someone remarked that the Polish Army was probably short of tea boys so they would be sure to take me. But nobody made wisecrack remarks wondering if my mother knew I was out and about on my own. I imagine none of them had seen their mothers for a while and they would all be wondering how their families were faring back home without them. It would be many years before I learned that by the time I reached the Mediterranean, both my mother and father had been dead for more than a year. Beelzebubska had been dead for more than two years. All were victims of the ghetto and illnesses which spread easily through overcrowded communities and the weakness induced by perpetual hunger.

There were six people in the Perpignan group to which I had attached myself, five men and a woman called Danuta. They had all collided with each other en route for Spain. All of them then went off into a huddle, leaving me on my own. I wasn't surprised or hurt. I could hardly expect them to take me into their confidence or share any important secrets with me. I had only just pitched up. Danuta later told me that she had said she would take responsibility for me and that she would not let me out of her sight until the crossing was complete. I was glad that Danuta had quickly decided to adopt me. It removed me from the spotlight.

It emerged that the group were planning to go over in a few days. The precise timing had not yet been fixed. The ringleader, a man who called himself Frans, had already made a connection with people in the French Resistance, and they would provide a guide to a remote spot in the mountains next to the border. From there, if there wasn't someone waiting from the Spanish side to guide us down, they would point out and describe the remainder of the route. We weren't to worry. It would all be obvious once we were there. But we would not be going over the mountains from anywhere near Perpignan. We would be taken further inland to make the crossing. Transportation to take us to the embarkation point had been arranged. Everything was in hand.

By this point, the group had been together for over an hour, so they decided to break up, go their separate ways and meet again the following day at another café a couple of streets away. The owner had a back room where we could talk without being overheard. We agreed to meet at 12 noon, and, except for Danuta and me, we were to arrive on our own and go straight to the back. Frans would already be there, watching out for us. I went off with Danuta and spent that night in her room, a pattern that was repeated over the following two nights. Danuta kept her word. She never let me out of her sight, and I had no problem with that. None at all.

Before splitting up to go our separate ways Frans reminded us that now the Germans were all around the town and the surrounding area, we obviously had to watch out for them and stay out of their clutches. However, the French police could not be relied on to help or turn a blind eye in respect of matters concerning enemies of, or apparent fugitives from, the Reich. Equally, the Spanish border guards who patrolled the lower and middle reaches of the Pyrenees varied a lot in their attitudes towards people they caught on their side of the mountains.

Some of them might ignore you and let you pass unhindered. Others, if they caught you, might be sympathetic or would accept a bribe, while others might either shoot and rob you or hand you over to the Spanish police and then it was anyone's guess where things would end up.

Frans emphasised that we should never be seen together as a group in the town or out on the road. We should travel singly, Danuta and me again excepted. People seeing us would think we were big sister and little brother. We agreed a rendezvous point some way out of town on a pathway that started behind a farm which had a gate that had been painted bright green. He said no one could miss it. We were to approach the rendez-vous point in staggered, roughly fifteen-minute intervals. Then onwards and upwards. Literally.

XV

One of the original six did not turn up. This was worrying, but everyone agreed it was no reason to ditch our plans. Obviously, he knew where we were assembling, but he did not know where we would begin crossing the mountain range, so there was no reason not to proceed. Frans led the way as we set off and walked for a couple of hours before descending on to a country lane where a truck with a canvas canopy was waiting. While in the truck that took us to our launch point, Frans told us that the Resistance had advised we abandon any fake IDs we had, and we should not carry any weapons. If any of us were caught with either, it would only complicate matters and not in a good way. And so began the penultimate leg of the escape that began with me killing the guard. From a physical point of view, it was also easily the most arduous. And it ended badly, at least for me.

When we got to the departure point, our *passeur* was waiting for us. He told us his group had not had a chance to coordinate with anyone on the Spanish side. Nobody would be waiting for us there, but it wasn't going to be a problem. We would be going downhill all the way. He told us he would leave us close to the border, then we would be on our own to make the descent. If we followed the path that he would point out to us, we would finally see a variety of small farms and farm buildings dotted about. As soon as we saw them, we would know for sure we were on the Spanish side and should split up, each going our own way singly towards wherever it was we had in mind. When Danuta asked if she and I could go down together, he simply shook his head and suggested we arrange to meet somewhere further into Spain. Two people moving together on a mountain were much easier to spot than one person doing the same.

Mercifully, the weather remained reasonably equable. In the higher reaches, it was extremely cold, but there was no snow or ice. The real challenge was simply the arduous nature of the climbing involved. It was relentless. We had to keep moving upwards. It was not what you could call mountain climbing. It was more like scrabbling across scree, negotiating dips and twists.

The driver of the truck that had brought us had left stout sticks in the back, so we had them to help us with the terrain, but even so at one point or another all of us except the guide himself lost our footing, tripped or fell, though the worst anyone suffered were scratches, bruises and grazes. We could not carry on during darkness. There simply wasn't enough light from the moon to show the way, and we didn't have anything with us to illuminate a pathway. Even if we had, advertising our presence would not have been a great idea. The guide took us to a sheltered spot in the mountainside in the lee of some large boulders, where we all huddled together and ate a large part of the little food we had brought with us then did our best to sleep.

The following day was a similar story. Then, in the afternoon of day three, with food stocks reduced to near nought, the guide told us that we had already reached and passed the summit and were now, technically, in Spain. We all let out a great cheer and imagined our guide would leave us straight away, which is what he'd said he would do. But he didn't. He took us a little way down on the Spanish side and then pointed to a pathway which he told us to keep in our sights all the way down. It wasn't going to descend in a straight line, but it wouldn't be difficult to figure it out. At some stage, as the ground ceased to be so steep, we would start to see the farmhouses and buildings a little way in the distance, and it was at that point we should disperse, staggering our departures so no one could see a group acting in concert or moving together along a defined path.

We all agreed this was a sensible plan. We assembled as a group for the last time before each of us set off, making no promises about meeting up again but with me holding Danuta's hand. One by one, the five started to go. I was the third.

I set off with a big wet kiss from Danuta on my cheek. Maybe there was an unspoken understanding I would wait for her down below, but it was unspoken, and it remained unrealised. The first person to depart had gone to the left, down at a fairly sharp angle; the second had gone to the right. Being the third, I also went to the left but back up the mountain a little before proceeding downwards at a more oblique angle, keeping that pathway in view at all times. It's hard to judge these things, but I think I'd been moving downwards for a good two hours when I reached a rocky outcrop which I had to circumnavigate. As I was doing so, I must have startled or disturbed a creature. Something brownish and furry with a white flash, probably a small goat, shot out and frightened the life out of me. I lost my balance, and my right foot slipped into a small crevice. The weight of my body falling over caused the ankle to twist. I let out an enormous scream of pain, my foot came back out of the crevice and I started to roll down the mountain. I don't think I rolled very far, eventually coming to a gentle halt at the bottom of a slight upward turn. However, my ankle was hurting like hell. I tried to stand up, but pain shot through me, and I fell down again. Maybe I had broken a bone. Either way, I was not going to be walking anywhere or putting any weight on the ankle for some time. I took my boot off to survey the damage, and the whole area around my ankle was starting to look red, angry and swollen.

I hoped maybe another of our party might come along as they made the same journey towards freedom. I would see or hear them and attract their attention. I hoped Danuta would sense I needed her. When darkness fell, I realised this was not going to happen. Danuta and the others would all be long gone by now.

Was this to be my fate? Naturally, I assumed the worst. All the scrapes and dangerous moments I had lived through hitherto were behind me and reduced to zero because now I was going to die of exposure or hunger for not paying sufficient attention to my feet, allowing a goat or whatever it was to get the better of me. I would never see my parents to wish them goodbye, never find Nathan, never rescue Srulek and my sisters. The blackness of the night matched perfectly the blackness of my soul. I had tried but I had failed.

That night, the temperature dropped substantially, and of course I had no one to cuddle up to for warmth. I had eaten practically everything I had brought with me and had very little water left. The pain around my ankle showed no signs of abating.

Several hours into the new day, I heard two voices speaking Spanish. I couldn't see who they were, and I had no idea what they would be doing on the mountain. I hoped they were shepherds. Regardless I felt I had no option but to shout and make as much noise as possible, banging my stick on the rock, hooting and hollering. Two men in uniform strode into view. Their rifles, hats and fancy badges on their jackets told me they were not shepherds.

I have no idea what I must have looked like sitting on the ground with my back up against a boulder, one boot missing, but I did not get the impression they felt I posed any kind of immediate threat to them. Even so, one of them stood back, pointing his rifle at me while his companion approached me and searched me, presumably looking for papers or weapons. He found nothing of interest.

Pointing at my ankle and explaining in French, they appeared to understand my predicament, although they made it clear they spoke no French. They then proceeded to debate what to do with me. At least that's what I think they were doing, with their frequent glances, and pointing and gesturing towards me. I guessed, trying to parse Spanish into Polish, that one of them wanted to shoot or leave me and the other didn't. In the end, I'm happy to say the good guy won. His companion disappeared and a while later reappeared with a colleague. They were carrying a stretcher. If I had been bigger, heavier or meaner looking, I wonder who would have won the argument?

The three of them took me down the mountain on the stretcher, dropping me twice as they rotated carrying duties, but they eventually got me to a small village at the bottom and brought me to a doctor. He spoke a little French and, inspecting my ankle, reassured me nothing seemed to be broken. However, my ankle was badly twisted and swollen, so it might be a while before I could rejoin the *corps de ballet* or play football. He strapped the ankle for me.

At the prompting of the guards, the doctor explained to me that, without papers, I would have to wait here in the village until some police officers arrived, and they would probably take me to Pamplona. That is exactly what happened, but my stay in the police station in Pamplona did not last long. I delivered the storyline I had hatched after my conversations with Pierre. I told them I was a French Canadian of Polish stock who had been separated from his parents in France after the Germans invaded Vichy territory, and rather than risk being interned as an enemy alien I was now trying to get to Lisbon to take a boat across the Atlantic. My interrogator could hardly have cared less. He told me I would be taken to the prison at Miranda del Ebro. At my pained and quizzical expression, he told me there was a hospital there and someone would take a further look at my ankle. The next morning, I was off, still in a lot of pain, but not as much as before. I avoided trying to stand on my right leg as much as possible and used an improvised crutch. When I had to move my body under my own steam, it was more of a skip than a step. Standing on my toes for a few seconds was just about bearable.

Miranda del Abro was a huge prison which, as far as I could tell, still held a lot of Spanish political prisoners from the Civil War and foreigners who had enlisted in one or other of the units recruited abroad to support the Spanish Republic. However, there were also lots of prisoners, including many children, who had, like me, been picked up by border guards and transferred to the prison for processing until a final decision could be taken about their destination. Some children were still being held there not because they had done anything wrong but because their parents had been incarcerated during or after the Civil War, and no one else had yet come forward to claim them, probably because there wasn't anyone.

I stuck to my story about being French Canadian of Polish stock. That puzzled them momentarily. They then informed me that because Canada did not have separate diplomatic representation in Spain, they would have to contact officials from the British Embassy in Madrid. The British handled all Canadian affairs at that time. I got the impression that because I looked so young and was a foreigner with no apparent political connections of any kind, they were simply keen to get me out of the jail and out of their hair as soon as possible.

A few days later, a man turned up from the British Embassy. He hadn't come specifically about me. This was a regular visit, because so many foreign nationals with British or Commonwealth connections were being held in the prison. He had been told about me, so here he was, sitting in a room with me, just the two of us. Speaking French.

I made a decision to throw myself at the mercy of this guy. Although I had rehearsed a few lines about Canada with Pierre's help, I didn't feel as confident about them as I did the earlier unused and untested claims about my identity. Really, I didn't know the first thing about Canada. Any kind of detailed questioning would quickly expose me as a fake, and if he concluded I was lying to him, how would that affect his opinion of me or his desire to help me get out of there? In the end my spiel went something like this: 'My name is Henryk Karbowski. I am Polish. A Jew from Lodz. Just over two years ago, I killed a German as I made my escape from the ghetto.

Lodz was then and remains incorporated into the Reich. On my journey from there to here, I did various other things which broke the law both in Germany and in France. I know there's a war on, but maybe these things still count to the German and French authorities. I want to get to Gibraltar so I can enlist in the Polish Army and fight the Nazis. Since the Poles and the Brits are allies, I really hope you will help me. Or let me put it another way: if you don't, I have no idea what will become of me. If the Spanish authorities discover the truth, I fear they will hand me over to the Germans, and I will probably be killed straight away or soon after. The Germans do that with Poles, and they definitely do that with Jews. Or if I am simply kept here in the prison until God knows when, I will go insane or die at the hands of one of the many people I have seen here who have already gone mad.'

It was probably a lot more jumbled and incoherent as it tumbled out, but that was the essence. The diplomat smiled, and after asking me various other questions about my journey, he finally announced he would go along with it, saying, 'This is highly irregular, but I cannot swear, hand on heart, I know what would happen to you if I refuse your request. You could be right. You might be summarily shot if the Germans get their hands on you. I feel sorry for you and believe your story, or at any rate most of it. I will have to go back to Madrid and check some things, make arrangements, but somebody will be back for you in a few days. I will tell the prison authorities that we accept responsibility for you and that I will return with some emergency ID papers.'

Looking back, this was another moment of fundamental importance in my life. Why didn't I tell him my real name? Why did I continue to suppress the identity of Chaim Herszman? I can only assume I had a deeply protective impulse where my family in Lodz was concerned. Anything which might allow me to be traced back to them could put them in danger. Whatever the reason, right there, right then, in a prison in Spain in January 1943, a few months before my seventeenth birthday, I had stumbled on to another path, another chain of events, which would have all kinds of long-term consequences I could never have anticipated. Not in my most twisted nightmares or deliriously happiest dreams.

A week later, I was in a car with British diplomatic plates being taken down to Madrid, where a person from the embassy checked me into the Hotel Mediodía opposite the Atocha Railway Station. The embassy official said they had reserved a room for me for seven nights, because they needed to make additional arrangements to get me to Gibraltar, and it was not yet clear how or when we would set off.

I later learned there was a lot going on in the British Embassy in Madrid. Downed RAF crews and other Commonwealth military personnel had made it to Spain. Their objective, like mine, was to get to Gibraltar. Normally, they did so by sea, evading collaborationist French, German or, occasionally, Italian patrols. The point was they were not supposed to enter Gibraltar by the land crossing at La Línea, because that would violate Spain's status as a neutral country. Yet things didn't always go smoothly, and embassy staff were known to take the odd person or two into Gibraltar concealed in the boot of a car or other vehicle with diplomatic cover.

The German government had a consulate in La Línea and were able to surveil most of the Rock during daylight hours. They were constantly pressuring the Spanish authorities to tighten up procedures, insisting that colluding or being careless about the transportation of military personnel or others intent on aiding the British was both illegal and very unfriendly, no doubt reminding Franco and his associates how they had helped them win power in the first place.

Maybe I was going to be smuggled over in the boot of a car. Nobody from the embassy told me anything about what was going to happen next. The embassy would sort it out and let me know when they came to pick me up to begin the journey. My gratitude to the British diplomat I had met in Miranda del Ebro knew no bounds, but I was still uneasy not knowing what my fate would be, not knowing exactly how things would proceed. In modern parlance, I had 'trust issues'. I imagined all kinds of bizarre twists to the ongoing tale that was my life.

I spent a pleasant week wandering around Madrid and its environs, my ankle having fully recovered by now. In my two weeks or thereabouts in Miranda, I had picked up some basic Spanish, and I managed to expand it further meandering in the capital. The embassy had given me a little money to pay for meals, and I had managed to steal some more to fund my other activities as a tourist. It felt strange to be in a place where there was no indication that the country was engaged in a war, although the signs of damage from the civil war were still all too abundant, as were Spanish military personnel and military police. There were also lots of Germans strutting about the place. I even spoke to a few of them, but they were full of shit about how well the war was going and how the whole of Europe would soon be benefiting from German rule. And the Jews? 'They are being dealt with. They won't trouble us again.'

On the sixth day, a guy from the embassy came to the hotel while I was having breakfast to tell me that he would come back twenty-four hours later to drive me down to Gibraltar.

There would be two drivers, as they hoped to make the 400-mile journey in a day.

That night in my room I fretted. Why were they offering to drive me all that way? Was this a trap? What could go wrong? Had the British changed their minds? Had they decided they would not help get me into Gibraltar? Could they be about to hand me over to the Spanish authorities with unknowable consequences for me?

I decided to skip town at first light and make my own way, working out my own route to the Rock. I was certain that if I could get to the Polish mission, all would be well. I got to La Línea without incident, using buses, and found a room in a place which was close to where I could observe the traffic into and out of the Rock. I was staggered. Every morning, thousands of Spaniards crossed over into Gibraltar, and in the evening the tide went into reverse.

Talking to people in various languages, I gathered some were shipyard workers, but a very large number were women who did a variety of jobs, such as cleaning, cooking and serving. As they walked to the gates, they held up some sort of document, but as far as I could see very few people were ever actually stopped on either the Spanish or British side to have their documents checked. The number of people moving in and out in a fairly compressed time frame was just too large. I gathered that occasionally someone would be pulled out for inspection, and even more occasionally, someone, including saboteurs, would be caught trying to bring in or take out something they shouldn't. However, this was rare.

I saw my way in. I stole some women's clothes, including a coat and capacious headscarf that all but obscured my features, and I mocked up something I could disguise and hold in my hand in a way that suggested to anyone casually looking that I was carrying ID papers. It worked. I shuffled into a crowd approaching the frontier, pushing and elbowing my way into the dense centre of it.

On 21 January 1943, nearly four years after killing the guard, I crossed into Gibraltar from Spain.

XVI

'Henryk Karbowski', Gibraltar, 1943

As soon as I got through the gates on the British side, I separated myself from the mass of humanity that was making its way to places of work and approached someone in uniform who looked like he was important. I removed the headscarf and woman's coat. The man looked a little surprised but not completely astonished. I don't think I was the first one to have pulled a stunt like this. I was a great deal shorter than he was, and with my hands in the air it was obvious I posed no immediate threat.

In broken English, I said, 'I am Polish. I want to kill Hitler.' He laughed and told me I wasn't the only one in these parts who felt like that.

I was taken to a police station, where I gave my name as Henryk Karbowksi. The policeman behind the desk smiled and said, 'We've been expecting you.'

It seemed the guys from the British Embassy in Madrid had still driven down to Gibraltar. Maybe there was someone else they also needed to deliver to the Rock but whether or not that was the case they had left a file on me with the local police assuming, correctly, there was a good chance I would pitch up there sooner or later. Thank goodness I had stuck with the Henryk Karbowksi name just now. The sudden introduction of a whole new, German-sounding name like Herszman might have set off alarm bells and cast doubts about my earlier account given to the diplomat.

There were a number of low-level questions conducted in reasonable Polish but by someone who was obviously a Brit. He was seeking to confirm the details they already had about me in the file from Madrid. I was then shown to a cell, where I stayed for the rest of the day and that evening. Like the holding centre I had been in, the door was not locked, but this time I felt no impulse or need to escape. I was well fed, and I slept like a log. With an enormous sense of relief I cried with happiness because I was no longer on the run, but these tears of happiness were mixed with tears of sadness and loss when I thought about my family back in Poland and Nathan, who could be almost anywhere, alive or dead. Me being alive and in an unquestionably safe place almost shaded into a rebuke. Of me.

The next day, I was escorted to the Polish military mission and handed over with another file and very little ceremony. My English was just about good enough to understand when the British policeman said to the Polish guy, 'This one is for you. Henryk Karbowski. Another "bird of passage". Interesting story about how he got here. It's all there in the file. Let us know what you make of him. We can always send him back.'

At this point, he laughed. I didn't, and neither did the Polish officer. As he walked away, the British guy adopted a more serious face, saying to my Polish guardian, 'Please let us have a transcript of your interrogation and interview. If we put him on a ship to Blighty, we need to know we are not allowing a spy into the country. I agree he doesn't exactly look like one – being just a kid – but appearances can be deceptive, and we don't want to take any chances.'

The Polish officer translated much of the last statement for me, and the word 'spy' sent a chill down my spine. Surely, they couldn't believe I might be a spy? Could I now be shot by my own people or the British as a German agent? That possibility had never occurred to me. It was both too ridiculous and too awful to occupy my thoughts for more than an instant. A Polish doctor gave me another medical, confirming my ankle was fine and appeared to have suffered no lasting damage.

There came a point that day when I had to sign something which was a promise to join the Polish Army. I did not hesitate for a moment. That was precisely why I was here.

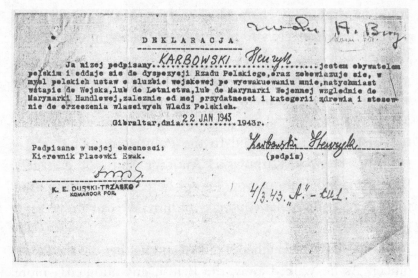

Declaration made by Henryk Karbowski, 22 January 1943

Bearing in mind what I had already told the Brits when they'd interviewed me in Miranda del Ebro, and yesterday when interviewed by the Polish-speaking Brit, it was clear I needed to continue with the same narrative, which was broadly based on my actual antecedents and what had actually happened during my journey. The truth is always the easiest thing to remember. Thus, while sticking with the name Henryk Karbowski, I also gave my parents' names as Adam and Jadwiga Karbowksi. These were indeed the names of Cesek and Mietek's parents, but, inexplicably, I gave my correct date of birth and correct place of birth, Zyrardow. I had hesitated on those points, but the guy hadn't picked up on it, and since these details were true I just registered it as one less lie for me to remember.

Having told the Brits I was a Jew to get them to help me be released from Miranda del Ebro, there would have been no point now trying to maintain I was a Catholic. For one thing, in the Free Polish Army there would be communal showers, so a certain tell-tale sign would be instantly obvious to everyone. In such intense and close proximity, it would just be too difficult to carry off the whole Catholic thing successfully all the time, and if there were any 'out' Jews, they would be very unlikely to be sympathetic towards me.

The Polish officer who had filled in the forms about my status saw the crucifix I was wearing. I explained it had been part of my disguise and had helped keep me alive. He nodded but then took it from me. That was the last time in my life I ever owned or wore a crucifix.

Over the next ten days or so, I must have been interrogated by eight or nine different people on at least a dozen occasions at various times of the day and night. It wasn't hard to work out what they were trying to do: catch me out in an inconsistency which could, in turn, suggest I was lying about something important. They told me other young Poles had made it this far, but if either they or the Brits were not satisfied with the accounts of their journeys, they would be taken to the UK and immediately interned to avoid any possible threat to national security. Such persons were likely to stay in an internment camp for the rest of the war.

There was a slight hint that not all of the Poles who fell into this class had in fact made it from Gibraltar all the way to the UK. Some had been known to have terrible accidents on the ship or had mysteriously 'fallen' overboard never to be seen or heard of again. I wasn't sure if this was being said in all seriousness or if the guy was trying to frighten me for the hell of it. It was unlikely to encourage me into making a confession. If I ever made it on to a ship heading for the UK, I resolved to stay away from the railings if any other people were nearby.

On 2 February, the Polish authorities handed me back to the Brits, who took me on board HMS *Letitia* that night. They told me the ship was heading for the UK, but they did not say where it would dock. I was shown to a bunk bed in a large dormitory room way below deck. In it were boys of about my age and men of a whole variety of nationalities across a broad spectrum of ages. It was good to be able to talk Polish over the next few days.

The ship left Gibraltar on 4 February as part of Convoy MKF8. I knew such ships had been attacked and sunk, including some quite recently in November 1942, but here I was truly in the hands of the gods. I just hoped the gods were on good terms with the British Navy and the RAF.

The ship was bristling with armed men. We were all free to walk about but I did not do much of that. I had never been on a ship at sea before. Worries about being thrown overboard and motion sickness meant I stayed in my bed quite a lot, clinging on to something solid.

HMS *Letitia*

The voyage took five days, finally docking on the Clyde at a place called Greenock on 9 February. I was escorted off the ship – which felt a little odd – and waiting for me at the other end of the disembarkation gangplank was a British police officer. He handcuffed me to himself and, via the good offices of a Polish interpreter who was with him, he explained that I was being taken to London on a train. This was not the kind of welcome to Great Britain that I had been hoping for. Was being 'taken to London' a euphemism for going to an internment camp? It wasn't, but at the same time it turned out not to be that far off.

I was decidedly spooked, and my sense of unease was not lessened when we were joined on the train by another person, this time in a British Army uniform. He spoke to me in German. He had in his briefcase a file which I assume was based on my interviews at Miranda del Ebro and in Gibraltar, but several times he complimented me on my fluency in German. I did the same in return, but perhaps the intended irony was lost on him.

When we got to London early the next day, the officer disappeared, and the policeman, to whom I was still handcuffed, walked me off the train towards a taxi rank. There were a few short but uncomfortable moments as, inevitably, we attracted some attention from members of the public. The policeman got a lot less of that attention than I did. I heard a couple of people talking Polish as we walked by. I tried to speak to them in Polish, but the policeman tugged on the handcuffs and frowned while the two Poles just stared at me. We climbed into a taxi and my companion gave the cabbie an address in Wandsworth. This turned out to be the Royal Victoria Patriotic School, a dark, forbidding Gothic construction which put me in mind of Dracula's castle.

Royal Victoria Patriotic School, Wandsworth

The school was an interrogation centre for people who were not British who had come out of enemy-occupied Europe. In my case, most of the interrogations were held in German, but there were the odd bits that were in Polish, so it was clear they had no doubts about the fact that I was a Pole. That was a relief. The interrogation served two purposes: principally, the interrogators were trying to obtain intelligence which might have some military value, but also, and very obviously, they were on the lookout for potential spies. The spy thing was real. Not a fantasy, a joke or a threat. Oh boy. Was a firing squad truly to be my fate? After everything I had been through, would I die on foreign soil without ever having had the chance to fire a shot in anger at any Germans? And before I'd even lost my virginity? The injustice!

I told them about various things I had seen while in Berlin, when I had journeyed to Metz and Nancy, while around Monhofen and Wappingen, and finally about how I got out of

Vichy France. I think that was the bit that amazed them most. I have no idea if anything I told them was of any value at all from a military perspective, but on the other matter I was in for a terrible shock. They did not say, 'OK, kid, you can go. We'll drop you off at the barracks of the Free Polish Army here in London. Sorry for all the fuss, but we can't be too careful.'

Instead, they acknowledged I had landed on British soil largely because of my own ingenuity and determination, but 'why did you run away before the embassy staff came to get you? Did you meet with anyone in Madrid before you set off for La Línea? Did anyone help you get down there?'

Then came the killing lines, 'You don't look Jewish. You were wearing a crucifix, and the story of your journey is so incredible, we are bound to have a question mark over you. You are obviously a very bright and resourceful young man. With your languages and your grit, you could be a great asset to the war effort, so we are at a bit of a loss at the moment. We are making more enquiries, but, for now at least, you have to stay here.'

This was shattering news. I dropped my trousers, showed the guy my dick and started to speak in Yiddish. That didn't really help: 'Thank you for showing me your penis, Henryk, but I am afraid it proves nothing. There are lots of Christians and others who are circumcised. Not having a foreskin does not prove you are not a Nazi agent.'

Sickened to my core, I was stuck in the Royal Victoria Patriotic School for nearly three weeks. Towards the end of my time there, a rabbi who was with the British Army – now there was a novelty – came to visit me. His name was Rabbi Israel Brodie, an Australian who after the war became the chief rabbi of the UK. In Yiddish, he apologised for having taken so long to get down to Wandsworth, but here he now was. He asked me to recite a few Jewish prayers, which I did, and then we talked about a number of things which made it clear to him that I was familiar with all kinds of details of Jewish rituals, Jewish holidays and Jewish life. It was obvious he had seen a version of my story, because that was what we mainly discussed. He was soon convinced the chances of me not being a Jew were vanishingly small, and the idea that I could be a Nazi agent was therefore preposterous. He apologised for me having to be held like a prisoner but said he hoped I understood the reasons for the precautions. Rabbi Brodie told me there had been a case of the Germans taking a young Belgian teenager down to La Línea with instructions to go across into Gibraltar and be accepted as a refugee. Nothing came of it, because the Belgian boy blurted out everything at the first opportunity. There was a chance I was made of sterner stuff than the Belgian boy, hence the third degree.

Even so, Rabbi Brodie's main interest seemed to be in my journey and how I had survived in all the different places I had been. More than once, he proclaimed his utter astonishment but then said something that gave me great heart and convinced me all would be well: 'I have met a good number of poor Jews who got out of Poland and other places after the Nazis invaded. If you have money or valuable, tradeable items, all kinds of things are possible. Nazi officials, ships' captains and railway workers can be bribed, but if you don't have those kinds of assets, if you're poor, and particularly if you are poor and young, the not-so-simple fact is every single story I have heard of how they managed to escape and get to Britain verges on the unbelievable, the fantastical. Your account is closer to the edge than most, but, as you've told it, it is nevertheless still believable. I believe you. Your looks saved you. If you'd looked Jewish, you'd be dead. This conversation would not be taking place. I am certain you will be out of this place before too long and that you will be granted your wish. You will be allowed to join the Free Polish Army. And the very best of luck with that.'

Wishing me luck with the Polish Army did not strike me then as being anything other than a throwaway line or a conversational pleasantry. I was about to find out it wasn't.

XVII

On 4 March 1943, just over a month before my seventeenth birthday, at the Polish Consulate in London, somewhere near Regent's Park, I signed up to join the Free Polish Army as a volunteer. I was certified as fit for service by Dr Anthoni Bednarski, my weight was recorded at fifty-six kilograms, just under nine stone, and my height recorded as 156 centimetres, just over

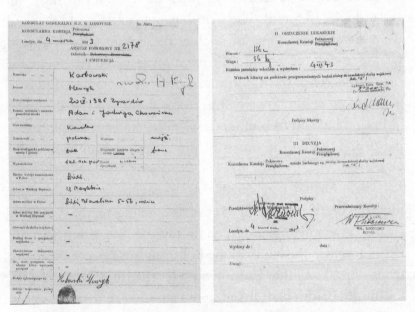

Registration at the Polish Consulate General, 4 March 1943

five feet. I would grow a bit taller as I got older, perhaps as a result of starting to get regular and more nutritious meals.

I was given a Free Polish Army uniform and assigned to a Polish military barracks, more of a hostel, in Marylebone. I underwent various aptitude tests and, along with other new recruits, was taken daily to a gym and for runs around Regent's Park. I stopped thieving. There were two main reasons for this sudden turn towards virtue. The regular meals in the hostel were one, and I was also getting wages of a sort. Not much, but this was the first time in my life I had ever had a regular income of any sort. Up until then, everything had been a hassle, a hustle or a crime.

It was explained that the Polish authorities understood many of us had endured all kinds of hardships and done all sorts of things to get to London. Our patriotic impulses to show up and fight did us proud. The British people understood that and were grateful, every bit as much as the Polish high command were grateful and proud. We were a great advertisement for the heroic Polish spirit. However, now we represented Poland in a foreign country, we had to think about not just the spirit of Poland but also its honour. If we didn't and got caught stealing or fighting in the streets or pubs, the punishments would be severe.

It was further explained that, recognising the size and importance of the Polish Forces assembling in the UK, the British government had agreed to leave de facto control of the Polish forces in the hands of the Polish authorities even though, strictly-speaking, they remained under British command. This meant the British had agreed, in effect, to keep their noses out of Polish military affairs. All of our officers would be Polish, our uniforms would be Polish and all communications would be in Polish.

I didn't know how long I would have in London before my first posting to an operational unit, so I resolved to make the most of it. I had never seen or experienced a city anything like the size or complexity of London. Berlin felt a lot smaller, and I never really felt like a tourist there. In London, I fell in love with Trafalgar Square and with the river, particularly near Parliament.

The damage from the Blitz was very much in evidence, particularly around the East End, where there was a large Jewish community. I visited several times. I didn't try to go to a synagogue or anything like that, but there were cafés and clubs populated almost entirely by Jews of varying degrees of orthodoxy, selling familiar food and drinks from Eastern Europe or approximations thereof. Yiddish was being spoken everywhere; Polish was also being widely used. It was almost like being at home.

It was in the East End in predominantly Jewish places that I first met other Poles wearing the same uniform as me. A couple were from the same hostel in Marylebone where I was staying, but the fact they were Jewish had somehow escaped me. I asked them if the army knew they were Jewish. Both of them winked and one of them said, 'Maybe we filled our forms in wrongly. Let's keep it that way. God knows we're Jews. We know we're Jews, and now you know it too!'

I used my time in London to improve my English, building on the slightly Americanised version I had picked up from Pierre in Voirons. At this point, I never envisaged a future living in the United Kingdom. After the war was over, I would go back

With a friend in Trafalgar Square, May 1943

to Poland to reunite with my family. If Nathan wasn't already there, we would wait until he got back from the Soviet Union, or wherever he had ended up, then we would all be off to Palestine. However, I was still far from convinced the war would end any time soon, so I could easily be in the UK for a year or maybe more. Learning English made a lot of sense, and it wasn't difficult. After the war, it might even come in handy. If things didn't work out in Palestine, I'd heard America was a good place for Jews, and they spoke English there too. Maybe I could go up to Canada and find Pierre. I knew so few people in the world, I felt I had to hang on to any I had brushed up against and liked.

On 24 March, I was notified that I had been posted to the 1st Polish Armoured Division, and the following day I learned I had been assigned to the 1st Tank Regiment, which I assumed was part of the division. This meant I was going back to Scotland. A couple of other guys from Marylebone had also been posted to different bits of the 1st Polish Armoured Division, so a few days later we all travelled by train together. None of us were in handcuffs. For me that was progress.

My base was in a place called Duns. I was there for less than three months before being sent at the beginning of June to a unit in Bury St Edmunds in Suffolk, back down in England, to train to be part of an infantry formation. In August 1943, I was sent back up to Duns, where I stayed for all of seven months. That was the longest I had been in the same place for quite a while. Of course I thought a lot about Nathan and my family back in Lodz but there was simply no way of getting any kind of reliable information about what was happening back home. Having said that, in Polish circles word was reaching the UK and the USA from the Polish underground about the conditions generally in Poland and specifically about what was happening to the Jews. None of what I heard was good or encouraging but I continued to cling to the hope that the Herszmans would come through it. Somehow.

I have happy memories of my time in Scotland. The locals were appreciative of our presence, and I managed to form friendships with a number of Poles about the same age as me or a bit older, including some from Lodz.

I vividly recall an occasion when a group of us were able to get some leave together and arranged transport down to Newcastle, a city in the north of England. The way the local people spoke down there was barely comprehensible, far worse than the Scots, but there was no doubting their friendliness, and in the various pubs and cafés we visited we were met with many expressions of thanks for being part of the effort to defeat Germany. Because this happened a lot, my usual answer was to say I was just grateful the British had stood up to the Nazi bastards and had done so in defence of my country. I was doubly grateful to have the opportunity to hit back both for England and for Poland simultaneously. Or words to that effect. That always went down really well.

We were in Newcastle for three nights, and on the third one of the guys insisted we go to what he called a 'knocking shop'. I was pretty sure I knew what one of those was, but I didn't raise any objections or ask any questions in case I showed myself up as the sexual innocent I actually was. When we got to this very large house, it became obvious the chap who had suggested it, and a couple of the others, were known and had been before. We were shown into a large waiting room. We all sat down, talking nonchalantly as if this was an everyday occurrence. Judging by the fidgeting and faux bravado, for most of them it plainly wasn't. Various young women came into the room, and one by one the guys disappeared. Except me. When I was the last one in the room, and before another young lady could come in, I got up, went out and waited around the corner. In about half an hour, most of the guys were outside on the pavement talking raucously about their exploits and with no apparent embarrassment. I heard them from my hiding place and managed to rejoin the group without anyone realising I had ducked out. I tried to behave as if I had just done exactly what I assume everyone else had, while being light on detail. I might have said, 'Peggy was fantastic,' then grinned, but that was as far as it went. Mercifully, nobody pressed me for any other elements of my encounter with my fictional Peggy.

Then I made a blunder born of naivety. I had noticed in the corner of the waiting room that there was a lady who was not exactly repulsive to look at but considerably older than the others. Nobody had approached her or said anything to her. She'd stayed in her seat, making no visible attempt to promote herself to any of us. I'd assumed she was just there to make sure no one tried to steal anything belonging to the brothel, but I asked if I had read that right. There was a roar of laughter, and one of the guys put his hand on my shoulder and said, 'She's in the same game as the rest of them, but she has a special talent. You could call it a gift. She has no teeth.' It was a while before that particular penny dropped. I felt very foolish. From time-to-time, I would think about that moment and inwardly blush about my innocence.

On 4 March 1944, I was assigned to the 3rd Transport Company of the Free Polish Army in Scotland, and eleven days later, on 15 March 1944, I left the Free Polish Army altogether. I had been in the uniform for almost exactly one year, and now I was out.

Happy though that episode down in Newcastle might have been, and there were several other great memories as well, happiness was not the dominant sentiment associated with my twelve-month sojourn with the Free Poles. Far from it.

While still in London, I'd quickly come to understand why those two Polish Jewish soldiers I'd met in the East End had been keen to keep their religious backgrounds quiet. I hadn't asked them how they'd managed in the showers or wash houses or what had happened at their medical. They had found a way through, so what was it to me? In the Marylebone hostel, everyone had been aware I was a Jew. The kind soul who'd made the initial introductions to my comrades had made a point of ensuring everyone knew: 'I know he doesn't look like one, but Henryk here is one of the chosen ones.'

This had been greeted by a mixture of laughs from those who did not believe what they were hearing, and horror from those who plainly did. However, the harassment and Jew-baiting I had experienced while in the small hostel in London was nothing compared to what I walked into when I was assigned to the large operational units in Scotland.

Obviously, I was not the only Jew who was the subject of verbal and sometimes physical attacks by their comrades in arms. There were supposed to be around 800 'openly acknow-ledged' Jews in the Free Polish Army. Even to write that tells you how bad things were, although I later heard Jews might have made up as much as ten per cent of all personnel serving in one or other of the Polish armed wings. Whatever the number, the great majority of the Jews in Polish uniforms seemed to be having it rough in just the same way I now was, or else for them it was even worse. My looks once again acted as a shield, at least insofar as they helped make my religious affiliations invisible to anyone who didn't already know the score.

As I was not the least bit bothered about the kosher laws, it was impossible for me to be embarrassed about anything connected with food, but this was not true for every Jew in the military, and while it was impossible to keep any kind of seriously Kosher regime in practical terms, my more religious brethren absolutely dreaded the days when bacon was served. This would provide our persecutors with no end of amusement. They would even sacrifice part of their own rations in order to force-feed bacon to a protesting Jew. Any NCOs and junior officers watching on rarely intervened to stop it: 'Just a bit of fun. You Jews need to learn how to take a joke.'

It wasn't that difficult for the Jews to find each other in the units I served with, in the Tank Regiment. We were the ones who were always being pointed to and having our religion mentioned. Non-Catholic Christian Poles also got the occasional dig, but nothing like on the same scale.

Sometimes I wondered if things wouldn't have been easier for me if I had stayed with the schtick of being a Catholic. Had I made a mistake by disclosing I was a Jew to begin with? But the die had been cast in the prison at Miranda del Ebro. There was no point continually beating myself up over it. I'd had no choice. I am sure telling the British diplomat I was a Jew is what got me out of prison and therefore kept me alive.

There was one slightly older guy on the base at Duns who spoke out strongly about the evil that anti-Semitism represented, how it was a Nazi tool and so on. Maybe he was a communist. I didn't ask. Because of his huge size, whenever he was around,

I stuck close to him so as to remove any temptation anyone might be feeling about assaulting me. This guy also had a piano accordion, and he decided to teach me how to play it. A visible act of solidarity. I guess my ear, the same ear that had produced my talent for languages, kicked in and helped me out, because I very quickly got it, and by the middle of the second week I was knocking out tunes that were recognisable and melodic, even if they were far from perfect. This caused a couple of the anti-Semites to soften their attitudes towards me, but it definitely did not win over all of them. To the hard core, I wasn't just a Jew; I was now also a smartarse Jew.

Rumours circulated about Jewish soldiers in Free Polish Army uniforms being found dead in circumstances which suggested it was very likely they had been murdered and the murderer could only have been someone in the same unit or one posted nearby. In one case, so the rumour mill went, a Jew was found dead with several rashers of bacon laid across his head. I had no idea whether any of these rumours had any foundation in fact, but they were persistent, and that alone spoke volumes.

Apparently ENSA, the organisation that arranged entertainment for the troops, had been told never to send an act to any Polish bases if it had any Jews in it. Some of us had been told at some point or another that once we landed on the Continent to begin the land battles with the Nazis, there would be two bullets in our comrades' guns: 'One for Fritz, and one for you, Hymie.'

We were getting fed up with the constant harassment. I was too junior, too small and too young to have acted as any kind of ringleader among us in uniform in Scotland, but when we gathered together I was absolutely up for doing something to end what felt like persecution. For many of us, the feeling that the people who could harm you, maybe kill you, were not only the ones opposite wearing a *Stahlhelm* and field greys or the black of the SS, but might also be at your side or behind you was deeply enervating and upsetting beyond words.

I heard Jewish soldiers who had been around longer than me say things had been getting worse in the ranks since Rommel's defeat in North Africa, because included in the thousands of soldiers captured were a great many *Volksdeutschen* from Poland who had been conscripted and forced to fight. Whatever their attitudes towards Jews before 1939, once in the Wehrmacht they had, inevitably, so the reasoning went, absorbed Nazi ideas and attitudes. I didn't know what to make of this, but it sounded plausible. These *Volksdeutschen* had started to arrive in the UK in larger numbers from late 1942 onwards and shortly afterwards began to be absorbed into fighting units of the Polish Army. The problem grew in intensity roughly from around that time.

Having failed to get any effective response to counter anti-Semitism through the established Polish channels or high command, some of the Jewish soldiers with better English had started to write to prominent people in Britain, church leaders and politicians, pointing out what a terrible time the Jews were having in the Free Polish Army and telling them that nothing was being done by anyone to stop it. They asked these prominent Brits to intervene. Letters were also sent to newspapers, but because of prevailing censorship rules, little, if anything, ever appeared either in letter form or as a press report. We were repeatedly told that because of the arrangements agreed with the Polish government in exile, it was impossible for the

British authorities to step in. This was a Polish problem; the Poles would have to sort it out themselves.

That was not an answer we were willing to accept, because it meant nothing would change. I heard the names of three British members of parliament being mentioned. They had agreed to be our champions. From what I gathered, most of what they had done hitherto had been behind the scenes. They were reluctant to speak publicly. It would have been a gift to Nazi propagandists and would generally undermine the war message of a united front against a common enemy.

One of the MPs was from the Labour Party, Samuel (Sydney) Silverman, who was Jewish. The second was Tom Driberg, who, despite his surname, was actually a devout Christian and at the time technically an independent MP, although he later became a Labour MP. The third MP was said to be a Conservative, Bob Boothby. They were being helped by a journalist called Michael Foot, who would become a Labour MP and leader of his party many years later. Finally, I heard mention of a prominent Methodist, an ordained minister called Donald Soper. I wasn't sure what a Methodist was, but it was great to hear at least one Christian leader was on our side.

The object of the campaign that emerged was to win the right of Jews in the Free Polish Army to transfer into units of the British Army without dishonour; that is to say, without any stain on their character or on their record. Groups of us were asked to obtain leave or absent ourselves from camp. We were to make our way to London to lobby MPs and talk to other influential people. I joined a group that met with Tom Driberg in the East End. Later, we attended a very large meeting in the Stoll Opera House on Kingsway in Holborn. It was all very exciting, and £1,000 was collected to help sustain our efforts. I had never been to a meeting like that before. Most of the speakers were British – Michael Foot, Eleanor Rathbone, another independent MP, and Driberg were among them – and while I did not understand everything they said, I definitely caught their drift.

It appeared to be the case that while nothing would be said or acknowledged publicly, both the Polish high command and the UK authorities had agreed to turn a blind eye and allow Jews who were so inclined to move over from Polish units to British units without any fuss or bother.

That all worked out fine for the first two groups of Polish Jews, numbering around 200 – I think I must have been in the second group – but everything went wrong for the third group. There were only about thirty in this group. As with those who had gone before, they made no secret of their intention to join the British Army, but it appears, in the meantime, the Polish authorities changed their mind about the previous, informal arrangements and were no longer willing to sanction any more Jewish transfers out. When this third group nevertheless went ahead, everything blew up.

In the first week of April 1944, British and Polish military police jointly raided the hostels and other places the thirty Polish Jewish soldiers were known to be staying in London. They were arrested for desertion. Trials were held in camera, and they were each sentenced to between one- and two-years' imprisonment. Bearing in mind that none of these individuals wanted to avoid fighting the enemy – on the contrary, they all wanted to go to active fighting units in the British Army – this finally prompted Tom Driberg to break cover by raising the matter in Parliament, getting it put on the record in Hansard on 6 and 26 April. The following month, he wrote a pamphlet that was published by the National Council for Civil Liberties called 'Absentees for Freedom'. That word 'absentee' was incredibly important. The men in this third group were just like us 'absentees', not cowardly deserters. We had wanted to absent ourselves from an anti-Semitic environment, but only so we could 'un-absent' ourselves to focus more effectively on the major anti-Semitic threat sitting across the English Channel and the North Sea.

Thus, while there might not have been massive awareness among the general public about this dreadful state of affairs, there was no question that among the governing elite of the United Kingdom the idea that Poland and the Polish people had a problem with anti-Semitism took a deep hold. This coloured a great many influential people's attitudes towards Poland for a long time after the war had ended.

I did not hear Tom Driberg speak in the House of Commons, but reports of what he said reached us in short order. His words were echoes of the speech I had heard him make at the Stoll Opera House. Some of my co-religionists who were leading the Absentees for Freedom campaign managed to acquire a bottle of cognac and get it to Mr Driberg as a token of their appreciation of his efforts. Being such a rarity in those days, we were all told it was gratefully received and enthusiastically consumed.

By then, I was wearing the khaki uniform of the British Army's Royal Regiment of Fusiliers, a company of infantry-men that had first been established in the seventeenth century. I had transferred into the Fusiliers after a brief spell in the Royal Pioneer Corps. Pioneers, apparently, could trace their roots even further back, to the fourteenth century. As a Jew, these timespans held no special significance, but there was something rather comforting about connecting with bodies of such antiquity, even with an apparent link to royalty. It suggested solidity, permanence and certainty, qualities which had been entirely lacking in my life of late. It was always a matter of great sadness to me that at a time when Poland itself was facing an existential crisis, ancient prejudices and hatreds still had such potency among so many, possibly even the majority of men who really should have been preoccupied with other things.

Part Four

Henry

XVIII

The Royal Pioneer Corps unit I joined in Buxton, Derbyshire, was a marvellously multilingual affair. There were foreigners everywhere. Collectively, we were often referred to as 'His Majesty's Most Loyal Enemy Aliens', or sometimes as 'Britain's Foreign Legion'. Among other things, the corps was used to provide an initial berth for people who wanted to fight against Hitler but who would not otherwise qualify in the conventional way to join an operational army unit; for example, because they were German or Austrian. Although some stayed with the corps for long periods of time, a great many, like me, were only there for short periods until they could be found an appropriate posting elsewhere.

England and the British Army were turning out to be full of surprises. In my bunk room in the barracks in Buxton, there were several Germans and Austrians, some of whom but not all were Jews. One was a socialist and another was an artist, a painter, seemingly with no strong political views, but he wanted everyone to know he was an atheist. He said he hated the authoritarianism, intolerance and anti-intellectualism of the regime now governing his people. I had never before met anyone who proclaimed and advertised themselves to be an atheist. That was novel and made me think. I'd told people I thought God was a con trick, or that I felt he wasn't paying attention, but I hadn't yet definitively concluded He wasn't actually there.

In the Free Polish Army, I had learned about firing a rifle, unarmed combat techniques and basic things of the kind you imagine every soldier would have to know. With the Pioneers, the same sorts of things remained part of the daily diet, but I was also able, if only briefly, to develop my carpentry skills in anticipation of the possibility that on the battlefield I might need to be part of a squad that helped create or improvise gun emplacements or other artefacts necessary to enable soldiers to fight in the safest and best conditions possible.

A tremendous sense of camaraderie developed among the non-Brits. We were drawn to each other and held together by very obvious and strong bonds. Not only were we all refugees or fugitives from our own countries, typically having made it here alone, almost all of us had done amazing things en route. We were all incredibly grateful to the Brits for taking us in, providing us with shelter and helping us get back at the regime that had ruined our lives, our families' lives and our countries.

There was also a shared comic edge to our plight. We were all simultaneously trying to improve our grasp of the English language, while also improving our understanding of the ways and traditions of the British Army and the ways and traditions of the British people among whom we were now living.

There were quite a few French speakers among the Pioneers, but if there was a lingua franca among the non-Brits, it was probably German, although, in the circumstances, wandering about Britain speaking the tongue of the hated enemy did not seem a terribly good idea. English was the preferred medium. If anyone hit an obstacle, if they didn't know how to say what they wanted to say in English, they would revert to their mother tongue, and if that was German, they tried to ensure nobody else overheard them.

My time with the Pioneers was very intense in terms of the military training I had to undergo. But against that, a major compensation was Buxton itself. It was beautiful, as was the surrounding countryside. In addition, finally being away from the Free Poles, the sheer relief of just being able to walk about in a place where I did not have to fear I could be killed or injured solely because I was a Jew was a joy. Now I was in a British Army uniform, I no longer drew sideways looks from curious passers-by. That was good too.

Another reason why I would never forget my time with the Pioneers was that on the day before my eighteenth birthday, I finally admitted to my friends I had never actually had sex with anyone. I had had a sweetheart, I had kissed a girl, Martha, but in a moment of total honesty I went for full disclosure and made this shameful revelation. I skipped over my near-sex experience in Newcastle.

That weekend, a few of my usual crew and I got passes to go to Manchester. There was a constant stream of trucks and buses heading there from the camp. We were off. One of the guys said he had heard of a new place that had some interesting things on offer, and he knew one of the people who ran it, so he could get us all in. I imagined we were heading for a pub or some sort of shebeen, so I happily agreed to go along. We ended up outside a building that looked like it had been a department store, a warehouse or something similar but had been bomb-damaged and abandoned. Many of the surrounding buildings appeared to have been similarly abandoned. Some now had stout fences to keep people out, presumably because the structures were unsafe or there was a risk of looting. But not this particular building. While the blackout meant there was no visible light from within to help anyone flying above or strolling by work out what was going on inside, there was a hubbub that indicated there was definitely something happening. There appeared to be a complex ritual for entering the building. It was negotiated by the guy who knew someone who worked there. When we were allowed in, it was clear all the action was taking place in a large and well-lit basement.

I soon realised what I had been taken to was a mixture of a brothel and a nightclub. These days it would be called a 'pop up'. We had been standing at the improvised bar for about ten minutes when a very attractive young lady, she never told me her name, approached and said she had been told to look after me. She took me by the hand and led me away as the rest of my party cheered me on, sang 'Happy Birthday' and made a variety of gestures which removed any possible doubt about what lay ahead.

I am not going to go into any details about what happened next, but all I will say is I was very sorry I hadn't done it before, and I very much looked forward to doing it again as soon as possible.

When I emerged, to more cheers and another rendition of 'Happy Birthday' from my pals still standing at the bar, we all moved to the far end of the large basement room to join an audience for what turned out to be a striptease show involving five young ladies in a variety of complex poses, some of which were highly anatomical in nature. When they walked off the stage, they were completely naked. I was beginning to get another insight into a world which, only weeks ago, I had no idea existed.

The following day, back in Buxton, I was notified I was being transferred to the Royal Fusiliers at the end of the week.

My new posting was only over in Blackpool, so I figured I ought to be able to get back to the same spot in Manchester and see if I could find the same lady. I got permission to spend a night travelling to Blackpool and found my way back to the same building in Manchester. It was completely deserted, no signs of life, not a sound emanating from the place. A friendly air-raid warden looked at me, shaking his head sadly, and said, 'Sorry, son. They've all gone.'

I was with the Fusiliers in Blackpool for three months. That was another great posting, because it was a major British seaside resort, and lots of soldiers from all over the northern parts of England and southern parts of Scotland would make their way there whenever they had the opportunity. Part of my time there was spent teaching a number of men and women from other units how to speak and read German, although in most cases they could already speak and read a bit, so I was really only helping them to improve. Sometimes an actual German or an Austrian would join us, and my spoken German was rarely corrected by them. This was very gratifying.

In July 1944, I was transferred to the Queen's Own Royal West Kent Regiment, and I got to see much of the UK. I was stationed briefly in Ashford in Kent, Lerwick in Shetland and Hastings on the south coast before transferring to the Royal Berkshire Regiment in February 1945.

With the Fusiliers and West Kents, it was a never-ending series of drills, training and grunt work, such as guard duty. My main distraction was upping my skills with the piano accordion and improving my command of both spoken and written English. I had managed to acquire my own accordion so as to continue practising, and I like to think I became quite an accomplished performer. Certainly, whenever I was around a call would go up for me to play, and I enjoyed the whole thing immensely. I might not know the words of the songs I could play – although they were coming – but I seemed to be able to get and replay the tunes usually after hearing them only once, and definitely after hearing them twice.

It was during my time with the West Kents that I made an important decision. Everything I was hearing about how the war was going in Eastern Europe made me think it was very unlikely I would ever again be able to live in Poland, which was now substantially, even wholly, occupied by Soviet forces that no one believed would simply turn around and walk back to Moscow, leaving a free and independent Poland behind. I would return but only long enough to reunite with my family before setting off with them for Palestine or America. If I ended up in Palestine, Chaim Herszman would reappear, but I would face that as and when it happened. For the time being, I decided to anglicise Henryk Karbowski. Henry Carr stepped on to the stage. This was partly an attempt by me to fade into the background a little and stop drawing attention to myself as a foreigner. Obviously, I had an accent that instantly broadcast the fact that I was not a native Brit, but for anyone to know that they would have to at least speak to me or hear me speak. Changing my name to something unmistakably British meant a foreign name would not be on my papers or sewn on to any identity tags. I made a mental note to explain all this to Cesek and his parents, assuming they were still alive. The Karbowksi ID had substantially served its intended and largely anticipated purpose.

Thus, when I transferred to the Royal Berkshires in February 1945, I did so as Henry Carr. Finally, I would get a chance to fire a weapon at Germans. I hoped all the ones I hit would be Nazis not Walthers

I discovered part of the reason why I was assigned to the Berkshires was because they were contemplating close engagement with the enemy in the near future and the idea, wherever possible, was to have people to hand who could read and speak German, both to deal with potential prisoners but also to examine and secure documents. These might be on individuals who were captured alive or found dead in field locations which we had overrun. Someone needed to be able carry out a rapid assessment of the likely value or importance of any paperwork that was to hand. We couldn't take every scrap and flood field command offices with them.

I joined the 5th Battalion of the Royal Berkshires, which was then in Lille in France and was moving to Waterscheide in eastern Belgium, where it was re-establishing itself after earlier heavy losses at Normandy and elsewhere. They would then be moving towards the Rhine, near the German village of Xanten, a little west of the river itself. Our task was to assist the 15th Scottish Division to cross the Rhine into what one might think of as mainland Germany.

Xanten, 1945

B Company, July 1945, Germany

And so it was that I found myself on German soil again, this time looking east towards and across the Rhine. On the first day, there were minor but still deadly skirmishes with German units who remained on our side of the river. I saw German soldiers dropping as a result of fire which had come from the direction of my platoon, although whether or not my weapon had done the damage was impossible to say. I like to think it did some. On the fourth day, my platoon was moving through houses and using them as cover to fire across the river at a German patrol that seemed intent on coming back over to our side to attack us, perhaps joining up with other units still here whom we hadn't yet flushed out. This time I was pretty sure I hit a couple of them, but they had light artillery support, and the house I was in was targeted. A couple of shells hit the ground floor. I was upstairs. If I didn't get out of there fast, I reckoned I would be killed. I jumped through an upper window just as another shell hit the top of the house.

I wasn't sure how long I was out, but when I regained consciousness, I was in a field hospital, concussed and my ears ringing. My right wrist was bandaged, strapped and hurt like hell. There was talk of me being sent back to Blighty to recuperate, but I made it clear I wanted to stay and carry on. I was exactly where I wanted to be, with a gun in my hand shooting at – and apparently killing – the enemies of Poland and the Jews. In the end, I was partially overruled and was sent to a hospital in Brussels. I heard that as my platoon had gone on a sweeping up action a little further north, one of my best mates had been killed in Emmerich, not so very far from where I had nearly met my maker. Another died triggering an unexploded landmine near to where my platoon had set up to make a cup of tea.

After the war, my wrist became very troublesome, and I was eventually diagnosed as having Kienböck's disease. The doctors said it was directly attributable to the injury I had sustained at Xanten. I was given a stiff leather sleeve with a steel spine. I wore it when my wrist and arm began to feel heavy and sore. The sleeve was meant to immobilise my wrist, and I kept it on until the pain wore off. My kids loved playing with it, so that was an unexpected bonus. But I'm getting ahead of myself.

As the German forces were cleared from the other side of the Rhine, so the British Army moved on towards Berlin, while the Royal Berkshires stayed in Xanten until the war ended. I was still in Brussels when news came through that Hitler was dead and the war was over. It was a wonderful moment. I lost count of the number of people I kissed or who kissed me that night, men and women of all ages – hailing me as a Tommy – and I was staggeringly drunk by the end of it, but nobody cared.

Brussels, May 1945

As the evening wore on, I once again shed an ocean of tears as I thought about all the things I had been through to get to this moment. Word had also been coming through thick and fast of the horrors and the scale of what the Nazis had done to the Jews of Europe in general and the Jews of Poland in particular. There had been talk of such things all the time through the latter stages of the war, but many people simply could not or would not believe it. Now they were no longer rumours or leaks. There was absolutely no dispute about the facts and it would not be long before the scale of what had happened became clear. The Soviets had liberated Auschwitz in southern Poland in January 1945 and then more recently, in April 1945, the British had reached Bergen-Belsen. Everyone knew what had been going on, and the enormity of the atrocities was starting to sink in.

My initial feelings of anger about how this had been allowed to happen turned to blind range at times, but I realised this would be unlikely to be useful to anyone, least of all me. I had to find out where Nathan was and find my family. Had he made it to the Soviet Union? Had he survived? What about my parents, Srulek and my three sisters back in Lodz? How the hell was I going to do that in the chaos and destruction that lay between me and Lodz?

I went back to my unit in Xanten but was still not considered fully fit so was put on light duties. I spent a lot of time running errands on a motorbike. My senior officers figured it would help strengthen my wrist, and they were right. It did. Towards the end of June, my battalion was disbanded. I transferred to another part of the regiment, but the work was dull beyond words.

It was around this time I had my first run in with the army's disciplinary processes. I was confined to barracks for fourteen days from 27 July 1945 for failing to enforce curfew restrictions on German civilians, associating with German civilians after the curfew and being absent without leave, the unauthorised leave being the time I spent drinking with the German civilians, none of whom, as far as I could tell, had fought in the war and all of whom damned Hitler with a degree of enthusiasm which I did not believe could be faked. Right enough, once Germany had been humiliated and reduced to rubble and starvation it wasn't hard to find and feel the genuine anger of German people about what the Nazis had brought upon them. We might all have regretted they hadn't realised this sooner and acted upon it, but we had to deal with people as we found them in the here and now, not as we would have liked them to be in the then and there.

I got into trouble again a few months later when I was caught posting a letter in the army post office for a German civilian. For this, I got sent to the detention unit from 20 October until 2 November. The petty nature of army life was getting to me. I was not cut out for it.

As a Polish Jew, I had no reason to feel any obligations of friendship or compassion towards Germans, but, equally, when you meet ordinary people and you have to engage with them face to face, it seemed to me just plain wrong not to extend normal courtesies and politeness to everyone unless and until they gave you a specific reason to do otherwise. And if some old guy wanted me to help him get a letter to his son who was a POW in England, what the hell? Who would it hurt? I knew, both from my time as a child in Lodz and more particularly from when I was on the run, that not every German was bad; indeed, Germans had saved my life more than once. The idea that a whole race or class of people could be branded and put in a box marked 'evil' just seemed to me to be so obviously wrong and stupid, I wanted nothing to do with it.

I did not feel so generous towards anyone with links to the SS or the Nazi Party itself, or anyone who still professed sympathy for Nazi ideas. Few and far between as they now were, they were not non-existent. Soon after the war had formally ended, there were rumours about an underground movement that had been developed and put in place by elements of the Nazi Party when they realised defeat was staring them in the face. This clandestine organisation had adopted the German name Werwolf. It was intent on conducting a guerrilla war until the German people rose up and threw off the yoke of decadent western-Jewish and Bolshevik oppression. But the predominantly old men and women I was drinking and chatting with and posting letters for? They were as war weary as anyone. No yokes, decadent, western-Jewish or otherwise, were going to be overthrown by them. Their sole preoccupations were securing a bite to eat, something to drink and finding a warm place to sleep where there was no danger of death falling from the sky, coming to the door or through the windows.

After I came out of the detention unit in November, I got sent back to the UK and was in London for Christmas and New Year. I very much enjoyed being in a place I now almost thought of as my second home. To all the world, I was a Tommy. I liked that. It conferred a kind of protective cloak.

London, 1946

Now began an extremely painful part of my life that would continue for many years. I started to try to trace my family, principally through the International Red Cross. I left my name with them, the names of my extended family in Poland and my then contact details. I did the same with the Polish authorities in London, but when I mentioned the names of the people I was enquiring about – Herszmans, Lewkowiczs, Levinsons and Blumowiczs – and that they had been in the ghetto in Lodz, they said absolutely terrible things had happened there, and I shouldn't hold out much hope. This much I had been expecting to hear, but that didn't make it any easier. It wasn't confirmation they were all dead but I was fearful that that is what it probably did mean.

Otherwise, I seemed to be constantly being lent out to different bits of the army or British civil service who needed people who could speak, read and write German. Then, in April 1946, I received orders to go back to Germany and report to the headquarters of the British Army of the Rhine, where Field Marshal Montgomery was in control, though not for much longer. HQ BAOR was in a town called Bad Oeynhausen on the Weser River, 240 kilometres east of Xanten. The beginnings of an idea started to crystallise.

None of the agencies I had contacted had sent me any word about any of my family in Poland or about Nathan. I was constantly badgering and pleading with them. Bad Oeynhausen to Lodz was a round trip of around 1,600 kilometres. It would be almost impossible to try to get there and back using trains and buses, and the roads would still likely be impassable for all but rugged or military vehicles. On the other hand, with a motorbike it might just be doable. It was summer, so if I had to sleep rough as I moved along, it shouldn't be too bad. Lots of Poles and others were making similar journeys. I asked for and got a week's leave, and my boss said if I didn't tell him I had borrowed a motorbike and two jerry cans full of petrol, he would never know about it. I was off.

Afterwards, when I watched films about the war and its immediate aftermath, my feelings of discomfort centred not just on how parts were glamorised but also how its sheer awfulness could never be properly conveyed. Pathé News managed to get close sometimes; Hollywood never did. My journey east from Bad Oeynhausen was a graphic and dreadful illustration of why I held that view. For a large portion of my journey, I was travelling through parts of Germany the Soviets had conquered. They had not held back. The scale of the devastation was immense. There were images that stayed with me for ever of queues at standpipes for water or outside feeding stations for handouts. With my British uniform, Polish tongue and a little Russian that I had picked up from prisoners in Miranda del Ebro, I made it to Lodz. Word had gone out across all the Allied Forces in the occupied zone to allow people like me an easy passage, so I encountered no major hold-ups or hassles on the way.

I was surprised by how little the main fabric of the city had been damaged. In fact, Lodz was at that time the de facto capital of Poland. The new Polish government had established itself there because so much of Warsaw had been flattened and rendered unusable. By contrast, the Soviet advance on Lodz had been so rapid the Germans had simply not had time to blow up the factories and main buildings as they'd retreated, neither had they dug in to defend it.

What was truly depressing from my point of view, however, was to learn that when the Russians arrived there were fewer than 900 Jews left alive in Lodz, and not all of them were actually from Lodz or indeed Poland. Several hundred of the 900 had been deliberately left alive when the ghetto had been liquidated by the Nazis so they could form part of a clean-up detail that would destroy any evidence of what had been happening there. However, their supervisors had fled as the Red Army got close. On top of the clean-up detail, the remainder of the 900 were Jews who had somehow managed to hide in the ghetto, plus a small number who had lived on the Aryan side for the duration and now finally felt it was safe to come forward and live openly again. I later learned that of the entire Jewish population of Lodz from before September 1939, only an estimated 10,000 survived by escaping before the Germans arrived or by going into hiding somewhere or other.

When I got to Lodz, a Jewish office had been re-established on Zachodnia, where previously there had been some Jewish communal buildings. They had no news they could give me other than to say that there was no record of any survivor by the name of Herszman, Levinson, Lewkowicz or Blumowicz. I should assume they were all dead.

Obviously, knowing what had happened to the Jews of Poland in Auschwitz, Chelmno, Belsen and so on, I had suspected there was a possibility that I would be told what I had just heard, but it was altogether a different thing to have it confirmed so categorically with so little room for doubt or hope. I asked specifically if anyone by the name of Nathan Herszman had been in touch or left word. I told them I thought he had made it to the Soviet Union. He hadn't contacted them, but they said Jews who had been in Russia were trickling back to Lodz in dribs and drabs. As with the Polish authorities in London, I left my contact details with them. No one from there ever got back to me.

Before leaving, I tried to find Cesek Karbowksi or his mum or dad or any of the non-Jewish Poles I had known before the war. I found nobody, but I learned a great deal more about just how bad it had been for the Poles left behind. Far more Poles than Jews perished during the war, but as a proportion of the total respective populations the Jews were almost completely wiped out: ten per cent made it; ninety per cent did not.

It became crystal clear that there was nothing for me in Poland any more. I then started to hear that as small numbers of Jews did make it back to Lodz some of them were being attacked and killed by Poles who had assumed they were dead and had decided to appropriate their properties. They did not want to give anything back to their rightful owners. When I got back to my British Army unit, I vowed I would never set foot on Polish soil ever again. That was a promise I kept and never regretted.

Returning to Bad Oeynhausen, I managed to prang the motorbike, and while I escaped injury, I knew I would be in trouble. Here was my next encounter with the army's disciplinary code. I acknowledged that I had been negligent with army property. The damage was estimated at over £50, but I was only ordered to contribute £3 by way of compensation, and this was deducted from my pay.

I spent four months at Bad Oeynhausen, where much of what I was involved with concerned the war trials that were being held under the auspices of the War Crimes Tribunal based in Hamburg. I was promoted twice, first to lance corporal and then to corporal. Then, in September 1946, I was posted to the Autobahn Control Unit at Helmstedt. One of the westernmost parts of Germany which had been reached by the Red Army in May 1945, this was one of the points where east met west. It was later destined to become a major border cross-ing into East Germany.

I was at Helmstedt through the most appalling winter conditions when almost no traffic of any kind moved in either direction, so all I did was hang about, avoiding getting cold. In February 1947, I got in trouble again. I lost a bicycle, valued at just over £5. I think initially it fell in the snow and got covered, only this time, unlike with the motorbike, I had to repay the full amount, which, again, was deducted from my pay, and I was held in open arrest. I was never entirely sure what that meant, because I carried on with my duties and activities as normal, only I stayed within the confines of the barracks and camp.

On that bicycle

I also had two severe reprimands placed on my record about this time. The first, on 9 May, arose from me being careless. An officer spotted a bottle of schnapps in my possession, and I refused to tell him how or where I had acquired it. For this, I was once again placed in open arrest. There was black-market trading and bartering going on between local Germans, the Russians and several Brits. No way was I going to rat on anybody and risk bringing it all to an end.

A week later, on 16 May, I was reported again for leaving my rifle unattended and in poor condition at the *autobahn* checkpoint and for making a remark about the stupidity of company orders. It was definitely time to move on.

Underlying my falling out with another officer was his extreme dislike of the Soviet soldiers and officials. He was a virulent anti-communist who could sometimes be heard muttering about how we are going to need the Germans to help us defeat the Reds so the sooner we got on with that the better it would be for all concerned. I was as anti-communist as the best of them, but I got the impression from this guy that skipping over even the most despicable and inexcusable Nazi war crimes was a price he was willing to pay to cement an early anti-Reds alliance. That was not how I saw things. The Nazis had to pay for what they had done. The fact I already spoke a little Russian and was very obviously improving my command of it as the days went by definitely annoyed him as well.

A few weeks before he definitively took against me, there had been what can only be described as a mysterious incident at the crossover point on the *autobahn*. Maybe this explained his obvious dislike of me. Late one night, when I was on duty, the officer in question turned up unannounced with a middle-aged man in plain clothes. It was impossible to tell who he was or why he was there. Nobody said. I didn't ask. He didn't speak.

The officer called me over and told me to escort this gentleman to the Russian checkpoint and leave him there. I asked if anyone or anything was to be brought back? 'Negative.' Did I need to sign anything? 'Negative. Just get on with it. They're expecting him.'

As is the way of things, word about what had happened got around. All kinds of rumours circulated about the identity of the man who had been handed over and why it had happened in such unusual circumstances. My favourite was that he was Georgian, from Stalin's home country, but he had been a senior officer in the Waffen-SS, a volunteer. Stalin had been told this guy was in British custody, and it was agreed we would short-circuit the normal processes because it would be regarded by Uncle Joe as doing him a huge personal favour if we just handed him over. I never discovered what the truth was, but assumed the guy was probably dead within an hour of being given to the Russians.

In September 1947, after a period of extended leave, I ended up about 110 kilometres away at Fischbeck at the War Criminals Holding Centre. The Nuremberg trials of major Nazi war criminals had attracted global attention in the media and were drawing to a close. More than twenty death sentences were carried out, but a far greater number were handed down following war crimes trials heard in many other parts of Germany, particularly in Hamburg, where the Allies commandeered the undamaged 'Curio-Haus' as their HQ. In those court rooms a catalogue of human misery and suffering poured out as concrete illustrations of what had been conjured up by the Nazis' hateful, racist ideology. The constant stream of denials by the accused and pleas of 'I was only following orders' were as utterly sickening as they were unbelievable.

Briefly a sergeant

On 23 January 1948, I was promoted to and paid as an acting sergeant, but it didn't last long. On 10 August, following an incident on 31 July, I was reduced to corporal again. This time

I had simply refused to help an officer move his car which had got stuck in the mud. That seemingly constituted a refusal to obey a lawful order. Open arrest again, but shortly afterwards I was once more sent to Autobahn Control Unit at Helmstedt. I knew I had had enough of being in Germany. Everything was too difficult and complicated. I needed to get back to the UK, get on with finding Nathan, get on with determining if all of my extended family really were dead and, if they were, how, when and where? If they were not all dead, where were the survivors? I had to get on with the rest of my life. It would not be in soldiering.

My last day in the British Army was 28 October 1948, although I stayed within their reach either in the Territorial Army or on the Active Reserve List until June 1951. Getting out was quite a convoluted process. Technically, I did not leave the Royal Berkshires until February 1949, by which time I was with the 15th Scottish Volunteer Battalion of the Parachute Regiment, part of the Territorial Army. The main thing was that I was out of Germany, across the North Sea to the part of the UK I probably knew best, which was Scotland.

Ending up in a parachute regiment, much less a Scottish parachute regiment, had never been part of the plan, although I loved the hard-man image that went with the Red Beret. It wasn't easy getting accepted by them, but it got me back to the UK, away from the scenes of devastation that were still the norm on the Continent and would be for quite some time.

Learning to jump out of aeroplanes with only a sliver of silk between you and certain death was definitely scary, but thankfully I never had to do it in true battle conditions, and being in a Scottish regiment allowed me, with at least a measure of legitimacy, to have a rather marvellous picture taken of myself in full Highland gear. I'm not sure if it was actually the prescribed uniform of my regiment or, even if it was, whether I was entitled to wear it, but the photographer's studio I attended in Aberdeen had it to hand and assured me it would be no problem: 'Lots of men stationed up here like being photographed wearing a kilt, and they rarely ask, know or care about the formalities. Be assured, within my shop there aren't any. But you are in a Scottish regiment, so you are definitely entitled to wear the tartan.'

On 1 November 1948, I received my Aliens' Registration Card, reference A285406, from the Aberdeen City Police. By the end of November 1948, I had been taken on by Winetrobe and Sons in Clyde Street, Glasgow, as a trainee tailor's cutter. Who'd have thought? A young Polish Jew ending up in the *schmatter* (clothing) business. I got the job, of course, by speaking Yiddish and telling the big *macher* (the boss) a little bit of my story.

Winetrobes prompted me to sign on at a night school on Sauchiehall Street to learn more about the finer points of cutting cloth and other matters connected with the clothing industry. I started around the beginning of 1949. It was at the night school that my life took yet another dramatic turn.

Into it walked a young Irish woman, Elizabeth Angela Cassidy, known to everyone as Angela. She was learning to be a seamstress. We first met and got talking in the canteen. Angela was a fraction taller than I was, a couple of years younger, slender, with shiny brown eyes, dark hair, creamy white skin and delightfully red cheeks over finely structured bones. I thought her the most beautiful woman I had ever met. Even the memory of Martha began to fade. When Angela started singing in the pub where we all used to hang out after classes, I thought I had died and gone to heaven and the lead vocalist in the Divine Ensemble was putting on a performance only for me.

The moment I realised how strongly attracted I was to Angela and recognised that there was at least a spark of reciprocated interest, I made it clear to her I was a Catholic. She never asked me a direct question about my religion, at least not then or for many years. In 1949, I pre-empted such a discussion by playing it as a Catholic from the start. A blond, blue-eyed Pole. What else would I be? There was no need for her to ask anything because I had answered it.

But I lived a lie with Angela, and right here is where that lie began. Why did I lie? There were two answers to this question. One is simple and obvious; the other was far from simple but becoming more obvious, at least to me.

The simple and obvious one was that I was in love with Angela. Smitten. Hook, line and sinker. She was bubbly, funny, sexy and smart. A dream come true. I could not face the possibility of losing her. I hated the idea of being alone again. I just didn't dare to put her feelings for me to the most extreme test imaginable to a devout Catholic by asking her to consider getting entangled with someone who was not only not a Catholic, but someone who wasn't even a Christian.

The less obvious reason why I thought it wise not to be too open about my religion was to do with developments in Britain. Incredible though it may seem, nationalist groups that were linked with or spoke warmly about the British Union of Fascists from before the war were on the rise and on the streets again. As early as 1947, there were reports in the Press of street fights between fascist groups and communist and Jewish organisations in a place called Ridley Road in Hackney in the East End of London. The backbone of the fascist organisation was a body called the British League of Ex-Servicemen and Women. The parallels with the early days of the Nazi Party in Germany were all too apparent, and there had always been talk that parts of the British establishment were not wholly unsympathetic to Herr Hitler's ideas, but, obviously, they had had to put them on ice once the war started. Now the war was over, who knew how these sorts of ideas might resurface?

As Jewish pressure grew for a Jewish state to be founded in the Middle East, Jewish agitators in Palestine started to take direct action. A paramilitary Jewish group, Irgun Zvai Leumi, hanged two British sergeants, Mervyn Pierce and Clifford Martin. The Jewish leadership in Britain condemned the murders, but the British Press went bananas. Soon after, on the August bank-holiday weekend of 1947, there was anti-Semitic rioting which was particularly violent in Manchester and Glasgow. There were reports of abattoir workers in Birkenhead refusing to process meat destined for Jewish shops. Several newspapers carried a particularly telling picture of a Jewish-owned business in Liverpool with its windows smashed in by the rioters. Echoes of Kristallnacht. Hard to believe, but there it was. Being identified as a Jew suddenly didn't look so smart. Again.

But back to Angela. The thing about a lie, particularly a really big one, is that it can very quickly take on a life of its own, becoming self-sustaining. Every day of non-repudiation adds to and deepens the original deception.

It was a whirlwind romance, and before long Angela announced she was pregnant. I was thrilled at the idea of starting my own family, and by now, settling permanently in the UK with Angela, a family, an English name and a British Army war pension did not seem too bad. With a family of my own, I believed I could perhaps create something I had missed because of Hitler.

Despite its ubiquity, pre-marital sex was frowned upon by the Catholic Church, so an unmarried pregnant girl would be bound to bring shame to her family. Angela and I agreed we had to do two things: get married and get out of Dodge, both as soon as possible.

We decided we were going to head to England, to Leeds in Yorkshire, where there was a large clothing industry, meaning we should both have no difficulty finding work. I would go down first in order to sort out accommodation. Angela did not tell her parents of her plans until moments before she departed. As she related it to me later, suitcase in hand, she simply walked into the kitchen of their flat on North Street to announce she was leaving for England because her firm had offered her a much better job down there. She refused to say where in England. Her father, John 'Pop' Cassidy, followed her to the railway station, pleading with her not to leave. It was only when they were on the platform standing next to the train Angela was about to board that she turned and told her dad she was pregnant. Good on Pop, he said that was no reason to desert her family. They would find a way to make it work. Angela turned a deaf ear.

On arriving in Leeds, Angela was sporting something that looked like a wedding ring. Naturally, everyone imagined we were husband and wife. This gave our relationship a deliciously naughty edge. But we weren't wed, and we had to put that right. I think Angela thought the jaws of hell might open up and swallow her if she gave birth to a child out of wedlock. We went to St Anne's Cathedral in the centre of Leeds and saw a priest. I explained I could not produce a baptismal certificate or any other kind of documentation to prove I was a Catholic, and I would not be able to get any such papers any time soon because they were in Poland, where they had probably been destroyed by the war anyway.

He took me off into a room on my own and asked me some questions about Catholic doctrine. He wasn't convinced by my act and we emerged from the room when, despite Angela's bitter protests, he refused to marry us. A month later, after getting married in the Leeds Register Office with two strangers from the street as our witnesses, we went back to the cathedral, where Angela spoke her mind to the same poor priest, who once more asked me to step outside with him.

In a small room, he repeated what a difficult position he was in. Many ex-servicemen were trying to marry British and Irish women just so they could stay in England, but he could see the evident and overwhelming distress Angela was suffering, and was worried it might even affect the child she was carrying, perhaps precipitating a premature birth and threatening the life of Angela and also putting the baby at risk! Heaven forbid that might happen this very hour, right here in the sanctified precincts of Leeds Cathedral.

The priest asked me if I minded if he baptised me now so at least I would then, technically, be a Catholic in the eyes of God. I told him I had no objection. He poured some water over my head, said something I didn't properly hear, then we went back to Angela, where he announced, 'I am now satisfied Henry is a Catholic. The wedding can proceed.'

And so, a little while later, on 5 December 1949, in St Anne's Cathedral in Leeds, Angela and I were married according to the rites of the Roman Catholic Church. Our son John was born exactly two weeks later. He was to be the first of six boys born to Angela and me, one of whom died within two days of being born. All were baptised into the Catholic Church.

Postscript

In 1957, my efforts to find Nathan finally paid off. He was married, living in Israel, had a daughter called Sarah, and would soon have three more children, two more girls and a boy.

Late in 1958, Nathan came to England. The visit was always going to present problems. How would I explain the existence of a brother called 'Nathan Herszman' living in Israel? The simple answer is, I wouldn't.

In a letter, I explained my situation and asked Nathan if he wouldn't mind becoming 'Michael Karbowski' for the duration of his stay with us in Leeds. Nathan replied, saying if I thought it would work, he would play along. He was also kind enough to tell me he had heard all kinds of stories about how thousands of Jews had survived during the war and made their way after it. Mine did not exactly establish a whole new class or category of artifice. He was just glad it seemed to have done the trick for me. That I had managed to maintain the facade for this long did give things a bit of a twist, but no more than that.

If anyone expressed an interest, we agreed Nathan would tell them he married a Jewish woman he had met in a displaced persons camp after the war. She had wanted to go to Israel, so that is where they both ended up. That should be enough. Few people who lived through it enjoyed talking about the war, certainly not in any detail. It ought not to be too difficult to fend off someone who showed signs of being too inquisitive.

The worry was not Angela or her family. Nathan couldn't speak any English, so that imposed a natural interrogatory limit of sorts. It was the other Poles who lived in the neighbourhood, many of whom had become friends and visited regularly. If they had any suspicions about my antecedents, these had not surfaced up to now, at least not in any way Angela or I knew about. Early on, I had made a point of attending a few Catholic Masses said by a Polish priest for the large Polish community in the city. I ensured I was seen by several of the Poles who lived near us before allowing my attendance at Mass to drop off. To zero. But with 'Michael' arriving from Israel? How would that play out? I would just have to roll the dice, as I was absolutely determined to be reunited with my big brother.

As you might imagine, when Nathan arrived in England, our first encounter was tear-filled and intense. It was the first time we had seen each other since as kids he'd waved goodbye on that street corner in Lodz in September 1939. We wept over lives lost, a family lost, a whole way of life lost. At that point, we still did not know the exact fate of our parents, sisters or Srulek, but we imagined all the Herszmans had died, either in the ghetto or in a camp. There was nothing new to be said. All we could do was hope that somehow one or more had escaped and survived somewhere and had not yet found a way to connect with us. This was a hope that was never to be fulfilled.

The bit of good news Nathan brought was that two of our

Lewkowicz cousins had survived. Heniek was now Henry Lee, living in the USA, while Yehuda was a policeman in Tiberias in Israel. He would eventually go to the USA and settle there as Irving Lee. Several years afterwards, Heniek and his wife Nadja (Nancy) Ginsberg came to see me in London, and a little while later his brother Yehuda, with his wife Regina Mandel, also paid a visit.

So that was it. No Levinsons had survived, and only two Herszmans and two Lewkowiczs made it, plus the Blumowicz who had left for Palestine before the war started.

Nathan and I talked about the horrific things we had experienced or witnessed during the war, trying not to dwell on too many 'what ifs'. There was not a word of reproach from Nathan about my leaving the ghetto. On the contrary, he thought I was mad for even thinking there might be. After all, Nathan had gotten out, and he too had been unable to do what he'd promised to do before he'd left. The war confounded everything for everyone, but above all for the Jews. It was a great comfort to hear Nathan say that, although it did not mean I would ever completely rid myself of feeling that had I stayed, things might have turned out differently for the Herszmans of Lodz.

Nathan had made it across the Bug River, where he had been picked up by Soviet border guards, and he'd then spent the rest of the war in Siberia looking after horses in stables belonging to the Red Army. This allowed him to eat some of the food meant for his animals. Nathan was certain if he hadn't been able to do that, like a great many others held against their will in Siberia during the war, he would have perished. To the Soviets, keeping horses alive was more important than keeping Jews alive.

After the war had ended, like me he had first gone back to Lodz to see if he could pick up any of the threads of our previous life, find any of our family or get news of them. We couldn't work out whether he had been there before or after me. We even wondered if we might have passed each other on the street. In my British Army uniform, Nathan would have had no reason to give me a second look, and there could have been any number of reasons why I didn't see or recognise him.

After a couple of weeks staying with us, Nathan went home. While sorry to see him go, at another level I breathed a huge sigh of relief. It looked as if my secret had held. My Jewish antecedents, my Jewish identity, had not been exposed.

I was wrong about that. Other Poles whom Nathan had met while staying with us simply did not buy into 'Michael Karbowksi'. After he returned to Israel, they soon told Angela the conclusions they had reached about him, and therefore about me.

I don't think my religion or my lie about it was a major factor in the separation and later the divorce. Lots of other things had gone wrong in our marriage by then. For more than ten years, I had been living in the middle of a small piece of Catholic Ireland that had been transported to England. Living a lie every day had taken a heavy toll. Towards the end of the marriage, I probably wasn't a very good husband or father. But that's a different story, for another day.

Before the divorce was finalised in September 1963, I had left Yorkshire, ending up in London, where I remarried in the late sixties. Hylja Muhonen had come to England from Finland to train as a nurse. We had two children together, a boy Paul and a girl Helen, but Helen died when she was five months old.

On one of his trips to Poland to research the background to my life story, John met and stayed with Cesek and his wife Zofia in Lodz. In 1988, Cesek and Zofia came to stay with me in London, later travelling up north, where four of my five children with Angela still lived, now in Holmfirth, a small town in West Yorkshire. Peter, the youngest, had just bought a property which he had named 'Hershman House'. Peter figured the English phonetic version of our family name would go down better than the original. The following year, Nathan came to the UK again. This time it was to London for a holiday, and he came as Nathan Herszman. There was no need for any kind of subterfuge. All that was well and truly over.

During his stay, we went to visit John at his home in Hackney, where, among other things, he showed us a photograph from *The Chronicles of the Lodz Ghetto* by Lucjan Dobroszycki. It was the picture of a man inside the ghetto. He was pulling a cart. Something about the man's face had caught John's eye. It reminded him of his brother Frank. The man in the picture was our father, Chil Herszman (see page 97). As such, it is the only surviving picture of any Herszman from Lodz at the time they lived there. Neither of us had seen it before. This provoked another prolonged burst of tears on both our parts, recalling the tragedies and the loss we had both suffered and the fate of our family. John was taken by the emotion of the moment as well, though perhaps not with the same intensity as Nathan and I.

I took Nathan up to Holmfirth to meet my Yorkshire-based sons, along with their wives and many children. Nathan was thrilled to bits to step into Hershman House. I made my one and only trip to Israel to visit Nathan and his family in 1992, and at different times two of his daughters with husbands and children also came to stay with me in London or with their cousins in Holmfirth.

I recognised that, in a sense, with the prolonged suppression of the truth about my Jewish history and family the Second World War ended later for me than it did for almost everyone else. Finding Nathan, seeing Nathan, visiting Israel and, in the course of my discussions with John, the whole truth coming out about the things I did on the way to Gibraltar and afterwards allowed me to process the previously unprocessed and draw some sort of line under it. My struggle and determination to survive did not bring back my parents, Srulek or my sisters, but in my new life in England and with my new British family I found peace and a great deal of happiness. Finally.

Chaim Herszman's descendants gather round
his memorial in Lodz, 2005

Heniek and Cesek at Cesek's *dacha*, near Lodz, 1988

Epilogue

My cultural roots are tied up with Ireland and Yorkshire. I was raised in the 1950s and '60s in the north of England, in Headingley, Leeds, within a relatively devout, closely knit Irish Catholic community. It was a community not entirely devoid of anti-Semitic sentiments, albeit of the unthinking, unoriginal and wholly passive variety. It therefore came as a bit of a shock to discover, when I was about eleven or twelve, that Dad was not a Catholic after all. He was, in fact, a Jew.

This was not the straw that broke the camel's back of my parents' marriage. Discovering Dad was a Jew certainly added a bit of colour to the proceedings, but by the time the truth came out the marriage was effectively over anyway. Nevertheless, I was curious to know precisely why Dad had lied in the first place then kept it secret for so long. Was there something about the lie and its longevity which would help explain what I felt was his lack of love for and distance from me when I was a child? I had to find out. Maybe 'curious' isn't exactly the right word. I was more driven than that.

In the run up to and in the years immediately following my parents' divorce, my relationship with my dad could hardly have been worse. I was frightened of him. He constantly praised me for being clever, a quality he valued highly, but at the same time he was unpredictable and irascible. Not a drinker, he was nevertheless quick to strike with his hand or a belt for any of the several high crimes and misdemeanours of which I was undoubtedly guilty.

After the divorce, Dad went to London and later remarried. I stayed in Yorkshire with my mum. Then I became an undergraduate at the London School of Economics and Political Science. Dad by then was living in an enormous flat on Rupert Street in Soho, within easy walking distance of my new seat of learning. He offered me a rent-free room and free meals whenever my energetic social life permitted me to be there to consume them. I could not refuse. Dad was reaching out. I recognised that and responded. I was reaching out too.

This was when the reconciliation between Dad and me began in earnest. Once, and only once, he asked me how I felt about discovering my father was a Jew. I assured him it was supremely irrelevant. He was my dad. That was the beginning and end of it. I was ill-suited to be either a priest or a judge, particularly in respect of matters which had grown out of or were the result of war. I am not sure Dad completely believed me. Not at first.

Although he never said it explicitly, it became clear Dad had been embarrassed by and ashamed of the part of his conduct which had led to his five Catholic sons being deceived about their heritage. Growing up as a Jew in Poland in the 1930s, he was, to say the least, fully aware of many Catholics' ambivalent attitudes towards Jews. Had I picked up on it? Had my brothers? Were any of us resentful, at least to some degree, to learn that an ostensibly important part of what we thought we knew about ourselves had to be adjusted, and not in a minor way?

I am happy to say that eventually, and it didn't take too long, Dad became completely, and rightly, convinced the 'Jewish connection' mattered not a jot to his sons. On the contrary, if anything, we all rather enjoyed the extra, exotic edge added to our otherwise unexceptional back-story. If any resentment did exist, it was resentment which had become indissolubly mixed up and entangled in the maelstrom of the divorce. It did not linger or persist.

As I began the business of writing this book, I got Dad to open up and tell me what you have read in these pages. If I was his therapist; he was also mine.

I retraced Dad's entire journey, from Lodz to Gibraltar, making stops at all the key points along the way. I made a visit to Israel, where I met the Blumowicz who had left Lodz before the war started and, of course Uncle Nathan, as he now was, having first met him as 'Uncle Michael' more than ten years earlier. I also made several trips to Poland. During one of these, I discovered when and where my grandparents had died and the location of their graves.

In making these discoveries, I was helped enormously by Heniek, by then a resident of San Diego. When I heard he was planning to go to Lodz in 1988, I arranged to be there at the same time. Heniek was able to speak Polish to the people in charge of the cemetery records.

Chil and Chaja-Sura Herszman had died within months of each other in early 1941. The exact location of their otherwise unmarked graves had been recorded on a grid kept by the Jewish authorities. Astonishingly, these records had survived.

Heniek and I visited Zagajnikowa and the ghetto area. During our time together on this trip, he told me the bulk of the story of Chaim's departure from the ghetto, although we met again several times afterwards, both in the USA and in London, where other details were fleshed out.

When I got back to London, I told Dad I had found where his parents were buried. He rarely cried in my presence. This was one occasion when he did. Taken together, all of this book-related activity grounded the new and much closer relationship which grew up between me and Dad. We had many lengthy discussions about his early life in Lodz, punctuated with lots of laughter, whereas his escape from the ghetto, journey to Gibraltar and experiences as a soldier hitting back at the Nazis rarely brought anything but the most fleeting of smiles to either of our faces.

After everything he had witnessed and lived through, Dad deserved not a free pass exactly, but understanding and unconditional acceptance. It is what it is. If anyone could say their life had been shaped by events beyond their control, it was Dad.

The whole Carr family benefited from a new air of contentment, a new family settlement which emerged as the work on this book progressed. Talking through everything in the way we did allowed Dad to feel comfortable in his skin. He became a Jew again. Not a Jew who went to the synagogue or kept kosher, but a Jew who grew a beard and sought out the company of other Jews; for example, in card schools and at the Freemasons Lodge, which he joined. At their annual 'Ladies' Night' dinner, after the loyal toast came a toast to the President of the State of Israel. No, I never joined the Freemasons. There are limits.

Major elements of the story – for example, the initial escape – were confirmed by eyewitnesses, by army records provided by the British Ministry of Defence, from contemporary newspaper accounts in Poland or other Polish records, from records of the Lodz Ghetto that survived the war, from the British Public Record Office or, last but not least, by Hansard, the record of the proceedings of the British Parliament. As I said at the beginning of this book, unquestionably my dad's story is remarkable. It is a story of a tenacious, quick-witted determination to live, of defeating enormous odds, often in novel ways. But then, any and every story of a Polish Jew who survived the Holocaust borders on the miraculous.

In 2005, on the tenth anniversary of Dad's death all the Carrs went to Lodz to put up a plaque on a wall in the main Jewish Cemetery. It reads: 'In memory of Henry Carr, born Chaim Herszman, 20th April 1926. Died London 22nd April 1995. And in memory of our grandparents and all the other Herszmans who died in the Lodz Ghetto or elsewhere during the Holocaust. Dedicated by Chaim's six sons, their wives, eighteen grandchildren and (so far) three great grandchildren'.

Dad had never wanted to return to Poland during his lifetime but to us, his sons, this seemed a fitting way to close a chapter of *our* lives and acknowledge the family we never knew. I'm pretty sure dad wouldn't really mind.

John Carr, London

Dad playing a piano accordion

A Very Incomplete Bibliography

I have not kept a note of every book or article I read when checking the background or doing research. I never thought of this as an academic piece of work where it would be necessary to cite sources. But here is an incomplete list of some of the many books I referred to while writing my father's story:

— *German Concentration Camps*, World War 2 Investigators Ltd

Adelson, Alan (ed.) *The Diary of Dawid Sierakowiak*, Bloomsbury

Adelson, Alan and Lapides, Robert *Lodz Ghetto: Inside a Community Under Siege*, Viking Press

Altman, Linda Jacobs Warsaw, Lodz, *Vilna: The Holocaust Ghettos*, Enslow Publishing

Antony, Beevor *The Second World War*, Weidenfeld & Nicolson

Bessel, Richard (ed.) *Life In The Third Reich*, Oxford University Press

Bielenberg, Christabel *The Past Is Myself*, Corgi Books

Boyd, Julia *Travellers in the Third Reich*, Elliott & Thompson

Breitburg, Victor with Krygier, Joseph *A Rage to Live: Surviving the Holocaust So Hitler Would Not Win*, BookBaby

Browning, Christopher *Ordinary Men: Reserve Police Battalion 101 and the Final Solution in Poland*, Harper Perennial

Bullock, Alan *Hitler: A Study in Tyranny*, Pelican Books

Carswell, Allan *For Your Freedom and Ours: Poland, Scotland and the Second World War*, National Museums of Scotland

Darling, Donald *Sunday at Large: Assignments of a Secret Agent*, HarperCollins

Dawidowicz, Lucy *The War Against the Jews, 1933–45*, Penguin

Dobroszycki, Lucjan (ed.) *The Chronicle of the Lodz Ghetto, 1941–1944*, Yale University Press

Driberg, Tom 'Absentees for Freedom', NCCL

Driberg, Tom *Ruling Passions*, Jonathan Cape

Foot, M.R.D. and Langley, J.M. *MI9: Escape and Evasion, 1939–1945*, Bodley Head

Foot, M.R.D. *Resistance*, Paladin

Gilbert, Martin *Auschwitz and the Allies*, Pimlico

Gilbert, Martin *The Holocaust: The Jewish Tragedy*, Fontana

Gilbert, Martin *The Righteous: The Unsung Heroes of the Holocaust*, Black Swan

Goldhagen, Daniel *A Moral Reckoning: The Role of the Catholic Church in the Holocaust*, Little Brown

Grabowski, Jan *Hunt for the Jews: Betrayal and Murder in German-Occupied Poland*, Indiana University Press

Heiber, Helmut *Goebbels*, Robert Hale & Company

Horwitz, Gordon *Ghettostadt: Lodz and the Making of a Nazi City*, Harvard University Press

Keneally, Thomas *Schindler's Ark*, Hodder and Stoughton

Kershaw, Ian *The End: Germany 1944–45*, Penguin

Koskodan, Kenneth *No Greater Ally: The Untold Story of Poland's Forces in World War II*, Bloomsbury

Manvell, Roger *SS and Gestapo Rule by Terror*, Ballantine Books

Moorhouse, Roger *First to Fight: The Polish War 1939*, Bodley Head

Moorhouse, Roger *The Devils' Alliance: Hitler's Pact with Stalin, 1939–1941*, Vintage

Overy, Richard *The Third Reich: A Chronicle*, Quercus

Roy, Jennifer *Yellow Star*, Marshall Cavendish Corporation

Sands, Philippe *East West Street*, Weidenfeld & Nicolson

Scheyer, Moriz *Asylum: A Survivor's Flight from Nazi-Occupied Vienna Through Wartime France*, Little Brown

Stourton, Edward *Cruel Crossing: Escaping Hitler Across the Pyrenees*, Black Swan

Sword, Keith with Davies, Norman and Ciechanowski, Jan *The Formation of the Polish Community in Great Britain, 1939–50*, School of Slavonic and East European Studies

Zimering, Sabina *Hiding in the Open: A Holocaust Memoir*, North Star Press

Acknowledgements

This book would not have been possible without the constant urging and support of my wife, Glenys Thornton. Before I did, Glenys saw the importance of telling Chaim's story as widely as possible. She heroically looked after our children while I went on prolonged excursions tracing the route Chaim took. Many other people helped me at different times, in particular Sir Mark Jones who agreed with Glenys. I am sad Rabbi Abraham Pinter did not live long enough to see the book published. He did not prod me as often as Glenys or Mark, but sometimes it felt like a close-run thing. The other huge prodder was Danny Silverstone. As a dear friend and a Jew he was invested in a different way. My Aunt Eileen Boyle (nee Cassidy) has a most astonishing memory. Her vivid recollections of things that happened before I was born and in my early childhood certainly illuminated several corners of Chaim's life in the UK after he met the woman he was to marry. Her older sister. My mother, Angela Cassidy. At a more practical level I have to thank Jutta Croll, resident of Hamburg and Berlin, Szymon Wójcik of Warsaw, and Agnieszka Wrzesien-Gandolfo of Warsaw and Paris. At key moments they each stepped in but none of them can be held accountable for any of my doubtless many authorial failings.